MILNER CRAFT SERIES

Jenny Bradford

Embroidery Collection

SALLY MILNER PUBLISHING

Cover photograph: chest of drawers and location courtesy of Kathy Kasz of Rustic Rumours, Randwick, NSW.
Colour photographs 23 and 30: perfume bottle, lipstick case, old spectacles, sewing case and scissors courtesy of Candle-Ends Antiques, Double Bay NSW.

First published in 1995 by
Sally Milner Publishing Pty Ltd
558 Darling Street
Rozelle NSW 2039 Australia

© Jenny Bradford

Design by David Constable
Diagrams by Don Bradford
Photography by Andre Martin
Photographs on cover and colour pages 1, 4, 5, 12, 22, 23, 26 ,27, 28, 29, 30 and 31 styled by Judy Barouch
Typeset in Australia by Asset Typesetting Pty Ltd
Colour separated in Australia by Sphere Color Graphics
Printed and bound in Hong Kong

National Library of Australia
Cataloguing-in-Publication data

Bradford, Jenny, 1936–
    Jenny Bradford Embroidery Collection.

    ISBN 1 86351 167 9.

1. Embroidery — Patterns. I. Title. II. Title:
Embroidery collection. (Series: Milner craft series).

746.44041

ACKNOWLEDGEMENTS

I hope all those I acknowledged in the original editions of my books will forgive me if I do not mention them individually for this publication but accept my thanks once again for their help and support. Where applicable their work is acknowledged in the text, as are all products and brand names of threads, etc. used.

Special thanks to Diane Neumann who inspired me to create the Australian Wildflowers design in wool. Diane commissioned me to do the design exclusively for her shop Truly Lois, Victoria Street, Hall, ACT 2618 (ph. (06) 230 2415), then kindly gave permission for the design to be published in this book. Kits for the cushion illustrated on page C30 are exclusive to Truly Lois and available direct from the shop.

Once again I am indebted to my husband, Don, for his constant support in preparing this book.

Finally, my thanks to Sally Milner for her vision and hard work in setting up and preparing this project. Her constant efforts to promote and establish Australian authors as a force in a highly competitive market are much appreciated and have created an occupation for me that I never expected to have.

Any queries for the author should be directed to:
Jenny Bradford
7 Noala Street
Aranda ACT 2614
Australia

CONTENTS

COLOUR CROSS-REFERENCE CHART

This chart has been formulated as a colour guide to give the DMC colours closest to the Kanagawa silk ribbon and silk thread, and the wool yarn colours.

Silk Ribbon	DMC No
1	white
2	891/666
4	black
5	819
8	776
15	726
20	3346
23	554
26	776
28	606
31	504
34	3047
39	754
45	824/825
48	891/892
49	304
54	725
58	762
60	703
66	841
77	918/356
91	899
93	347
94	704*
98	3755
107	301
111	818
112	223
116	3766
119	445
120	307
125	3652
140	801/632
154	369
156	746
157	3713
163	3354
179	3740

* no close match

Silk Thread	DMC No
4	817
5	606
7	224
10	321
16	746
17	445
19	972
52	640
54	3790
79	729
91	3712/223
93	760/3708
94	761/754
104	3755/813
113	3345
114	3364/3013
117	791
140	818
157	3011/3052
160	471/472
161	733
165	563/562
169	891/892
170	316/3688

Wool Paternayan		DMC No
716	cream	746
845	apricot	3824
932	deep pink	3712
933	pink	760
934	pale pink	761
A604	green	3363

Rowan Botany Wool		
123	blue	964

Torokina Yarn		
211	pale pink	818
213	mid-pink	3688
214	dark pink	3687
251	light olive	3013
253	olive green	496
272	light brown	841
273	dark brown	839
371	light green	320
	cream	712

Marta's Yarn		
67	very dark red	815
106	bright red	349
107/2	dark red	304
203	mid-brown	420
205	red-brown	632
221	mid-green	987
301	gold	734
371	light green	3363
401	yellow	445
415	blue	322

INTRODUCTION

The work chosen for this book is drawn from four different types of embroidery: silk ribbon, bullion, Brazilian style and wool embroidery. Many of the stitches selected are used in more than one area.

Much of the work in this book has been selected from my earlier publications on *Silk Ribbon Embroidery, Bullion Stitch Embroidery* and *Textured Embroidery*. However, there are some previously unpublished designs included, particularly in the area of wool embroidery, with a selection of Australian wildflowers. Pansies have been added to the range of flowers in the textured embroidery section.

Basic instructions for handling each different style of embroidery are given, together with step-by-step instructions for each stitch, flower and project detailed, making this book ideal for the beginner to these freestyle types of embroidery.

Most of the designs detailed concentrate on one type of embroidery, as they were originally designed for a book on a specific form of embroidery. However, careful selection of flowers and techniques from the different sections of this book will offer the experienced embroiderer an almost inexhaustible range of designs and ideas. The opportunity is there to combine the different types of embroidery to create variety of texture within individual pieces.

CHAPTER 1

RIBBON EMBROIDERY MATERIALS

RIBBON

Silk ribbon has been used for all the ribbon embroidery projects in this book. It is softer and more pliable than any other type of ribbon available. As a result of this the work produced can be extremely fine and delicate.

Pure silk ribbon is currently available in approximately 185 shades in 4 mm width. Many of these colours are also available in 2 mm, 7 mm and 13 mm widths. It can be purchased from specialist embroidery and craft shops.

There is a synthetic ribbon very similar in appearance to the 4 mm wide silk ribbon but this is not as widely available as the pure silk and the colour range is very limited.

The difference between the two ribbon types can be likened to that between natural fibre fabrics which crush much more readily than synthetic fabrics. The synthetic ribbon has much more 'bounce' than the silk and therefore will not compact to the same degree, resulting in coarser work. This may be an advantage in some designs; however, the main criterion for your choice of ribbon should be that it is the one with which you personally enjoy working, as that is usually the ribbon that will suit your own style best.

This last statement also applies to the width of the ribbons selected for a design. The scale of a design can be increased by using wider ribbons, or decreased by using narrower ribbon. I find so much variation in individual student's work, due to natural differences in working tension, that the best advice I can give is for you to experiment with the various widths until you are satisfied with the results.

NEEDLES

A selection of crewel, tapestry, chenille and milliner's, or straw, needles in various sizes will be most useful.

Crewel or embroidery needles have a sharp point, a short thin shaft and a long slender eye and can be purchased in a packet of assorted sizes 3 to 9.

Tapestry needles have a blunt point, short shaft and long enlarged eye. Also available in assorted size packets. Sizes 18 to 24 will be most useful.

Chenille needles are very similar in appearance to tapestry needles except that they have a sharp point. Also available in assorted sizes from 18 to 24. In all cases the higher the number the finer the needle.

Milliner's (straw) needles have sharp points and fine eyes in long constant diameter shafts. Available in assorted sizes from 3 to 10, this type of needle is excellent for working colonial knots, and other embroidery highlights, in thread. The very finest of these is also excellent for sewing on beads as they are stronger and more durable than beading needles.

The choice of needle depends on the following:

• The type of stitch to be executed.

Any stitch requiring the needle to pass *between* a ribbon stitch and the base fabric should be worked with a tapestry needle to avoid snagging either the ribbon or the base fabric. If this is not practical (see next point), use a chenille needle and pass the needle eye first under the ribbon.

• The type of fabric you are working on.

The background fabric may influence the choice of needle. A tapestry needle may pull threads on fine silk or be hard to get through closely woven fabrics, and it may be necessary to use a chenille needle. As a rule, the tighter the weave, the larger the needle. This can often lead to the feeling that you are using a 'crow bar' and are going to leave unsightly holes in the fabric. However, the fact that the ribbon works easily this way and looks so much better soon overcomes this concern.

In general, I use sizes 18 to 22 tapestry or chenille needles for most of my work.

• The width of ribbon used.

The eye of the needle must be large enough to accommodate the ribbon comfortably and make a hole large enough for the ribbon to pass through easily.

THREADS

A selection of your favourite embroidery threads will be needed for highlighting the ribbon work. Stranded cotton, rayon and silk are all suitable. But sometimes even a single strand of these threads may be too heavy for some flower centres, in which case machine embroidery thread will prove useful.

FABRICS

There is a wide variety of fabrics suitable for ribbon embroidery provided they are not abrasive in any way. If the base fabric is hard or stiff, it may cause stress on the ribbon. If this is the case, try washing the fabric, using a fabric softener, prior to use.

The projects in this book have been worked on shantung, silks, cotton, linen, synthetics and hand-knitted garments.

Some fine and most loosely woven fabrics may require a stabiliser in the form of a second layer of the same fabric, silk organza, fine cotton or fine batting.

Suitability of design and stitch choice play an important part in the success of a project and should always be taken into consideration when planning your work.

EMBROIDERY HOOPS

I find many students dislike the thought of having to use an embroidery hoop, as I did myself at first. It is, however, essential to use one for most ribbon work. Keeping the fabric taut in a frame makes the process of 'spreading the ribbon' easier and greatly assists in working flowers evenly.

One reason many students find hoops clumsy and awkward is that there is a tendency to use too large a hoop. For this reason I prefer the small plastic and metal spring hoops that are available in 7.5 cm (3") and 10.5 cm (4^1/$_8$") diameter. These hoops are easy to move around and there is a section of fabric between the spring handles that does not get clipped into the frame. If the fabric is positioned carefully, finished embroidery can be passed through this section without squashing it in the frame.

The use of a small hoop makes it easier to reach the stitching area with both hands in order to manipulate the ribbon correctly.

FABRIC MARKING PENS

There are two types — water soluble and fadeable. Some people prefer not to use these pens as the long-term effect of the chemicals in them is unknown. However, I find them very useful for putting very light guide marks when positioning the main flowers in a design. (See 'Transferring a Design to the Fabric' on page 210.)

CHAPTER 2

BASIC TECHNIQUES
AND HELPFUL HINTS FOR EMBROIDERY WITH RIBBON

It is all too easy to rush over chapters on basic technique in our enthusiasm to get on with the task. How many times are we all reminded of the saying 'when all else fails read the instructions'. Our hectic lifestyle and lack of time seem to make this almost a daily cry. However, if we make the effort to master the basics thoroughly it does save time and effort in the long run.

EQUIPMENT AND WORKING CONDITIONS

As with any specialised field, the 'tools of the trade' and working conditions are extremely important. The degree of involvement will generally dictate the amount of investment you will need to make in equipment.

It is important to pay attention to the various types of needles and embroidery hoops recommended. Only pure silk ribbon will give results similar to those depicted in the photographs.

Having considered these factors, give careful thought to good lighting and clear vision. For me the best answer is a Luxo Examiner K Mag lamp. The fluorescent lamp gives a cool light (no hot and sweaty hands) and the magnified area is excellent. The lamp is easily adjusted to give a comfortable working position. A cheaper alternative is another Luxo lamp, the Argus-1, which is very good except for the heat radiated by the incandescent bulb; but that is not always a problem. There are also many portable magnifying glasses available from needlework shops or opticians and these can be utilised together with a good lamp.

STARTING AND FINISHING

The length of ribbon used in the needle may vary according to the stitches being worked. Because overworked and worn ribbon is much harder to manipulate I suggest using short 30 cm (12") lengths. This is particularly important where 'spreading the ribbon' is an essential part of the technique.

THREADING THE NEEDLE

The nature of the ribbon allows it to be threaded and locked into the eye of the needle thus making the maximum use of the ribbon length. This prevents accidental loss of the needle but makes unthreading difficult. The use of a separate needle for each colour being used is therefore recommended.

To thread the needle, pass the end of the ribbon through the eye of the needle. Thread this end of the ribbon onto the point of the needle, piercing the ribbon about 12 mm ($^1/_2$") from the end. Pull back on the long end of the ribbon until the ribbon locks firmly into the eye of the needle.

STARTING

Leave a small tail hanging at the back of the work. Pierce this tail with the needle as the first stitch is taken. This stitch can be the first one of the design or taken as a tiny backstitch to be hidden under the subsequent stitching. Weaving the needle behind previously worked stitches is not to be recommended, as the large needle will distort the surface stitches.

Be careful if you skip from one part of the design to another that the ribbons will not show through when the work is finished.

FINISHING

Cut off the ribbon leaving a tail to be caught in as the next thread is started, as with 'Starting'.

MANIPULATING THE RIBBON

It is impossible to overemphasise the importance of learning how to manipulate the ribbon correctly.

There is little point in using ribbon for embroidery if it is going to end up looking more like thread than ribbon. The simple basic techniques described here should be practised with care until they become an automatic part of your routine stitching. Learning to perfect the stitches will save time, effort and ribbon.

SPREADING THE RIBBON

Spreading the ribbon is very important for some stitches.

This technique is designed to give an even spread of the ribbon as it passes through the base fabric. Allowing the edges of the ribbon to fold over or under means that the stitch, when completed, will not show the full face of the ribbon.

- Bring the needle up at the required point.
- Keeping the ribbon flat, hold it firmly between the thumb (on the surface) and the first finger (under the fabric) of the left hand.
- Slide the needle under the ribbon and pull up on the needle as you slide it back to the exit point.

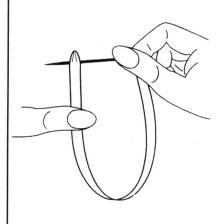

If the ribbon fails to spread evenly, turn it over and try again as it may be twisted where it passes through the base fabric. (See 'Preventing Twists' below.)

This process should not be difficult providing the needle used is large enough to create a hole of sufficient size to accommodate the ribbon easily.

PREVENTING TWISTS

Some stitches worked with ribbon require the full face of the ribbon to be laid down smoothly without twists. The following points will help ensure this:

- Keep ribbon lengths short, as recommended. It is easier to see and remove twists from shorter lengths.

- Hold the ribbon flat against the fabric under the left thumb while you take the stitch (diag. 1), after spreading the ribbon as described above. Keeping the thumb in place while you tighten the thread firmly over the thumb will, in most cases, remove all the twists from the ribbon, enabling the stitch to be completed smoothly (diag. 2).

- An alternative to this method is to work the loop over a second needle held in the left hand. (Use a large tapestry needle to avoid snagging the ribbon.) Tension the loop as you work by pulling up firmly with the second needle as the first needle is pulled to the back of the work. (See diag. 3.)

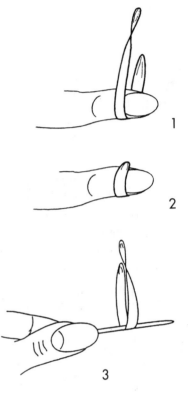

1

2

3

The point of this process is to remove twists before the stitch is completed. Poking and prodding with a needle after the stitch is set will snag and fray the ribbon. If you do need to adjust a stitch, use a tapestry needle to loosen the ribbon carefully before repeating the process.

TENSION

Ribbon work is delicate and a very delicate touch is required to achieve just the right tension. Pulling a stitch a fraction too tight will result in the stitch losing its form and fullness.

The best way to avoid this problem is to brace your hand against the underside of the hoop as you complete the stitch and work the ribbon down very gently until the correct look is achieved. Should you accidentally pull a straight stitch too tight, don't panic; you can rectify the situation by working a second stitch directly over the top, instead of unpicking the mistake.

CHAPTER 3

PREPARING
TO WORK A PROJECT

Careful consideration of the many factors that influence the end results of your project before starting will often help to avoid the frustration and disappointment that results from a project that turns out not quite right.

CHOICE OF FABRIC

This is particularly relevant to the final construction techniques. When choosing the fabric ask yourself the following questions:

- Is the fabric the best weight for the project? A medium to heavy fabric weight is ideal for a handbag; however, the same fabric may be very difficult and bulky to handle when covering a hairband or working a box top.

- Is the weave appropriate for embroidery? The ribbon will be easier to work on a fabric with a weave that is not too loose or too tight. Fabric such as taffeta has a very dense weave and may need special consideration. On the other hand, knitted fabrics often have too loose a weave to hold the ribbon securely. This problem can be overcome by backing the area to be embroidered with a very fine non-stretch fabric such as voile or silk organza.

- If the project will require laundering, are the laundering requirements of the fabric suitable? Remember that the fabric you choose has to be washed according to the most delicate fibres, which usually relates to the silk ribbon. For example, using a towel as a base for ribbon embroidery is not a good idea. A towel normally requires the use of stronger detergents and hotter water than you would use on silk fibres. It is also a pity to ruin the lovely three-dimensional properties of silk ribbon embroidery by choosing fabrics that require heavy use of an iron. For example, handkerchief linen is a very beautiful and popular choice of fabric for collars; however, it requires the use of a very hot iron and firm pressing after laundering. I prefer to use a fabric that has drip dry qualities and does not require so much ironing.

My favourite fabrics include raw or noil silk. Most dressmaking fabrics, including silks, synthetics and good quality homespun, cottons, voile and batiste, are suitable. Regular evenweave embroidery fabrics such as lugana, linda and hardanger 22 are also easy to use.

CHOICE OF STITCHES

Whether the item you are embroidering will require laundering or not is an important consideration when choosing stitches.

All stitches and flowers described in the silk ribbon designs are interchangeable. For example, designs shown using looped stitch flowers could all be worked using roses or straight stitch flowers for projects where laundering will be required. The choice of flat straight stitch flowers will ensure that the embroidery is not spoilt on fabrics such as handkerchief linen that require very firm pressing.

The amount of time you wish to spend on a project is an important consideration when making your choice of stitches and complexity of design. Projects such as Christmas decorations, cards and gift tags should be quick and simple. A minimum amount of embroidery combined with a clever use of fabric, lace, braid and beads can make such projects fun to do and a pleasure to give.

PREPARING THE FABRIC

1 Pre-wash all fabrics that will be laundered later.

2 When using lightweight fabrics, such as voile or batiste, it may provide a better working surface to back the fabric. Although not always necessary, I use a backing of fine Pellon whenever I can; I do this for the following reasons:

- It helps to keep the surface fabric smooth and makes the mounting process of the finished work easier.

- It ensures that the ribbon ends left on the back of the work do not show through to the front.

- It helps to minimise the marks left by using an embroidery hoop.

When working on clothing, the use of Pellon is not always practical, but it is sometimes possible to use a second layer of fabric for the same purpose.

When working on stretch fabrics the embroidery will sit more evenly if you back the area with a fine non-stretch fabric such as voile or silk organza. This enables the work area to be mounted in a hoop and holds the ribbon in place more securely.

The use of batting can also turn a lightweight fabric into a medium or heavyweight fabric, particularly if it is quilted.

3 Quilting your own fabric can be very effective and is not difficult if you refer to the section 'Machine Quilting' on page 212. Quilting reduces the amount of ironing required on some fabrics.

CHAPTER 4

SILK RIBBON FLOWERS

This chapter contains instructions on how to work each of the flowers used in the silk ribbon designs featured in this book. The flowers are grouped according to the stitches used to work them. Where more than one type of stitch is required, the flower is listed under the most difficult stitch. As the stitches are listed in order of increasing difficulty, beginners are advised to start with the straight stitch flowers.

References are given to the sampler, depicted in colour on page C1, wherever applicable; and the ribbon colours and widths quoted are those used to work the sampler.

Symbols used to depict the flowers in the design drawings are shown beside each flower name.

In the accompanying stitch placement diagrams, bold lines are used to indicate the stitch placement being described, whereas lighter lines and broken lines show previously completed steps.

ARRANGING PETALS EVENLY

If a specific variety of flower is to be depicted, care must be taken to choose a colour as true as possible to the flower variety. The shape and number of petals worked is also important as is the size in relation to any other flowers used in the design.

Many flowers have an uneven number of petals, generally five, rather than an even number such as four or six. Beginners will find it easier to arrange an even number of petals in a circle, but five are not difficult with practice.

To arrange five petals evenly around the flower centre the following image may help. Imagine the flower as a clock face and position petals as shown in the diagram.

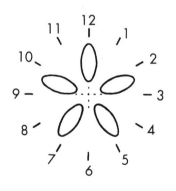

Working the petals so that they radiate evenly from the centre of the flower can be a problem. I find the following method helps to prevent petals from slipping sideways and distorting the shape of the flower.

- Mark the centre of the flower.
- Work the first petal at 12 o'clock, then bring the needle back through the fabric at the base of the next petal.
- Now *turn the work* so that the petal to be worked is now in the 12 o'clock position. Complete this petal and position the needle at the base of the next petal before turning the work again.

Working each petal in the same position makes judging the length easier and ensures even radiation from the centre.

Always start the petal at the point at which the stalk joins the flower and work towards the tip of the petal. This means open flowers such as daisies, columbines, etc. are worked out from the centre, bell-shaped flowers from the top down and tulips from the bottom up.

Be prepared to turn your work so that you are drawing the ribbon directly towards you, according to the requirements of the stitch being worked, rather than pulling the ribbon sideways and making it difficult to manipulate.

Finally, the centre of the flower is worked last and should overlap the inner edge of the petals so that they appear to go behind the centre, which is the way a flower grows. Working the centre first results in the petals looking as if they are tacked on to the outer edge of the centre and gives a very flat unnatural look.

STRAIGHT STITCH

Stitch Glossary page 239.

ROSE BUDS
Illustrated in colour on the sampler: 1A.
4 mm ribbon No 91 pink.
Washable.

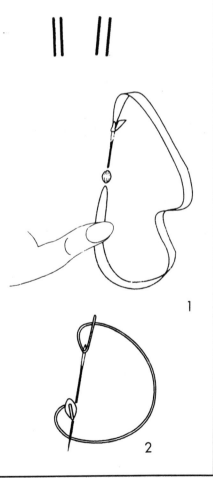

- Working from the base to the tip of the bud, lay a single straight stitch of length equal to the width of the ribbon being used.

- Cover this stitch with a second straight stitch starting immediately below and extending just beyond the tip of the first stitch (diag. 1).

- Using stranded thread, single strand for 2 and 4 mm ribbon, two strands for 7 mm ribbon, come up at the base of the bud and take a single straight stitch two-thirds of the way up the centre of the ribbon stitch. Bring the needle back up on the left-hand side of the bud, in line with this point. Take the needle down on the right-hand side of the bud and out at the base, with the thread looped under the needle (see diag. 2). Anchor with a tiny straight stitch or use this thread to form a stem for the bud.

1

2

TINY BLOSSOMS — FOUR PETAL FLOWER

Illustrated in colour on the sampler: 1A.
4 mm ribbon No 26 pink.
Washable.

These tiny four petal flowers are quick to work, make a useful fill-in for larger designs and are very pretty used on miniature pieces, such as jewellery.

- Mark a very small dot for the flower centre.
- Work four straight stitch petals, slightly shorter than the width of the ribbon used, in the order shown in diag. 1.
- Fill the centre with a single colonial knot worked in 2 mm ribbon or embroidery cotton.

SMALL FLOWERS — FIVE PETALS

Illustrated in colour on the sampler: 1A.
4 mm ribbon No 125 blue.
Washable.

- Mark a small dot for the flower centre. The finer the ribbon the smaller the dot required.
- Keeping the base of the petals close to the marked spot, position five petals as shown in the diagram on page 10.

A good guide to the petal size is to make them the same length as the width of the ribbon used.

Remember to turn the work as described on page 10.

SNOWDROPS AND OTHER BELL-SHAPED FLOWERS

Illustrated in colour on the sampler: 1A.
4 mm ribbon No 1 or 3 white.
Washable.

In order to start the petals where they join the stem of the plant, the work should be turned upside down.

- Work a single straight stitch for the centre of the bell, making it slightly longer than the width of the ribbon used (diag. 1).
- Work a petal on each side of the first petal, starting each one close to the centre at the stalk end and fanning them out at the bottom of the bell (diag. 2).
- Work a fourth petal directly over the first petal, starting just below the previous petal and finishing through the same point as petal 1.
- Work tiny straight stitches in green cotton thread at the tip of each petal and finish the top of each flower as described in step 3 of the rose buds on page 11.

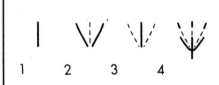

Other bell-shaped flowers can be created by varying the colours used and the stitch length. Use very short stitches to create lily of the valley and longer stitches to form the elongated bells of heath or correa.

WATTLE

Illustrated in colour on the sampler: 1A.
4 mm ribbon No 15 yellow.
Washable.

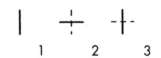

- Work one 2 mm vertical stitch from 6 to 12 on a clock face.
- Bring the needle up at the 9 o'clock position, as close to the side of stitch 1 without piercing that stitch as possible.
- Turn the work and complete a second stitch over the first stitch.
- Come up again at 9 o'clock, turn the work and complete stitch 3 to cover stitch 1.

Note: The stitches must be small and compact so that the final stitch closes over the first two stitches to form a smooth bobble.

SIMPLE SMALL LEAVES

Illustrated in colour on the sampler: 1A and 3A.

Washable.

Variation in the shape and size of straight stitch leaves can be achieved by varying the width of ribbon and the length of stitches used. Extra strength and durability can be achieved with the addition of a vein worked down the centre of the stitch with embroidery thread.

Twists and folds can be achieved by couching the ribbon in place using matching embroidery thread, allowing the stitch to change direction (see page 223).

LARGE LEAVES

Illustrated in colour on the sampler: 4A.
2 mm ribbon No 20 green.
Washable.

Straight stitch using 2 mm ribbon works well as a fill-in, as can be seen from the heart-shaped leaves I have used in several of the designs featured in this book.

Each stitch is worked so that it just overlaps the preceding stitch. The use of a fine silk thread (Kanagawa Silk Stitch or No 50) or a fine metallic thread, in a fine stem stitch, helps to smooth the outline. Veins may be added and are particularly useful on larger leaves, as they are stitched over the ribbon and help to hold it down firmly.

It is very important to spread the ribbon carefully for this stitch so that the edges do not curl in any way.

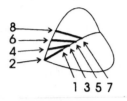

- Draw the leaf outline, including the centre vein.
- Using 2 mm green ribbon, work a straight stitch at the tip of the petal as shown in 4A.
- Fill in one side of the leaf, working out from the centre line to the outer edge (4A).
- Starting from the top, fill in the other half of the leaf, again working away from the centre.
- Using fine thread a shade lighter or darker, according to preference, outline the leaf with small stem stitching. Use straight stitch for the veins, couching in place where necessary.

COLONIAL KNOTS

Stitch Glossary page 222.

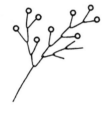

BABY'S BREATH

Illustrated in colour on the sampler: 1B.
2 mm ribbon No 156 cream or No 1 or 3 white.
Washable.

- Using a single strand of green stranded cotton, work stems in uneven feather stitching (see page 228).
- Scatter single colonial knots among the stems.

BILLY BUTTONS

Illustrated in colour on the sampler: 1B.
2 mm ribbon No 15 yellow.
Washable.

These flowers are formed by working colonial knots into a very tight circle, causing the centre of the cluster to be raised.

- Work a single knot for the centre.
- Work six or seven knots in a tight circle around the centre knot.
- Work a second circle around the outside of the centre cluster. It is important to pull the knots of this row in towards the centre of the flower by working the needle at an angle, sliding it in and out under the edge of the previous row. This helps to push the centre of the flower up, giving the finished flower a more rounded look.

LILAC

Illustrated in colour on the sampler: 1B.
2 mm ribbon Nos 23 light mauve and 179 dark mauve, or Nos 1 white and 34 cream.
Washable.

This flower works best if you use two shades of mauve, or white and cream mixed, to form the flower heads.

- Scatter small colonial knots as shown in the sampler.
- Fill in the spaces, using the second colour. Pack the knots very closely so that the flower head is raised up on the fabric.

BOTTLEBRUSH

Illustrated in colour on the sampler: 1B.
4 mm ribbon Nos 54 brown and 20 green.
2 mm ribbon No 49 or 2 red.
DMC stranded thread No 3031 brown.
Kanagawa 1000 silk thread No 54 brown (for bullion stitch).
Washable with care.

It is not possible to depict a bottlebrush in full flower, but flower heads that are just coming into bloom make an ideal subject.

- Work the branches using whipped running stitch, or long bullion stitches couched into shape. I use 50 to 60 wraps for bullion stitches; however, these can be worked in shorter stages as the joins are easily covered with the nut clusters.

- Old nut clusters form on the same stems as new flower heads. Using brown 4 mm ribbon, work clusters of nuts in colonial knots up the bottom half of the branch. Change to green ribbon, and repeat with clusters of green colonial knots towards the top of the branch.

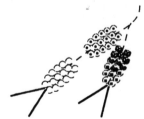

- Using two strands of DMC brown thread and a fine milliner's needle, work a colonial knot in the centre of each brown ribbon knot.

- Using 2 mm red ribbon and a fine crewel needle, work the ribbon into the centre of the green knots. Work a tiny looped straight stitch into the knots at the tip of the cluster. Towards the bottom of the cluster, take the ribbon down through the knots from the front of the work, leaving a short tail. Back stitch firmly at the back and bring the needle back through to the front, through the same knot. Cut the ribbon and fray the ends with the point of a sharp needle. Trim the ends until they are short and fluffy.

- Add ribbon stitch leaves, making them long and slender.

A circle of rubber (cut from a rubber glove) or a 'grabit' (available from patchwork supply shops) will help reduce stress on the fingers, if used to pull the needle through the knots when working this last step.

FANTASY FLOWERS

Illustrated in colour on the sampler: 4A.
4 mm ribbon No 26 pink.
2 mm ribbon No 8 pale pink.
Washable.

These pretty flowers can be varied in size according to the size of the bead used for the centre. A tiny pearl has been used for the centre of the flower on the sampler.

- Surround the pearl with six or seven colonial knots worked in 2 mm ribbon a shade darker than the outside petals.

- Divide and mark the outer ring into six equal sections as shown in diag. 1.

- Using 4 mm ribbon, back stitch two straight stitches, one directly over the top of the other, between each of the sections marked (diag. 2).

STEM STITCH

Stitch Glossary page 238.

STEM STITCH ROSES

Illustrated in colour on the textured embroidery sampler (page C20): 3B.
4 mm ribbon dark pink.
2 mm ribbon pale pink.
Not recommended for frequent washing.

This is yet another way to work a rose or camellia. It is quick and easy to do, but not as durable on clothing as the rolled roses.

- Using the darkest shade of ribbon, work four colonial knots in a tight circle.

- In pale pink work a row of small stem stitches around these knots, bringing the needle up through the fabric between the knots and the loop of ribbon. Tighten the stitches gently, leaving a soft loop for each petal.

- Work a second row of stem stitches around the outside, leaving each in a soft fold.

BULLION LAZY DAISY STITCH

Stitch Glossary page 220.

FLANNEL FLOWERS

Illustrated in colour on the sampler: 2B:
4 mm ribbon No 156 cream.
2 mm ribbon No 31 green.

- Draw a circle about 6 mm (¹/₄") in diameter.
- Work 9 to 11 bullion lazy daisy petals, each between 9 mm and 11 mm (³/₈" and ¹/₂") total length, around the centre. Wrap the ribbon two or three times for each bullion.

  Note: A more natural shape will be achieved if some of the stitches are slightly off-line. To create a smooth stitch, make sure the ribbon is laid flat at all times and spiralled up the needle when working the bullion wraps. Hold the stitch firmly under the thumb as the needle is pulled through the fabric, and tighten the ribbon by pulling firmly on the ribbon while keeping it close to the fabric. *Do not push wraps down with the thumb.*

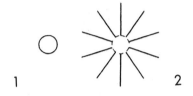

- Fill the centre with colonial knots in green.
- Using green, work a back stitch over the tip of each petal. Bring the needle up through the fabric under the tip, wrap the ribbon neatly around the tip, and return the needle to the back of the work through the same hole. (Slipping a spare needle under the ribbon as the stitch is tightened will ensure the ribbon lies flat over the bullion.)

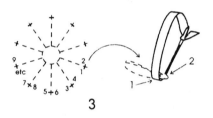

RIBBON STITCH

Stitch Glossary page 236.

Ribbon stitch can be substituted for straight stitch when working small flowers such as daisies and leaves. In the flowers detailed below, ribbon stitch is used in conjunction with other stitches. It is not washable unless overstitched with thread.

BELL-SHAPED FLOWERS

Not illustrated on the sampler: refer to tulips.
Washable with care.

Use a large crewel or fine chenille needle and 2 mm ribbon. Turn your work upside down so that you start each petal at the point at which the stalk will join the flower.

- Work a single straight stitch as shown in 1A.
- Work a bullion lazy daisy stitch — wrapping the ribbon once around the needle — on each side of the straight stitch to create a tiny fan shape. Pull the stitch firmly and anchor the point of the bullion into an outward curve.
- Work a ribbon stitch over the centre of the bell, covering the first straight stitch completely.
- Hang the bell from the stem with a short straight stitch worked in thread.

TULIPS

Illustrated in colour on the sampler: 4B.
4 mm ribbon No 39 apricot.
Washable with care.

- Depict tulips by working a bell-shaped flower the other way up and anchoring the bullion lazy daisy stitches straight, instead of pulling them to one side.

LOOPED STRAIGHT STITCH

Stitch Glossary page 239.

A guide for maintaining even-sized loops when working flowers in looped straight stitch is useful. It is possible to work these loops over a large tapestry needle but this requires accurate judgement to maintain even length. A more accurate guide is to use a small section of a knitting needle, 7 cm (3") is ample, provided it can be cut and smoothed properly. Other alternatives are cable knitting needles or the end pieces from circular knitting needles which can be cut from the flexible wire section and smoothed with sandpaper or a nail file. I use a size 5 mm cable needle for 7 mm ribbon roses or poppies and also 2 mm ribbon daisies.

BRIAR ROSES OR POPPIES

Illustrated in colour on the sampler: 2A.
7 mm ribbon No 157 pink or 2 red.
Not washable.

- Mark a small circle approximately 4 mm ($^{1}/_{6}$") in diameter.
- Work the first petal, coming up at the base and going down about 3 mm ($^{1}/_{8}$") from this point, adjusting the loop over the spare needle — a size 5 mm cable needle.
- Work a second loop over the needle without removing the needle from the first loop.

- Slip the first petal off the needle before working the third petal. Note that keeping the previous petal on the spare needle each time helps to avoid pulling the petal loop tight accidentally.

- When all petals are worked, thread a fine milliner's needle with machine embroidery thread, yellow for roses, black or green for poppies.

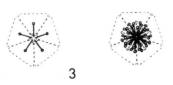

- Work the centres in pistil stitch (see page 235). Arranging the petals as you work, make one pistil stitch down the centre of each petal to hold them firmly in position.

- Continue working pistil stitches of various lengths around the centre, over the base of the petals. Fill the centre with colonial knots.

Buttercups, small roses and poppies are worked in the same way using 4 mm ribbon and starting with a smaller centre, with the loops made over a size 3 mm cable needle.

DAISIES
Illustrated in colour on the sampler: 2A.
2 mm ribbon No 98 blue.
Washable.

These need many more loops than the briar roses to complete the flower.

- Draw a small circle about 4 mm ($\frac{1}{6}$") in diameter and start the petals close to the centre.

- Eight petals form the base row, evenly spaced around the centre circle. Work a second row of petals in the gaps between the first row, adding as many petals as are needed to fill all spaces.

- Using gold or brown embroidery thread, work a circle of colonial knots for the flower centre, working well over the base of the petals to secure them firmly.

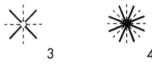

NARCISSUS
Illustrated in colour on the sampler: 4B.
4 mm ribbon No 156 cream or 13 gold and 39 apricot or 15 yellow.
Washable when worked in 2 or 4 mm ribbon.

- Mark a small circle for the centre of the flower. Work six straight stitch petals around the outer edge of the centre circle in cream or gold.

- Using apricot, yellow or gold, work four or five looped straight stitches for the trumpet.

- Using a single strand of embroidery thread, fill the centre with half colonial knots, carefully working over the base of the looped stitches to hold them firmly in place.
- Work leaves, using couched twisted ribbon stitch.

BANKSIA NUTS

Illustrated in colour on the sampler: 4A.
4 mm ribbon No 54 brown.
Washable.

Use a fine chenille or medium crewel needle.

- Draw a cone-shaped nut and mark small straight lines at random over the area.
- Fill in the nut with half colonial knots, leaving small gaps at each line mark.
- Work two looped straight stitches on each marked line. These should look a little like a slightly open mouth.
- Finish by working one or two half colonial knots between the looped stitches to hold them firmly in place, taking care not to disturb the looped stitches.

COLUMBINES

Illustrated in colour on the sampler: 2B.
4 mm ribbon No 163 pink.
7 mm ribbon No 156 cream.
Not recommended for repeated washing.

- Mark a small circle of approximately 2 to 3 mm ($^1/_{16}$"
to $^1/_8$") in diameter for the centre of the flower. If desired the petal positions can also be marked as shown in the diagram.

  Refer to page 10 for spacing for five petal flowers.

  A chenille needle should be used for all ribbon stitches.

- Using 4 mm ribbon, work five bullion lazy daisy petals, each being made by taking a stitch about 4 mm ($^1/_6$") long and wrapping the ribbon twice around the point of the needle.
- Using 7 mm ribbon, work five looped straight stitch petals around the centre circle. Take care as these stitches are easily disturbed until secured with the centre colonial knots. Use a single strand of DMC thread to work a cluster of colonial knots for the centre, covering the base of the centre petals to hold them firmly in position.

LOOPED RIBBON STITCH

Stitch Glossary page 236.

PAPER DAISIES

Illustrated in colour on the sampler: 2A.
2 mm ribbon No 1 white and 157 pale pink, or No 157 pale pink and 163 dark pink.
Not recommended for repeated washing.

These little daisies are similar to those detailed on page 19, but this way of working ribbon stitch gives a more delicate finish to the tips of the raised petals.

A crewel needle is used throughout.

1

- Draw a small circle for the flower centre.

- Work the base row of petals, as shown in 2A, using flat ribbon stitch.

2

- A second row of raised petals is added, working looped ribbon stitch inside the centre circle. Each petal is formed by first passing the needle through the ribbon at a point that will become the tip of the petal when the stitch is complete (approximately 4 mm ($^3/_{16}$") from the point where the ribbon emerges from the fabric). Continue pulling the needle through the centre of the ribbon until all the ribbon has passed through the hole. Complete the stitch as for a looped straight stitch, hooking a second needle into the loop as you pull the ribbon through. Control the loop with the second needle until the previously formed point is at the tip of the petal. Work eight to 10 of these shaped petals around the centre circle before anchoring them carefully with a cluster of tiny colonial knots, using a single strand of DMC embroidery thread.

3

4

WHIPPED STITCH — SINGLE

Stitch Glossary page 242.

DAISIES

Illustrated in colour on the sampler: 3A.
2 mm ribbon No 98 blue.
Washable.

The number of stitches used to form this daisy can be varied considerably. They look beautiful with tightly packed stitches forming a neat circular flower; but 15 petals of tightly worked ribbon take a considerable amount of time and ribbon to produce. Ten petals were used for each flower on the christening gown and the teddy bear, using method 1 given below.

The daisies can be worked in two different ways.

Method 1

The petals can be arranged around a marked centre, leaving room for a bead or a cluster of knots for the centre.

- Work each whipped stitch from the centre out, wrapping the outer end of the stitch a little more than the inner end.

Method 2

For working a daisy as shown in 3A.

- Use a stiletto or large needle to make a hole in the base fabric.

- Working from the *outside* into the centre, lay down a straight stitch, coming up at 1 and going down through the centre hole and back out at 1. Pull the stitch firmly and then wrap it, working in towards the centre and back out to the outer edge. The stitch should be fatter on the outer third. Anchor the stitch by passing the needle to the back of the fabric, gently pulling the stitch into a slight curve.

- Bring the needle up at point 3 and repeat the process.

- Continue working the stitches close to each other in a tight circle. You will need 14 to 16 petals to complete the circle.

THREE PETAL FLOWERS

Washable.

These flowers are not intended to represent any specific type of flower, so choice of colour and ribbon size will depend entirely on the type of design chosen. They are comparatively quick to work, economical on ribbon and will wash and wear well.

- Commence with a tiny dot for the centre.

- Work three whipped stitches in a darker shade of ribbon at 12, 4 and 8 o'clock.

- Using a lighter shade of ribbon, work one whipped stitch on each side of each dark stitch, first on the left then on the right, extending them to just beyond the tip of the first stitch. Work all the wraps on the outside stitches in the one direction from the base to the tip of the petals, taking the final wrap of the second outside stitch over the point of the first outside stitch to draw them together.

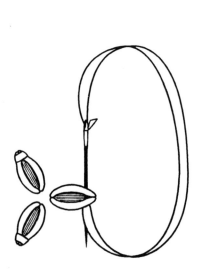

- Work a single colonial knot in 2 mm ribbon for the flower centre.

ONE-SIDED ROLLED ROSE

Illustrated in colour on the sampler: 3A.
4 mm ribbon in two selected shades.
Washable.

- Start the rose, using the darker shade of ribbon, with two straight stitches, one directly over the other, for the flower centre. Make these stitches equal in length to the width of the ribbon.
- Work one whipped straight stitch down each side of the centre stitch (1-2, 3-4 on diag. 1).
- Place three whipped stitches around the base of the flower, working the centre stitch first, then one stitch on each side (5-6, then 7-8 and 9-10 on diag. 2).
- Using the lighter shade of ribbon and commencing at point 1, work five overlapping stitches around base of flower and up to point 3 on the left-hand side (diag. 3).

Note that the needle always comes up on the odd numbers and goes down on the even numbers, then comes back through the fabric at the odd number point to start the wrapping process.

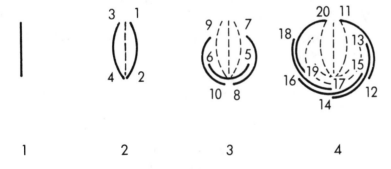

1 2 3 4

ROSES

Illustrated in colour on the sampler: 3A.
Washable.

These roses are very firm and strong and wash and wear well. The stitches are positioned in the same way as they are for bullion roses. They can be worked using any width ribbon in one, two or three shades.

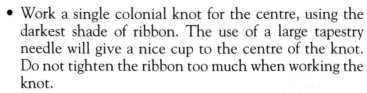
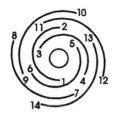

- Work a single colonial knot for the centre, using the darkest shade of ribbon. The use of a large tapestry needle will give a nice cup to the centre of the knot. Do not tighten the ribbon too much when working the knot.

- Work three whipped stitches in a clockwise direction around the centre knot, using ribbon of a lighter shade if desired. Position the stitches as shown in the diagram. Bring the needle up between the row you are working and the centre knot, halfway along the stitch just completed. Anchor each stitch into a slight curve.

- Work four or five whipped stitches around the previous row. The ribbon can, once again, be a lighter shade. Position these stitches in the same way as in the previous row, starting each new stitch halfway back and on the inside of the previously worked stitch. Anchor each stitch into a slight curve around the previous row.

WHIPPED RUNNING STITCH

Stitch Glossary page 241.

KANGAROO PAW

Illustrated in colour on the sampler: 3A.
2 mm ribbon Nos 49 red and 20 green.
Washable with care.

This distinctive looking flower is easy to work and looks very realistic.

- The stems are worked in whipped running stitch. Using 2 mm red ribbon, work the ribbon firmly to form a smooth stem.

- Using 2 mm green ribbon, work single whipped straight stitch, as shown in the diagram, for the flower head. The green stitches should touch the red stem at their base.

- Using 2 mm red ribbon, work a back stitch over the base of each green stitch where it joins the stem, as described in step 4 of flannel flowers on page 17. Complete with leaves worked in 2 or 4 mm green ribbon, using couched twisted ribbon stitch (see 'Couching' in the Stitch Glossary, page 223).

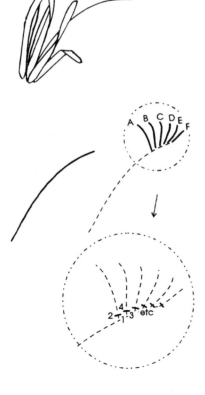

Portuguese stem stitch

Stitch Glossary page 235.

GUM TREE

2 mm ribbon Nos 140 brown, 77 tan and 20 green.
Madeira gold/black thread No 5014 (used for outlining).
Not washable.

- Fill in the tree trunk with lines of Portuguese stem stitch, continuing some of the lines on to form the main branches. Add some side branches in thread before working clusters of leaves in ribbon stitch, using green ribbon.

- The Madeira thread is couched along some of the lines of stem stitch as a highlight.

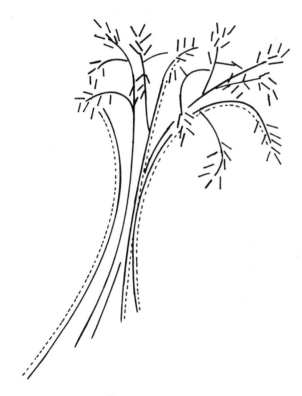

Rosette chain

Stitch Glossary page 237.

LAVENDER

Illustrated in colour on the sampler: 3B.
2 mm ribbon Nos 31 pale green and 178 lavender.
Washable.

Individual stitches of rosette chain can be used to represent stems of lavender.

The ribbon is firmly twisted and therefore may be used in wash and wear situations.

- Using stranded embroidery thread, work the stems in couching.
- Using 2 mm ribbon, thread a fine tapestry needle with one length each of pale green and lavender ribbon.
- Holding the work upside down, work a row of single rosette chain stitches up each stem, starting each stitch on the stem.

PUSSY WILLOW

4 mm ribbon No 66 brown.
2 mm ribbon No 156 cream.
Washable.

- Work twig-style stems in whipped running stitch using brown 4 mm ribbon.
- Using 2 mm ribbon in cream, work single rosette chain stitches at intervals along the stems.

ROSETTE CHAIN FLOWERS

Illustrated in colour on the sampler: 3B.
Washable.

These may be worked in a variety of ways using 2, 4 and 7 mm ribbon, single or double strand. Double strands can be of shaded or contrasting colours.

- Draw a circle for the centre of the flower. Make a tiny mark on edge of the circle for the base of each petal.
- Work rosette chain in to a circle, starting the base of each petal at the marked points.
- Work colonial knots for the centre of each flower.

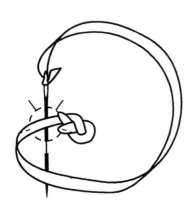

CHAPTER 5

SILK RIBBON BUTTERFLIES

Butterflies are always popular with embroiderers and they offer such a variety of shapes and colours, making the possibilities of design endless. The butterflies used in the designs shown in the silk ribbon section of this book fall into two categories:

1 Butterflies copied from nature; as used on the clock face and embroidery caddy.

2 Tiny fantasy butterflies; worked on evenweave fabric from charted designs.

All these butterflies are worked using the same basic straight stitch, so that each new stitch worked just overlaps the previous one, thus covering the background fabric completely.

It is very important to pay careful attention to spreading the ribbon for each individual stitch, so that the ribbon lies flat and does not curl at the edges.

Many of these stitches are quite long and their wearability has been increased by working over the top of them using fine silk thread (Kanagawa No 50 is ideal) or fine metallic thread. Machine embroidery thread can also be used for this purpose.

The fine top stitching can be worked in a random design, or in straight lines that run across the direction of the ribbon stitching.

I find the 2 mm ribbon easier to work than the 4 mm; however, the colour range is more limited, so it may sometimes be necessary to use 4 mm ribbon in order to obtain the required colour. This was the case for some of the butterflies copied from nature: the Cairns Birdwing butterfly (12 o'clock on the clock face), for example.

For a natural blending of colour the stitches can be interleaved so that the ends of the stitches overlap. This is shown clearly in the overlap between red and black on the Red Lacewing butterfly (6 o'clock on the clock face).

The tiny butterflies are also worked in straight stitch, using evenweave fabric, and, as detailed in the individual project instructions, the designs can be counted out square by square.

Butterflies are also very effective used as an applique design, decorated with a variety of outline stitches and beads.

BUTTERFLIES FROM NATURE

Good reproductions can be achieved by copying accurate colour pictures as closely as possible. (Good colour photographs of the first four butterflies detailed here are to be found on page 190 of *Australia's Wilderness Heritage Vol 2 — Flora & Fauna*, published by Weldon Publishing.)

The easiest way to transfer these butterfly pictures is to carefully cut a template, from a tracing or photocopy, and trace the outline directly on to the fabric, using a fine point fadeable marker or water erasable pen.

GENERAL INSTRUCTIONS

All butterflies are worked in long straight stitch, all small stitches such as spots are worked over the top of the base layer. These help to anchor the longer stitches and make the work more secure.

Veins also help to anchor long stitches firmly; make sure they are worked across rather than in line with the base stitching.

The body of the butterfly is divided into sections and, working satin stitch using a single strand of embroidery thread, each of the sections is filled in turn.

The feelers are worked with Kanagawa silk thread No 50 or any fine black thread such as machine embroidery thread. Couch a long straight stitch into place and finish with a short back stitch at the top of the feeler.

Cairns Birdwing (Ornithoptera priamus euphorion) _____

Ribbon required:

4 mm	yellow	No 119
	green	No 94
	black	No 4
2 mm	black	No 4

Thread required:
   black (body and feelers)

- Trace the outline carefully.
- Using green, work three long stitches along the front edge of the front wings.
- Change to black and continue to fill in with long straight stitches.
- With yellow, work over the black, two stitches along the inner edge and three short stitches towards the back edge of each front wing.
- The back wings are worked in yellow, overlaid with a few green stitches and three tiny black dots along the back edge.
- Finish the front edge of the front wings by working a row of whipped running stitches in black along the edge of the green stitches, pulling the stitches tight to form a very thin line.
- Edge the back wings with a row of palestrina stitch, using 2 mm black ribbon.
- Use black embroidery thread to fill in the body area with satin stitch.
- Work feelers.

Mountain Blue (Papilio ulysses) _____

Ribbon required:
  2 mm   blue   No 116
         black   No 4
         white   No 1

Thread required:
  brown (body)
  black (feelers and veins)

- Trace the outline and also mark the outline of the blue section.

- Fill in the blue area with long straight stitches.

- Work the outer black area, overlapping the stitches between the ends of the inner blue area.

- Finish the front edge of the front wings with a thin row of whipped running stitch in black.

- Work in black dot in the blue area towards the front of the wing.

- Edge the back wings with palestrina stitch in black. Using white ribbon, work a tiny looped straight stitch in each indentation along the outer edge.

- Fill in the body with satin stitch in brown thread.

- Work veins and feelers in black.

Lacewing (Cethosia cydippe) _____

Ribbon required:
  2 mm   blue   No 45
         pink   No 157 and 112
         brown   No 140
         white   No 1

Thread required:
  gold (body)
  black (feelers)

- Trace the outline carefully and mark the outline for the pink section.

- Fill in the inner wing area with pale pink.

- Work the outer area in blue, making the stitches meet but not overlap.

- Add white patches through the blue area.

- Work tiny spots of deep pink in the blue area of the back wings. Outline the pale pink wing sections with tiny straight stitches in the darker pink, working across from the pink to the blue stitching.

- Finish the front edge with a row of thin whipped running stitch in brown.

- Edge the remainder of the wings with palestrina stitch, working looped straight stitches in white along the outer edge in each indentation. Further looped stitches are added inside the brown edging at the back of the wings.
- Fill in the body with satin stitch in gold embroidery thread, and work feelers.

Red Lacewing (Cethosia cydippe chrysippe) _____

Ribbon required:
2 mm red   No 48
      black   No 4
      white   No 1

Thread required:
black (body and feelers)

- Trace the outline and also mark the outline for the red section.
- Fill in the inner wing sections with red ribbon.
- Work the outer wing sections in black, overlapping the two sections.
- Work the white flashes over the black stitching.
- Finish the front edge of the front wing with whipped running stitch and edge the remainder of the wings with palestrina stitch.
- Fill in the body with black and work feelers in black.

Lesser Wanderer (Danaus chrysippus) _____

Ribbon required:
4 mm black   No 4
      white   No 1
      gold   No 54
      tan   No 107
2 mm black   No 4

Thread required:
brown (body)
black (feelers)

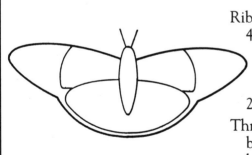

- Trace the outline.
- Work the inner front wing section in tan.
- Fill in the back wing with gold.
- Fill in the outer edge of the front wing in black and overstitch the white flashes.
- Work the front edge with fine whipped running stitch in 2 mm black ribbon and edge the remainder of the wings with palestrina stitch.
- Work the body in brown and the feelers in black.

CHARTED DESIGN BUTTERFLIES

The charts show the stitching pattern for these little butterflies. They can be varied in size according to the evenweave fabric used.

- Start each design at the front of the front wing and work both front wing sections before working the back wing sections.

- The body can be worked with a single wrapped straight stitch in brown ribbon or a bullion stitch worked in Kanagawa 1000 No 52 or 54.

- Feelers are worked in fine black thread, using a long straight stitch with a short back stitch at the tip.

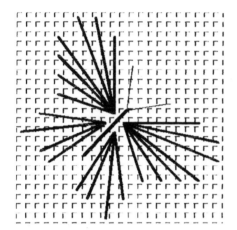
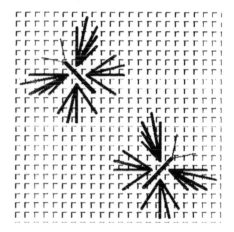
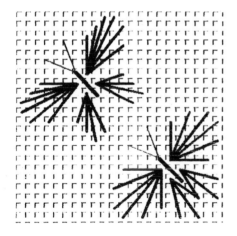
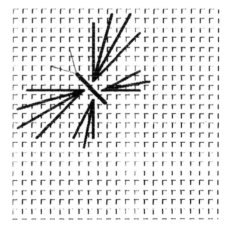

CHAPTER 6

RUCHING RIBBON

This has been used on the patchwork bag for the initial and the opal cluster. It can also be used for outlining a design or making flowers.

- Using a fine straw or crewel needle and fine silk thread, run a gathering thread of tiny stitches in zigzag pattern through a length of 4 or 7 mm ribbon.

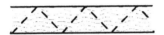

- Pull up gently until the ribbon is nicely gathered.
- Arrange and tack into place before ending off the gathering thread so that you can adjust the amount of ribbon required for your design.

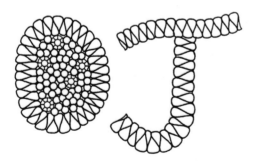

The opal cluster has been formed with ruched ribbon surrounding colonial knots and diamantes and the initial by ruched ribbon on its own.

CHAPTER 7

INITIALS

The use of lettering or initials can add a personal touch to your embroidery, with many sources of design for cross stitch lettering available that can be combined with silk ribbon work.

The alphabet included in this book offers the possibility of working letters in applique and then using ribbon work for further decoration, in a similar way to that mentioned for the butterflies.

Letters can be filled in with straight stitch and overstitched with highlight thread, as used on the butterflies and illustrated on the bottom right-hand corner of the embroidery caddy. These initials were worked in ribbon hand-dyed by Mary Hart-Davies.

Another use would be to outline the shape of the letter with one of the outline stitches and then fill in the shape with flowers or an abstract design.

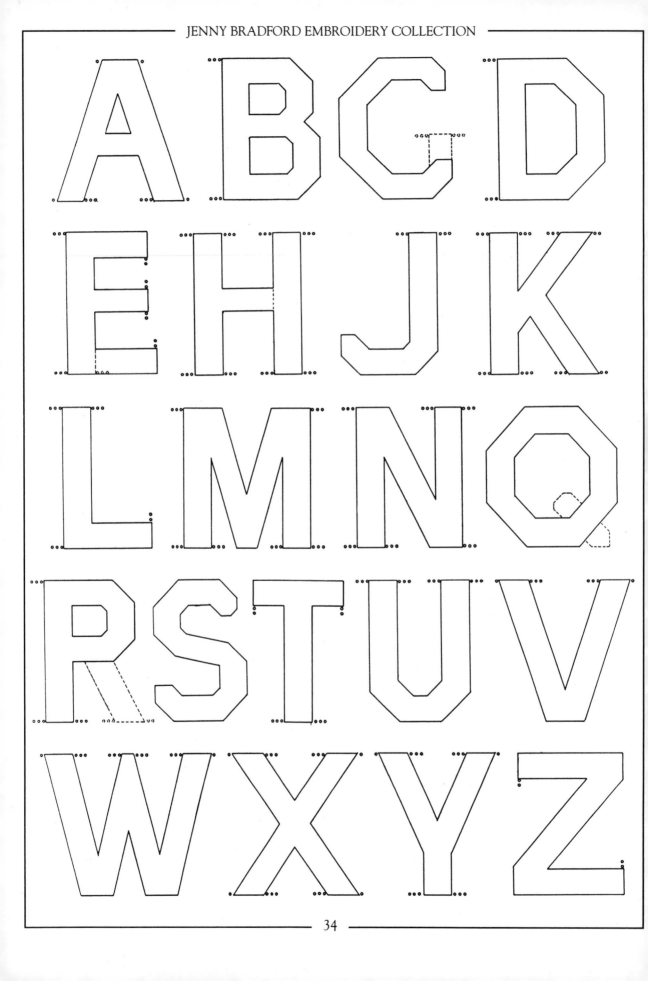

CHAPTER 8

CONSTRUCTING SILK RIBBON FLOWERS

FOLDED ROSES

Folded roses are very popular as they can be used in many forms of decoration. Worked in silk ribbon, they are very soft and delicate and, because of the fineness of the ribbon, a lovely shaded effect can be achieved by sewing together two ribbons of different colours. 7 mm ribbon is used for the posy brooch, but it is possible to make folded roses from 2 and 4 mm ribbon. The narrower ribbons are ideal for miniature work, but, being so tiny, they do need very nimble fingers.

There are many other types of ribbon that are also suitable, so once the technique is mastered the possibilities are endless.

I prefer to stitch the ribbon at the base of the flower as I work. It is also possible to use glue to stabilise the petals. The same techniques can be used to make the flowers on wired stems. Stick or sew the first fold of the ribbon over a wire stem, after bending the end of the wire over, and proceed as described below.

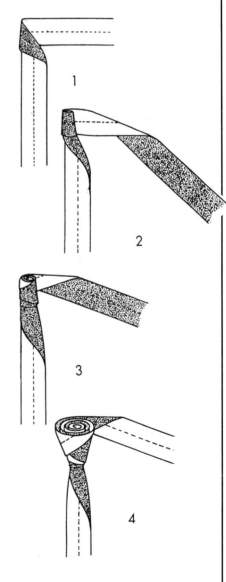

- Take two pieces of 7 mm silk ribbon in complementary shades and place one directly on top of the other. Using machine embroidery thread in a matching colour, sew down the centre of the strip by machine.

- Holding a short length, about 5 cm (2"), in the left hand, fold the ribbon at right angles (diag. 1).

- Roll the ribbon around this fold two or three times to make a tightly rolled centre. Stitch at the base of this roll (diag. 2).

- Fold the ribbon again by turning the ribbon back and down. (diag. 2.)

- Continue rolling, *lifting* the fold up to the top of the roll as it is wrapped around the rolled centre (diag. 3). Stitch in place at the base.

- Continue folding, rolling, *lifting* and sewing until the rose is large enough.

- Finish by sewing the end of the ribbon at the base of the flower (diag. 4).

- The ends can be trimmed if the roses are to be glued into place, or they can be used to sew the roses into place as described for the brooch project (page 195).

CARNATIONS

These pretty flowers are easy to make and can be used in two ways but washing and ironing are not to be recommended.

They are made before being applied to the fabric and can either be sewn on to the base fabric or attached where required with fabric glue.

- To make each flower, take two 10 cm (4") lengths of two shades of 7 mm ribbon.

- Lay the two ribbons together with the darker shade on top and allowing 1 mm of the lighter ribbon to show along the bottom edge.

- Using a matching thread, run a gathering thread along the bottom edge of the darker ribbon through both thicknesses (see diagram).

- Pull up the gathers and tie securely into a tight circle, taking care to leave the raw edges of the ends of the ribbon at the back of the flower behind the darker ribbon.

- Re-thread the needle with one end of the thread and bring the needle up through the centre of the flower and sew on tiny beads for the flower centre if required.

- If sewing the flowers onto the background, leave the ends of the gathering threads attached for this purpose.

- If the flowers are to be glued in place, knot the threads again after attaching the beads and trim the ends.

- If desired seal the raw edges of the ribbon with a light application of fabric glue to prevent fraying.

WIRED FLOWERS AND LEAVES

The flowers pictured on the wedding hat and the corsage or hair decoration (page C3) are made with a wired edge so that they can be shaped and moulded as desired.

MATERIALS REQUIRED

Suitable fabric — silk organza, georgette or any very lightweight silk or polyester fabric
Fine cotton-covered wire and stamens — both obtainable from most craft and cake decorating suppliers
2 or 4 mm silk ribbon to match the fabric
Computer paper or similar for patterns
Matching machine embroidery thread
Presser foot with a groove or hole designed to guide a cording thread
Florist stem-binding tape

METHOD

To make leaves and petals:

- Using a marking pen that will show through the fabric, trace the required number of petals and leaves from the patterns onto the paper allowing at least 1 cm ($\frac{1}{2}$") clearance between each one.

- Set up the machine with matching machine embroidery thread and the appropriate presser foot and a close narrow zigzag stitch.

- Place the fabric on top of the paper pattern, thread the thin wire through the hole or groove in the presser foot and, commencing at the base of each petal, work over the wire and stitch through fabric and paper around the outline of each petal.

- Cut out each petal leaving a 3 mm ($\frac{1}{8}$") turning.

- Tear paper away carefully.

- Using silk ribbon cover the edges of each petal with overlapping whip stitches.

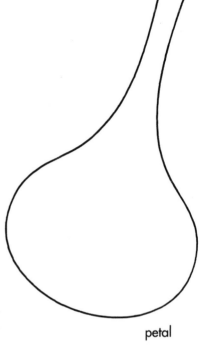

petal

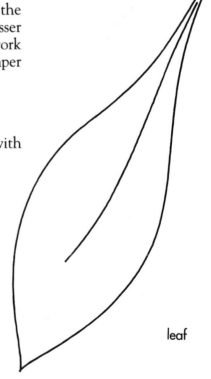

leaf

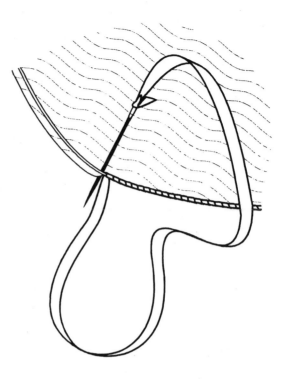

To construct a flower:
- Fold a small bundle of stamens in half and bind firmly with fine wire.
- Arrange four petals around the centre and bind together with the thin wire.
- Neaten the stem by binding firmly with stem tape, stretching the tape as you roll the stem.

The flowers and leaves may be sewn onto a hat or hairpiece as desired.

For a corsage, arrange the flowers with leaves and bind together firmly with tape.

CHAPTER 9

SILK RIBBON DESIGNS

Details for the projects mentioned in this section are to be found in the 'Projects' chapter starting on page 143.

DECORATIVE BEADED PANEL

This design is featured on the bag pictured in colour on page C2. It is suitable for bags, boxes, cushions and clothing.

MATERIALS REQUIRED

Fabric panel backed with batting if possible
4 mm silk ribbon Nos 91 and 93 pink (2 shades), and 60 green
Small beads in pink (2 shades) and green

METHOD

- Prepare the fabric panel as described on page 9.
- Trace the pattern on the following page onto thin paper. Centre the design carefully on the fabric (see page 210).
- Outline the design with whipped running stitch (see page 242) in chosen colours.
- Fill the inner petals with a mixture of shaded colonial knots and beads.
- Outline the centre petals and fill with green beads and colonial knots.
- Fill the centre with beads and/or colonial knots.

Decorative Panel Design

BOX TOP AND CARD DESIGNS

Daisies and Buttercups _____

The daisies, shown on a 7 cm (2³/₄") diameter box (page C2), have been worked on pure silk and the buttercups, shown on a 4 cm (1¹/₂") box (page C2), have been worked on silk shantung. Both designs are exactly the same except for the size of the flowers. The daisies are worked in 2 mm cream (No 156) or off-white (No 1) with 4 mm green (No 20) for leaves. Daisy centres could be yellow, gold, tan or green. Buttercups are worked in 4 mm ribbon (No 15 or 120) with 2 mm green (No 20) for leaves. Centres are a deeper shade of gold thread for colonial knots.

Start with the centre flower then position six more flowers in a circle around the outer ring. Add green loop stitches between the flowers for leaves and feather stitch greenery around the outside circle if desired.

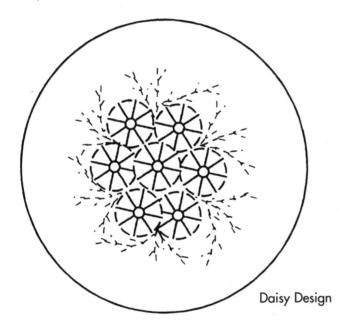

Daisy Design

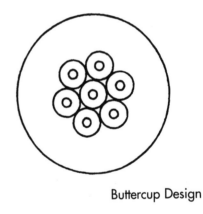

Buttercup Design

Poppies _____

The following design, featured as an insert on a wooden box top on page C2, is worked on silk fabric. It consists of poppies in 4 mm ribbon (No 2 or 28), three petal flowers in 2 mm blue (No 125) for outer petals and gold (No 15) for inside petals, and pussy willow with stems in 4 mm brown (No 66) whipped running stitch and buds in 2 mm cream (No 156) single rosette stitch. Green leaves in 4 mm (No 20) and green feather stitch are used to fill in around the main design.

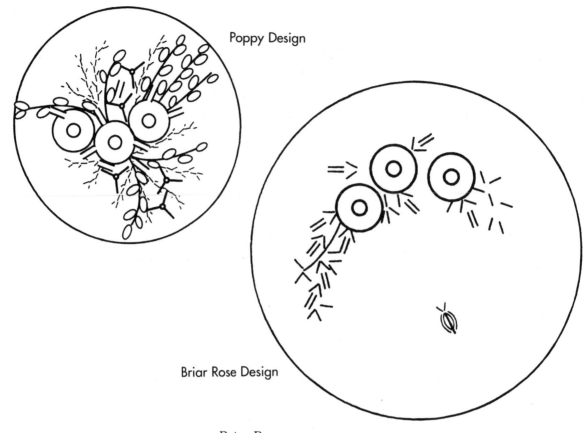

Poppy Design

Briar Rose Design

Briar Roses

The above design is featured on top of the metal music box by Framecraft, on page C2. It has been worked on fine deep green silk overlaid with olive green silk organza. The design consists of briar roses worked in 7 mm ribbon in pinks (Nos 5, 8 and 111) and straight stitch buds and leaves in 4 mm ribbon. The tiny beetle is worked in whipped stitch using 4 mm ribbon.

Lace Flower Bouquet

The following design is shown on a card on page C4. The card is worked on cotton batiste, and a fine 1 cm (³/₈") wide lace is used to form the flowers.

- For each flower gather about 6 cm (2¹/₂") of lace into a tight circle and sew in position.
- Work three petal flowers (page 22) over the lace using 4 mm ribbon.
- Add stems and feather stitch greenery to the background. For an added sparkle overlay the green feather stitching with fine gold feather stitches.
- Add baby's breath using 2 mm ribbon and colonial or half colonial knots.

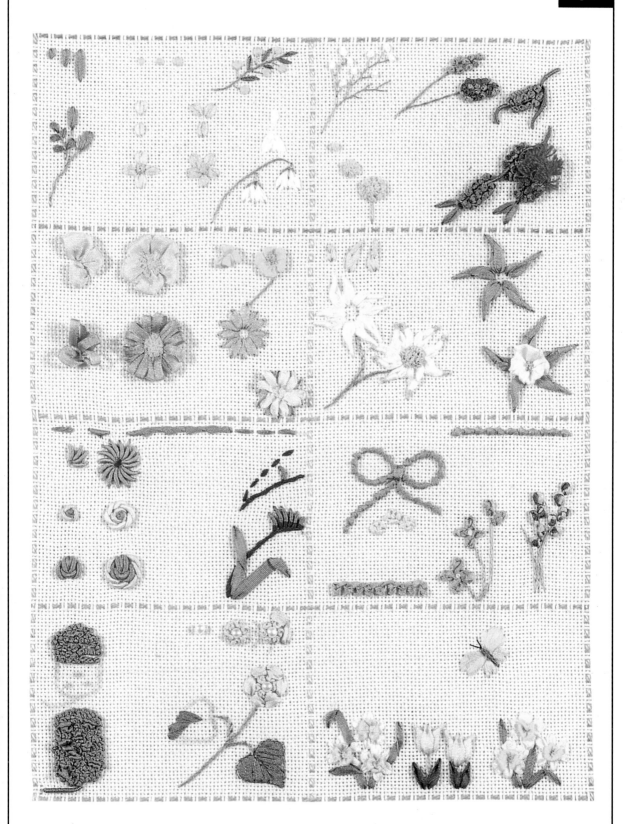

SILK RIBBON EMBROIDERY SAMPLER

BAG WITH DECORATIVE BEADED PANEL

BOXES WITH DAISIES, POPPIES, BUTTERCUPS, BRIAR ROSES

GIFT CARD, HORSESHOE AND WEDDING HAT

LACE FLOWER BOUQUET CARD AND BABY'S COLLAR

FOLDED ROSE BROOCH, CARD AND MATCHING BROOCH,
INITIALLED HANDKERCHIEF

ALICE BAND, EARRINGS, GIFT CARD, WIRED FLOWERS
AND LEAVES

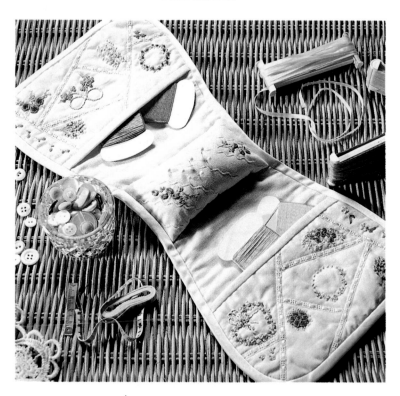

ARMCHAIR SEWING CADDY

BLACK VEST DECORATED WITH FLOWER SPRAYS

DETAIL OF HEART ON BACK OF VEST

DRESS WITH EMBROIDERED FLOWER SPRAYS ON COLLAR, BUCKLE AND SLEEVES

TEDDY BEAR, CHRISTENING GOWN AND MATINEE JACKET

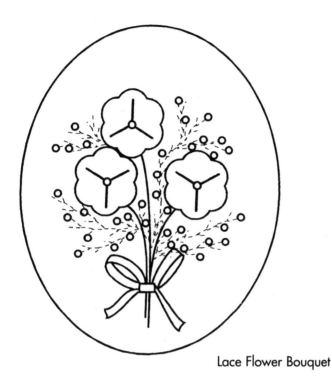

Lace Flower Bouquet

ROLLED ROSES

Shaded rolled roses are featured on the wedding card and on the horseshoe on page C3. These designs are also suitable for a prayer book cover or a photograph album. Both are worked on silk dupion, and both include four petal flowers and pearls as well as rolled roses.

MATERIALS REQUIRED
Stranded embroidery thread — green
Gold thread (optional)
4 mm silk ribbon in two or three shaded colours
Pearls

METHOD
- Work feather stitching using one or two strands of green thread.
- Work a second layer of feather stitching in gold if desired.
- Work roses in 4 mm ribbon.
- Add rose buds and tiny flowers in 4 mm ribbon.
- Scatter pearls through the design.

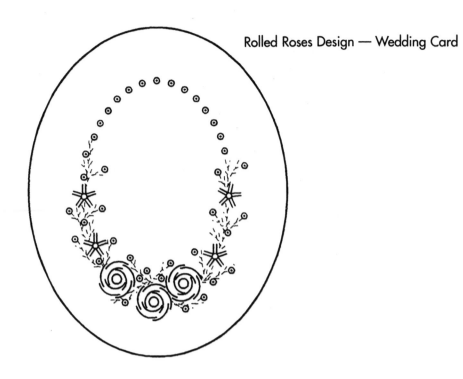

Rolled Roses Design — Wedding Card

Rolled Roses Design — Horseshoe

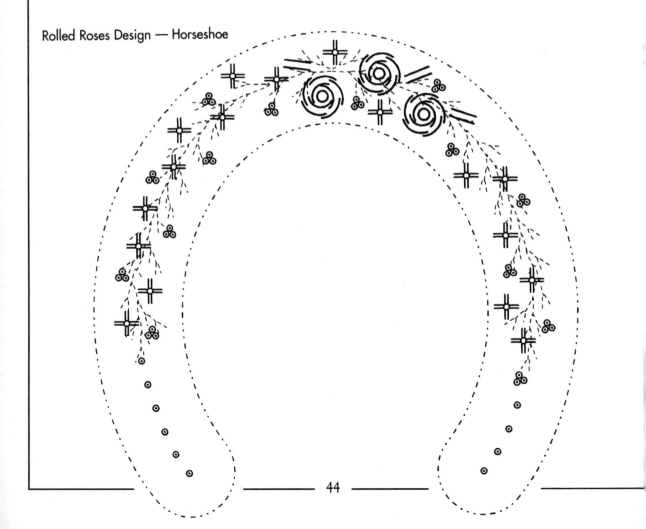

EMBROIDERY DESIGN FOR CARD AND BROOCH

This design has been used to create a matching card and brooch (see page C4), which can be displayed together. The charts for the butterflies are shown on page 31. The design is worked on hardanger 22 evenweave fabric and mounted into a purchased card mount. A piece of wadding, cut to the exact size of the window shape, is inserted between the fabric and the backing sheet of the card to allow the brooch to be pinned to the card easily.

More detailed instructions on making and mounting cards can be found on pages 189 to 190.

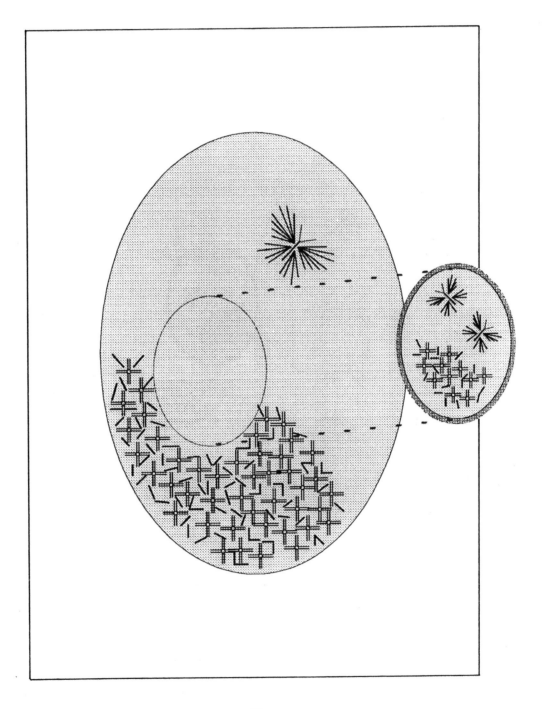

ALICE BAND DESIGN

This is featured in colour on page C5. Refer to page 197 for preparation and construction of Alice band. The design shown can be used as a guide, and was designed for a hairband 38 cm (15") long and 3.5 cm (1³⁄₈") wide in the centre. (Hairbands vary considerably in length and width.) Use a tracing of your pattern piece to draw out a suitable arrangement of flowers.

MATERIALS REQUIRED

Fabric
Purchased Alice band
Stranded cotton — green
7 mm silk ribbon in chosen colour
4 mm silk ribbon in green
Pearls

METHOD

- Embroider stems in stem stitch or couching, using two strands of green cotton.
- Using 7 mm ribbon, embroider looped straight stitch flowers based on the briar rose but stitch a single pearl for the centre of each flower.
- Add straight stitch rose buds in 7 mm ribbon and leaves in 4 mm ribbon.
- Finish with clusters of pearls at the tip of each curled stem.

Alice Band Design — half size

FLOWER SPRAYS

The small sprays illustrated below have been used to decorate various items photographed, such as the black vest, collar and cuffs, ready-made clothing and the embroidery caddies.

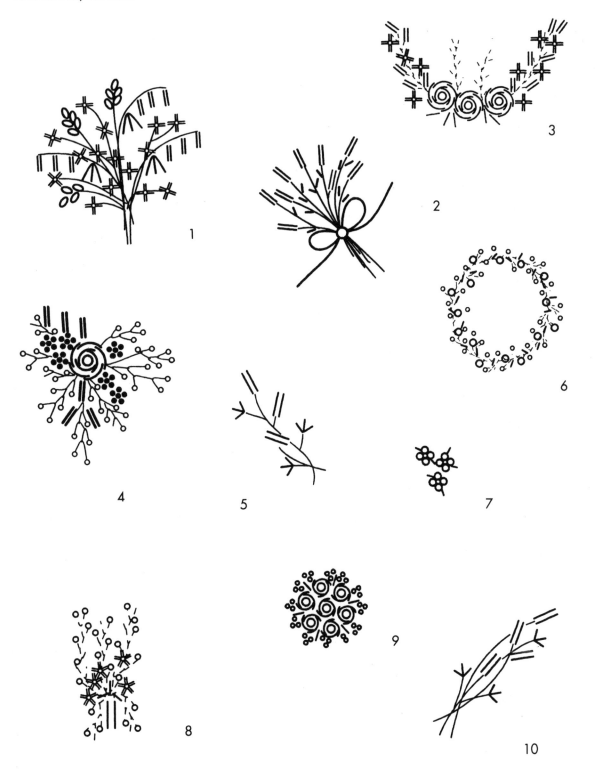

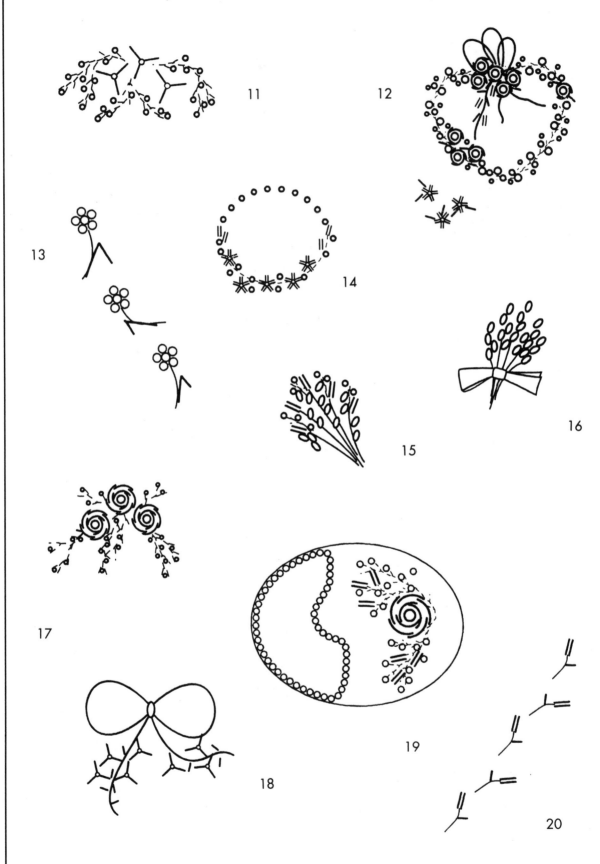

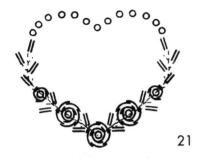

21

22

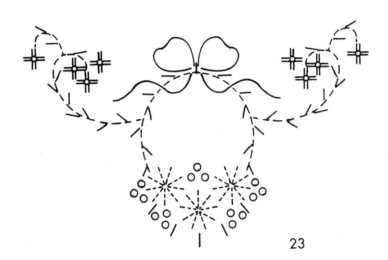

23

The above design can be seen in colour on the matinee jacket on page C8. The original is worked in:

2 mm silk ribbon

No 8 pink — daisies and bow
No 31 or 154 green — leaves
No 1 off-white — daisies and tiny four petal flowers
No 98 or 126 blue — forget-me-nots

DMC stranded cotton

green — stems
pink — stamens

- Couch the stems into place, laying two strands of thread with a single strand of matching thread.

- Work the bow using whipped running stitch.

- Work the tiny four petal flowers (page 12).

- Add whipped straight stitch daisies together with tiny clusters of blue colonial knots.

- Finish the embroidery by adding straight stitch leaves along the stems.

24

The above is a very simple design, shown on the hem of a christening gown on page C8, but equally suitable for use around the bottom of a lady's petticoat or across the yoke of a nightgown or blouse.

The design is worked in a lovely cream silk thread Kanagawa 380 No 97 and white silk ribbon No 1. The embroidery area is backed with a panel of white silk organza (see page 9).

The flowers are whipped stitch daisies (page 21) with a tiny pearl at the centre of each one. Feather stitching in cream thread completes the design.

25

Embroidery Caddy Flower Spray

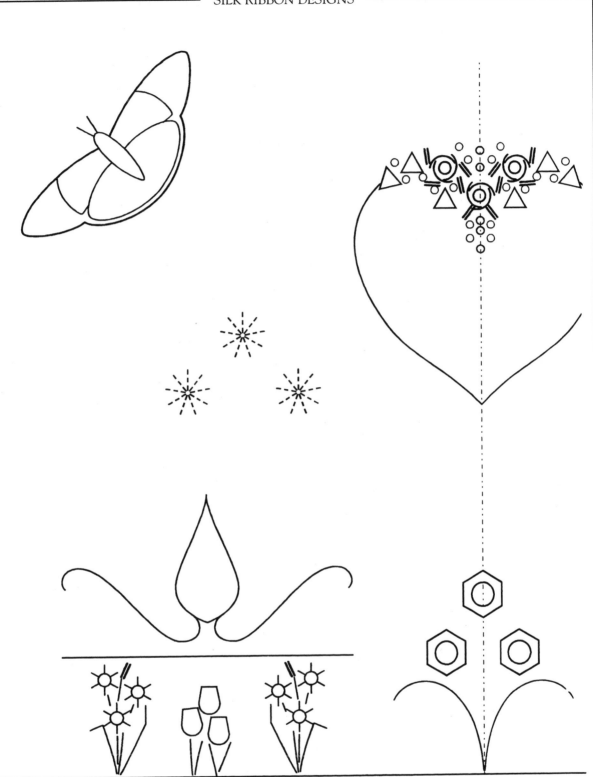

26   Embroidery Caddy Design

HEART

This heart could be used as decoration for clothing, cushion, quilt, basket lid, wedding album cover, picture and, no doubt, many other projects.

To work the heart, transfer the outline of the heart and the ribbons (page 53) to the fabric as detailed on page 210, backing the fabric with batting where necessary.

- Work the ribbons in whipped running stitch, working loops over the top of each other where they cross to give a more three-dimensional effect.
- Outline the heart with a single row of feather stitch.
- Add some side stems in feather stitch.
- Work rolled roses or chosen large flowers.
- Now fill in with smaller flowers. Working a few of each type in a scattered design will help to give a good overall random effect to the finished work.

Small flowers used in the heart are:
— Straight stitch rose buds and four or five petal flowers,
— Rosette chain lavender stems,
— Colonial knot baby's breath.

Heart Design

DESIGNS FOR KNITTED VESTS

The following two designs have been created specifically to decorate knitted vests, and can be seen on page C12 of the colour section.

Instructions for preparing the knitted vests for embroidery are given on page 188.

Abstract Floral Design

The flowers used in this design are of an abstract design and the size will depend largely on the size of the beads used for the centre of each flower.

The original design shown on page 55 is worked in 4 mm ribbon in the following colours:

No 58 grey
Nos 8 and 157 pink
No 154 green

Also used:

42 seed pearls 3 mm ($^1/_8$")
Silk organza as required

- Trace the design onto the prepared organza neckline facing and tack the facing in place.

- Transfer the main design lines to the front of the work by means of tacking thread, and working with small stitches from the reverse side.

- Work the curved lines using Portuguese stem stitch.

- Complete the remainder of the design with fantasy flowers (page 16), straight stitch leaves and the pearls.

- Slip stitch one edge of the facing to the neckline ribbing. The other edge should not need sewing down.

Abstract Floral Design for Knitted Vest

Flannel Flower Design

The original design is shown in colour on page C12, and is worked in:

4 mm silk ribbon
    No 156 cream
    No 15 yellow

2 mm silk ribbon
    No 31 green

DMC stranded cotton — green (for stems)

- Cut facing 7 cm (2³/₄") wide and tack in place.
- Using two strands of cotton, start at the shoulder line and work feather stitch stems at random down to the base of the V. Repeat for the other side of the neckline.
- Embroider flannel flowers (page 17) at random over the stems.
- Work wattle (page 13) along the feather stitch stems.
- Slip stitch the facing to the ribbing at the neckline.

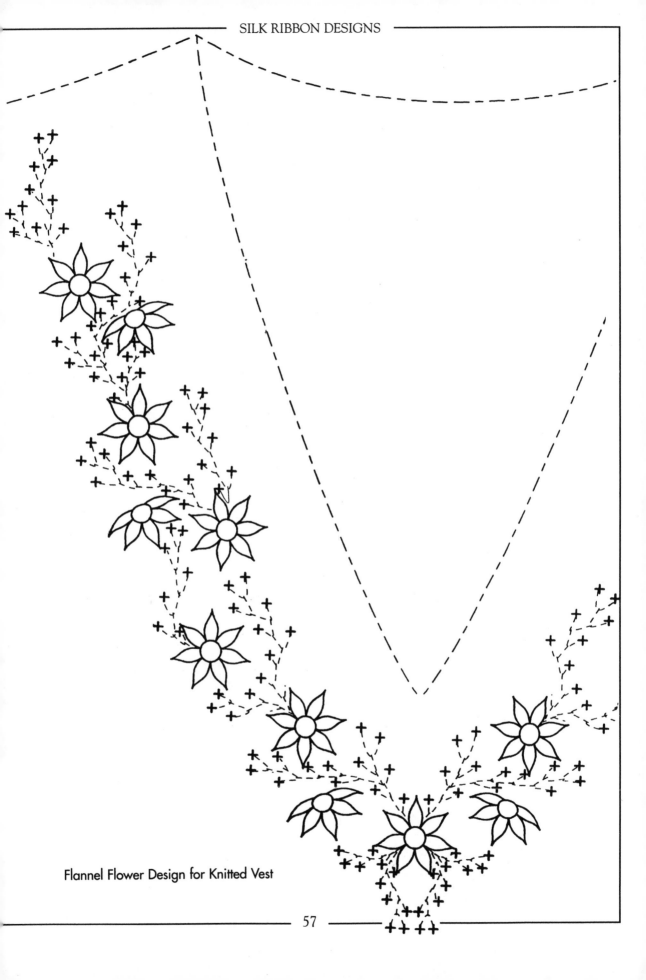

Flannel Flower Design for Knitted Vest

CUSHION PANEL

This cushion would make a pretty wedding ring pillow. The heart design can be worked in many different ways; a single heart on a tiny pillow stuffed with pot pourri makes a pretty sachet. The three corner hearts can be used on a collar or yoke or on the front of a purse or lingerie bag.

The hearts are outlined in whipped running stitch. The flower sprays are worked as charted on the pattern.

AUSTRALIAN THEME CRAZY PATCHWORK DESIGN

Silk ribbon embroidery is particularly suitable for the embellishment of crazy patchwork and, with the exception of the spider's web, all the decorative stitching on the following design is ribbon embroidery. It can be seen in colour on a bag on page C13. The same treatment could be applied to a cushion or a jacket.

References to the decorations used in the design are:

1. Kangaroo paw — page 24
2. Bottlebrush   — page 15
3. Gum tree   — page 25
4. Banksia nut   — page 20
5. Initial   — page 33
6. Whipped running stitch — used to apply guipure lace edging.
7. Straight stitch — used to overstitch and further embellish lace edging.
8. Palestrina stitch embellished with beads.
9. Single wrapped straight stitch.
10. Opal cluster — coloured diamantes interspersed with ruched ribbon (page 32) and colonial knots.
11. Earrings, stick pins, lapel tacks, charms, tiny pendants and other 'do-dads'.

Crazy Patchwork layout — shown half size

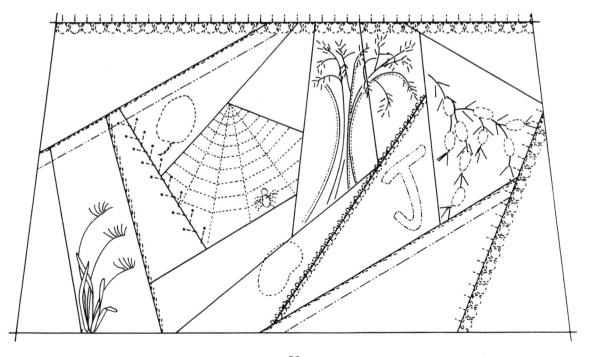

CLOCK DESIGN

This design, featured on page C14, is Australian based, depicting four of our beautiful butterflies together with billy buttons and paper daisies. It would also be very effective as a cushion panel, a framed picture or a padded box top. The background fabric is noil silk with a backing of Pellon fleece.

See page 170 for instructions on how to make up the clock.

- Mark the main design lines from each floral spray onto the prepared fabric as detailed on page 210.

- Work the embroidery, following the details given for the flowers (Chapter 4) and butterflies (Chapter 5).

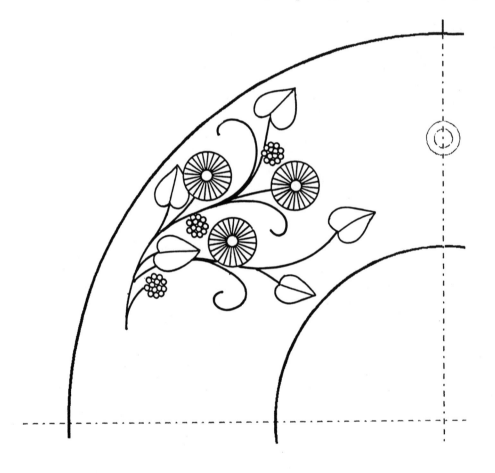

Chapter 10

TEXTURED EMBROIDERY MATERIALS

Threads

The choice of threads available for textured embroidery is ever increasing as the overall range of embroidery threads on the market steadily grows.

Many people tend to use the threads they are most familiar with and have readily available, usually stranded cottons. Unfortunately, these are not always the most suitable choice for the types of stitches used in textured embroidery.

For example, I find the easiest way to work bullion stitch is with a single strand of firmly twisted thread. The single strand must be heavy enough to produce the desired texture and, preferably, be smooth and silky in order to slide with the least resistance. The use of a single strand thread eliminates the possibility of any unevenness in the bullion wrap due to an uneven combination of several strands of thread. The choice of a smooth silky thread results in reduced resistance, making it easier to pull the needle through the wraps and tighten the stitch more smoothly.

Taking these factors into consideration, it will be obvious that the choice of thread will play a very important part not only in the look of the embroidery but also in the ease and speed with which one can work. A low resistance smooth silk thread is far less likely to result in aching fingers than a high resistance thread such as a low sheen cotton.

Conversely, when working other embroidery stitches, the slippery threads are harder to handle and it is much easier to maintain an even tension when using low sheen, high resistance threads. With this in mind I strongly recommend varying the type of threads used on any one project to give the best results.

The roses shown in section 1A on the textured embroidery sampler (page C20) are an excellent example of the variety that can be achieved by varying the choice of threads. Coton Perle No 8 has been used for the flower on the top line, the three roses on the second row are worked in wool (single strand of Paternayan), DMC Flower thread and Isafil machine embroidery thread respectively.

Note that wool threads and stranded cotton have a dull finish compared with the Coton Perle, silk or rayon threads. Further variation in size from that shown in the sampler can be achieved by the thickness of the wool chosen and the number of strands used when working with stranded cotton.

The following list of threads is intended as a guide for the beginner but all the stitches chosen for the flowers depicted will work well with almost any of the enormous variety of threads now available on the market. It is important to use threads that you enjoy working with and also to remember that varying the threads used in a design can add interest, texture and contrast.

SILK THREADS

There are many silk threads currently available that can be used for the embroidery in this book. Silk threads have a high sheen and will add a luxurious touch to your work. Some are easier to use than others and the laundering requirements of the finished article should be taken into consideration when choosing to use silk. Always remember that you should wash the article according to the most delicate threads used. For example, silk embroidery of any kind worked on a towel will require the towel to be washed as if it were silk. Cotton threads would be a better choice for the embroidery.

Kanagawa Silk Threads _____

High sheen, low resistance thread.

These threads come in various thicknesses and are quite lovely to use (attractively packaged and sealed with cellophane against dust and damage). The No 16 silk thread (Buttonhole Twist) is, in my opinion, the easiest thread of all to use for bullion stitch. The colour range is not as large as for some of the other threads listed, but I have found it quite adequate for the projects illustrated in this book. All of the Kanagawa range consist of very firmly twisted high sheen threads which I find less prone to catching and snagging than some other silk threads.

- No 16 silk thread — Buttonhole Twist (referred to throughout as Kanagawa 1000) Available in over 200 colours conveniently packaged in 20 metre lengths on neat easily stored cards. One strand is equivalent to approximately three strands of stranded cotton.

- No 30 thread — Silk Stitch Available in 80 colours and packaged on 50 metre reels, it can also be used for machine embroidery.

- No 50 thread This thread is very fine. Mainly intended for machine embroidery, it comes on reels, 100 metres per reel. It is useful for embroidering the centres of flowers. One strand is equivalent to approximately one strand of stranded cotton.

Other Quality Silk Threads _____

Also available at the 'Au Vere a Soie' range. All threads are attractively packaged in tiny plastic bags for protection against dust and damage.

- Soie D'Algere Stranded silk, medium sheen, medium resistance, sold in 2 gram hanks. This seven strand thread is available in a wide range of beautiful colours. A single strand is slightly thicker than a strand of stranded cotton and is strong enough to be used individually for very fine work.

- Soie Gobelins Sold on 50 metre reels, this is a high sheen, twisted single strand thread, easy to use and good for fine work. The available colour range may be limited. Similar to Kanagawa Silk Stitch.

- Soie Perle Also sold on 50 metre reels, this is a heavier thread, similar to Kanagawa No 16 Buttonhole Twist.

Over-dyed Silk Thread _____

Mary Hart-Davies (Kacoonda) has a range of hand-dyed silk threads available in various thicknesses.

Another beautiful range of over-dyed stranded silk is available under the brand name of 'Waterlilies' from the Caron collection.

COTTON THREADS

Stranded Cotton

There are several different brands available in this most commonly used embroidery thread. I personally prefer DMC as it is readily available in a superb range of colours and is of excellent quality.

Reference is made throughout the book to a range of stranded hand-dyed variegated threads marketed under the name of Minnamurra Threads. Hand-dyed in Australia, they are a small range of beautifully coloured threads using DMC stranded cotton for the base. There are many other over-dyed and variegated stranded threads now available from specialty embroidery shops, most of them coming from the USA.

Always remember when using the stranded threads to strip the thread before threading the needle. Separate each individual thread by pulling up in the line of threads as shown in the diagram. Smooth them back together and then thread in the needle.

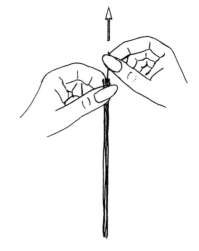

Stripping stranded thread

Pearl Cotton

Available in four different thicknesses, No 3 (thickest), No 5, No 8 and No 12, this is a shiny cotton thread that does not feature as much as I feel it should in embroidery in general. The main brand available is the DMC Coton Perle, with an excellent colour range in plain and variegated thread. Minnamurra Threads have a similar colour range available in Coton Perle Nos 5 and 8 as in stranded cotton.

Over-dyed Coton Perle Nos 3, 5, 8 and 12, from the USA, is also available in some specialty shops.

Flower Thread

This is a lovely, smooth 2 ply fine cotton thread with a firm twist by DMC, available in a good range of colours, most of them numbered in line with the stranded cotton shades.

Crochet Cottons

Many produce very even bullion stitch. They are strong and hard wearing and can work well for single colour flowers on items such as towels.

Knitting Cotton

There are various weights and types available. Some are high sheen, firmly twisted and easy to use. They wash well and are excellent for work on towelling items where bulk is sometimes important.

WOOLS

The many wools suitable for textured embroidery are discussed in detail in the 'Wool Embroidery Materials' section on pages 108 to 109.

RAYON AND SYNTHETIC THREADS

Once again the choice is large. The main properties of these threads are that they are usually very springy, making them difficult to control, and have a very high sheen.

Marlitt (or Decora) _____

A four strand thread, difficult to handle when working with more than two strands.

Isafil and Madeira _____

Machine embroidery threads, excellent for miniatures and jewellery but very fine and slippery. Work in a hoop, use a very fine milliner's (straw) needle and maintain a tight tension to keep the thread under control and the tension even.

Ribbon Floss _____

Another very high sheen, heavy synthetic thread which may be used for this type of embroidery.

Brazilian Embroidery Threads _____

These threads are rayon and vary from fine silk-like thread, to heavy boucle and straw-like threads. They are very springy and come in fairly bright plain and variegated colours.

Note that Down Under Designs (of Sydney, Australia) is one source for all the over-dyed threads imported from the USA referred to in this chapter.

NEEDLES

Milliner's (straw) needles are the best needles to use for bullion and detached buttonhole stitch.

A milliner's needle has an extra long shaft and an eye consistent in width with the shaft. The long shaft accommodates the wraps of stitches more easily and the lack of enlargement at the eye of the needle means it can be pulled through the wraps smoothly. The only restriction on the use of a milliner's needle is the size of the eye, which can be difficult to thread with the heavier threads.

Large-eyed needles such as tapestry (blunt point) or chenille (sharp point) will be required when working with heavier wools and Coton Perle Nos 3 and 5.

See notes on individual stitches for the best needles to use for specific techniques.

FABRICS

Almost any fabric is suitable for textured embroidery. The main criterion to be considered is that the fabric chosen is substantial enough to support the weight and density of the embroidery. Careful consideration of the following factors make it easier to achieve a professional finish to your work.

- Consideration should be given to necessary laundering if working designs on clothing, etc.

- Ironing is not recommended for highly textured flowers such as roses, fuchsias and sweet peas. Make sure the base fabric will not require ironing.
- The weight and texture of the fabric chosen will govern the choice of threads to be used. A fine delicate fabric will need a fine thread. A heavy textured fabric, such as towelling or velvet, will require a much heavier thread in order to give the embroidery sufficient bulk to stand out. The daisy design shown on the robe featured in the colour pages is worked in knitting cotton and is bold enough to stand out well on the rough texture of the towelling. The same daisies are used on strips of cotton batiste in the baby quilt (page C19), worked in Kanagawa 1000 silk thread, and on silk dupion on the lid of the powder bowl (page C16), worked in Silk Stitch. Embroidered in these finer threads the daisies become more delicate in shape and form.

EMBROIDERY HOOPS

Much of this embroidery can be worked without the use of a hoop, however, certain stitches, for example colonial knots and long, couched bullion stitches, are easier to work if the fabric is held taut in a hoop.

If the hoop is to be hand-held, make sure you use the smallest practicable hoop. If it is necessary to use a large hoop, try to use one on a stand to leave both hands free to manipulate the needle.

FABRIC MARKING PENS

Water erasable and fadeable pens are very useful for marking the main features of a design on to the fabric. Remember to use the lightest touch possible to avoid marking the fabric too heavily. Restricting the design marks to the heaviest areas of embroidery will also ensure that these marks will be well hidden on the finished work. A double-ended water erasable pen is now available, with a fine tip at one end and a bold tip at the other.

Chalk pencils used for dressmaking are useful on dark fabrics. Make sure that they are well sharpened to give good results.

Transfer pencils are available and should be used accordingly to manufacturer's instructions.

See page 210 for instructions on how to transfer a design onto fabric.

CHAPTER 11

TEXTURED EMBROIDERY FLOWERS

Flowers detailed in this section are grouped according to the stitches used. Where more than one stitch is used, the flower is listed under the most prevalent stitch.

References are given to the bullion stitch sampler or the textured embroidery sampler whenever applicable. The thread colours quoted are those used to work the samplers.

Symbols used to depict the flowers in the design drawings are shown beside each flower name.

In the accompanying stitch placement diagrams, bold lines are used to indicate the stitch placement being described, whereas lighter lines and broken lines show previously completed steps.

BULLION STITCH

Stitch Glossary page 218.
All references to the sampler in this section are to the bullion embroidery sampler on page C15.

SMALL ROSE BUD

Illustrated in colour on the sampler: 3D.
Kanagawa 1000 Nos 93 and 94.

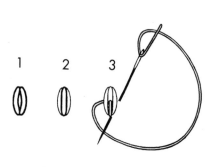

- Using the pale shade, work two bullion stitches, starting and finishing in the same holes (diag. 1). The original sample was worked with ten wraps over 5 mm ($^3/_{16}$'').

- Using the darker shade, work a third bullion *between* the first two stitches, wrapping eight times and starting and finishing in the same holes again (diag. 2).

- Finish the base of the bud with green thread, working a straight stitch coming up at the base of the bud and going down halfway up the centre bullion. Bring the needle back up on the left-hand side of the bud, down on the right and out at the base with the thread under the needle to form a 'V' stitch (see diag. 3).

LARGE ROSE BUD

Illustrated in colour on the sampler: 3 A-C.
Kanagawa 1000 Nos 91, 93, 94 and 114.

- Using the darkest shade, work a fan-shaped centre in satin stitch. Use three or four straight stitches all originating from the same base spot and spreading slightly at the top (diag. 1).

- Using the medium shade, work one 8-wrap bullion stitch on either side of the satin stitch (diag. 2).

2

- Using light thread, work two 10-wrap bullion stitches from the centre of the base around the outside of the previous two bullions (diag. 3).

3

- Using green thread, work one 8-wrap bullion up each side of the bud, starting at the centre of the base.
- Work two satin stitches from the base to halfway up the centre of the bud (diag. 4).

4

- Add a couched stem and leaves as desired (see page 224).

ROSES

There are many ways of working roses. Once you have mastered the basics of forming a well-shaped flower, your own individual variations will be more satisfying than copying someone else's ideas. Roses may be graded up or down in size by varying the choice of thread.

The good, rounded shape of the rose is easy to achieve, provided you overlap each petal sufficiently and pay careful attention to the stitch positions given in the diagram. However, the high-domed shape of a good rose may require a little more practice, but is not difficult provided you maintain a clear picture in your mind of the direction in which you are working (normally clockwise for right-handed people and anti-clockwise for left-handers) and you keep to it.

Study the diagrams carefully and follow the instructions step-by-step. Emphasis has been given to the points where students usually have difficulties.

You will require two or three shades in your chosen thread colour.

Bullion Rose 1 _____

Kanagawa 1000 Nos 91, 93 and 94.

- Using the darkest shade (Kanagawa 1000 No 91), work three straight bullion stitches side by side, using 8 wraps for each stitch (Nos 1 to 6 on diag. 1).

- Starting just outside this and using a shade lighter in thread, work one 10-wrap, slightly curved stitch from 7 to 8. Note this stitch goes from the lower right corner to the top left corner. Make sure it is the right length, as indicated in diag. 2; there is a tendency to underestimate the length required. To start the next stitch, bring the needle up halfway along and on the *inside* of the stitch just completed (No 9), take the needle down at 10, an equal distance past the end of

1

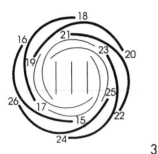

2

3

the first stitch. Continue overlapping the stitches in this way until the circle is completed with stitch 13-14 (see diag. 2).

- Start the second circle of stitches, using the lightest shade thread, by laying down one 10-wrap bullion *outside* the previous circle (Nos 15-16). Note this stitch is not overlapped by any stitch from the previous row. Continue working stitches according to the numbers on diag. 3, noting that the number of wraps used for each stitch is the same, but at least one extra stitch is used in each succeeding circle.

- *Always* come up on the *inside* of the petal just worked in that circle, and *always* work in the same direction — I teach right-handed people to work in a clockwise direction and left-handed students to go anti-clockwise. Working this way means that each time the needle passes under the back of the work it is passed across the centre of the flower, and this is an important factor which helps to lift the centre of the rose. Likewise bringing the needle up on the inside of the previous bullion helps to keep the stitches compact and tight.

- Note that the last but one stitch in each circle should almost meet the starting point of the first stitch of the same row in order to allow the correct overlap of the final stitch in the circle.

Bullion Rose 2 _____

Illustrated in colour on the sampler: 1 A-D.
Kanagawa 1000 Nos 91, 93 and 94.

This is a larger version of the previous rose and is worked in exactly the same way except that the centre three bullion stitches have been worked over with satin stitch, resulting in a slightly larger centre which is surrounded with six 8-wrap bullion stitches.

The second circle consists of eight 9-wrap stitches.

A third circle has been added to produce a larger rose consisting of ten 10-wrap stitches.

Bullion Rose 3 _____

Illustrated in colour on the sampler: 2 A-D.
Kanagawa 1000 Nos 91, 93 and 94.

This rose is a one-sided rose and illustrates how shape can be varied by altering stitch placement.

- With the deepest shade, work three 8-wrap bullion stitches side by side (diag. 1).

1

- Using the second shade, work three 8-wrap bullion stitches in a triangle around the centre three. Note that these stitches do not overlap each other in any way. The stitches meet end-to-end and must therefore be worked in the order shown in diag. 2.
- Using the palest thread, work four overlapping 8-wrap bullion stitches, commencing halfway along stitch 3-4 and working in a clockwise direction around the base and halfway up the other side (diag. 3).
- Work the final row using eight 8-wrap stitches, commencing close to the top of the rose just short of point 4 (diag. 4). Note that the direction in which this rose points is dictated by the angle at which the first three bullion stitches are worked.

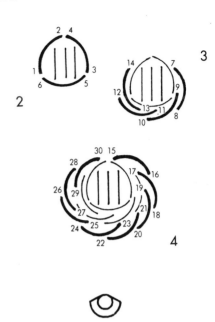

TULIP-SHAPED FLOWER

Illustrated in colour on the sampler: 4 A-C.
Kanagawa 1000 Nos 4 and 10.

- Using the darkest shade, work two 8-wrap bullions close together (diag. 1).
- Using the lighter colour, work an 8-wrap bullion on either side of the first two (diag. 2).
- Work a second 10-wrap bullion on either side of the last two, starting each one at the centre of the base of the flower and ending each level with the top of the other stitches (diag. 3). These stitches will lie on top of the bottom section of the stitches already worked.
- Work one more 10-wrap bullion on each side of the flower, starting each one at the centre point at the base of the flower (diag. 4). These stitches will lie under the bottom section of the previous two stitches, thus supporting the shape of the flower.
- Using green thread, work a 6-wrap bullion stitch around the base of the flower, followed by a second 8-wrap stitch directly over the top of the smaller green stitch and curving in around the base of the petals to give further support (diag. 5).
- Add a couched stem and leaves as desired (see page 224).

TINY PETAL FLOWERS

Illustrated in colour on the sampler: 4D.

These flowers can be worked as tiny roses or any other type of flower. The flowers on the sampler are worked in two shades of blue, with a yellow centre. For a rose use three shades of the same colour.

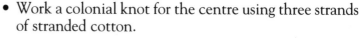

1

2

- Work a colonial knot for the centre using three strands of stranded cotton.
- Work three 6-wrap overlapping bullion stitches in a tight circle around the knot (diag. 1).
- Work three 8-wrap stitches around the outside. These stitches do not overlap each other but meet end-to-end around the circle and will shape the flower better if they are centred over the joins in the previous row (diag. 2).

DAISIES

Illustrated in colour on the sampler: 5A and 5B.

These flowers can be worked in any colour and, as only one shade is required, the choice of suitable threads is wider.

It is essential to have a focal point for the centre of the flower when working petals that radiate out from the centre, otherwise petals may be laid down off-line, producing a oddly shaped flower.

- Mark a tiny spot for the flower centre and imagine this as a clock face.
- Using Kanagawa 1000, work four 6-wrap straight bullion stitches at 12, 6, 3 and 9 o'clock, starting each one close to the centre dot (diag. 1).
- Position two more bullion stitches between each of the stitches already worked (diag. 2).
- Work a colonial knot in yellow for the centre and add a couched stem (see page 224) and bullion leaves as desired.

To make a larger daisy, start with a larger centre circle and work petals in a corresponding size in the same order, adding more than two petals in each quarter section if required. Work a cluster of colonial knots to fill the centre.

TINY HANGING FLOWERS

Illustrated in colour on the sampler: 5C.

These can be worked either in two shaded colours or one single colour.

- Work a single 8-wrap bullion stitch.
- Work 20-wrap looped bullion stitches around the single stitch as follows. Start and finish at the top of the stitch, picking up a very small amount of fabric on the needle. Wrap the needle 20 times and tighten the stitch, forming a loop. Use a single couching stitch

1 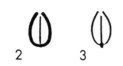 2 3

over the middle of the loop, to hold it in place around the straight bullion stitch.

- Using a single thread of green, work a fly stitch at the top of each flower and couch in a curved stem.

RAISED BULLION BUDS

Illustrated in colour on the sampler: 5D.

These buds may be worked hanging down like bells or straight up as buds.

- The bud or bell is based on three overlapping bullion loop stitches (see diagram for stitch positions). Work each loop with 20 to 25 wraps, tightening the stitch until the loop stands firmly on the fabric.
- Two small 6-wrap bullion stitches cover the base of the petal stitches.

CAMELLIA, PEONY OR OPEN ROSE

Illustrated in colour on the sampler: 6 A-C.
Kanagawa Silk Stitch No 140.

This flower is very effective and not difficult to work, provided a low resistance thread is used.

It is easy to make this flower larger by using heavier thread and/or more wraps and rows.

- Start the flower by marking the centre — approximately 2 mm ($^1/_{16}$") in diameter for the sample shown.
- Work six overlapping 20-wrap bullion loop stitches in a circle around the centre mark (diags 1 to 4).
- Start a second row outside the one already completed and work eight 25-wrap overlapping stitches to complete this circle (diag. 5).
- Add a third circle using 11 30-wrap loop stitches.
- Fill the centre with colonial knots worked in machine embroidery thread (see page 222).

Note that each row starts under the loops of the previous row so that the bases of the loop stitches are hidden. Also the number of petal loops in each row is not critical to the look of the flower, provided the petals overlap sufficiently, and the number of wraps is increased with each row worked.

BLOSSOM

Illustrated in colour on the sampler: 6A and 5D.

Work as for the start of the camellia, working one row of looped bullion stitch only (diags 1 to 4). Work colonial knots in brown or yellow for the centres.

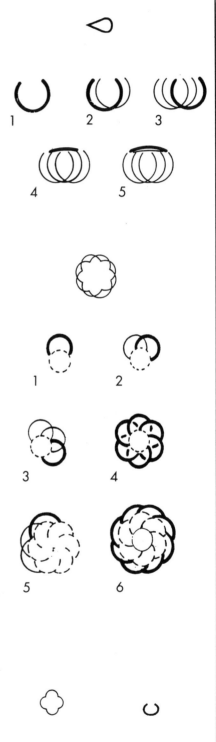

TINY FORGET-ME-NOTS

Illustrated in colour on the sampler: 6D.

These can be used to fill in around *larger* flowers or massed together to form delicate little sprays.

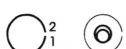

- For each flower, work a bullion loop stitch in Kanagawa Silk Stitch thread with 20 to 30 wraps, picking up just two threads of the fabric between points 1 and 2.
- Tighten the stitch firmly into a circle and pass the needle to the back of the work through point 1 instead of point 2.
- Use a single couching stitch directly opposite this point to anchor the bullion into a circle.
- Fill in the centre with a single colonial knot in yellow or cream.

LAVENDER

Soie Gobelins Nos 1813 green and 3333 mauve.

The stems are straight and upright and should be couched in first. Work the lavender heads using two strands, one green and one mauve, in the needle at once. Starting with a centre bullion stitch at the top of the stem, work six or eight more stitches, tightly packed and alternating down each side of the stem.

LEAVES

Illustrated in colour on the sampler: 2D, 3C, 4C, 5B and 6C.

Leaves may be worked in a variety of shapes and sizes, as will be seen from the samples in the photographs. Stitches can be laid side by side to form a solid leaf (2D) or shaped into a curve to form a hollow leaf shape (3C and 6C). Single stitches can be laid straight (5B) or extra wraps added and the bullion couched into a curve (4C).

BULLION STEMS AND BRANCHES

Work as many wraps as you can handle (I use 40 to 50 at a time), remembering that stems are never very smooth so some unevenness in the wrapping will not matter. This also applies to joins if you wish to work fewer wraps and join several stitches together. Make sure you overlap the start and finish of each stem so that there is no actual break in the line.

If you do use a large number of wraps, it will be necessary to slide the wraps off the needle as you fill its length.

BULLION STITCH AUSTRALIAN WILDFLOWERS

These flowers are clearly depicted on the clock face pictured on page C18. Reference positions are given for each flower.

It is easier to embroider flowers if you have a clear picture of the flower in your mind. You may find it helpful to refer to accurate pictures of the flowers as you follow the instructions. These may be found in gardening or pictorial books, cards, calendars, etc.

BLUE TINSEL LILY

Illustrated in colour on the clock face: 6 o'clock.

Stitches used:
Bullion stitch — flowers and leaves
Couching — stems

Threads:
Kanagawa 1000 No 117 — flowers
Kanagawa 1000 No 160 — leaves
Kanagawa Silk Stitch No 17 — flower centres
DMC stranded cotton No 840 — stems

- Mark a small dot for the centre of each flower.
- Work six 10-wrap bullion stitches, evenly spaced around the centre, working the first two at 6 and 12 o'clock. The other petals will be placed at 2, 4, 8 and 10 o'clock.
- Using Silk Stitch in yellow, work three 15-wrap, looped bullion stitches for the centre of each flower.
- Using three strands of DMC cotton for each stem, couch in place with a single strand.
- Work 8-wrap bullion stitches for leaves up the stems.

BLUE BELL

Illustrated in colour on the clock face: 10 o'clock.

Stitches used:
Bullion stitch — flowers and leaves
Couching — stems

Threads:
Kanagawa 1000 No 104 — flowers
Kanagawa 1000 No 160 — leaves
Kanagawa Silk Stitch white — flower centres

The blue bell has five petal flowers — see page 10 for hints on positioning petals.

- Mark a small centre spot for each flower.
- Work each petal as follows: one 8-wrap bullion for the centre. Work a second bullion using 12 wraps, starting the stitch at the same base point and finishing it just above the first stitch.
- Work a third bullion, using 16 wraps around the outside of these two stitches. Complete five petals for each flower.
- Work a white centre bullion in Silk Stitch, using 14 to 16 wraps, starting in the centre and finishing between two petals.
- Use a single thread of Kanagawa 1000 couched into a slight curve for each stem.
- Leaves are worked in the same Kanagawa 1000, using 15 to 20 wraps couched into curving shapes.
- Buds can be worked using a single petal formation of three bullion stitches.

PINK BORONIA

Illustrated in colour on the clock face: 8 o'clock.

Stitches used:
    Bullion stitch — flowers and leaves
    Colonial knot — centres of flowers

Threads:
    Kanagawa 1000 No 140 — flowers
    Kanagawa Silk Stitch No 161 — leaves
    Kanagawa Silk Stitch No 93 — flower outline
    DMC stranded cotton No 726 — flower centres
    DMC stranded cotton No 772 — flower centres

Pink boronia has only four petals, making it easy to position the petals at 12, 3, 6 and 9 o'clock.

- Start each petal as described for the blue bell, using 6, 9 and 12 wraps.
- Work a fourth bullion stitch, using 12 wraps, along the other side of the petal.
- Each petal is outlined with a fly stitch in darker pink, starting and finishing at the widest point of each petal.
- The flower centres consist of a colonial knot using two strands of pale green cotton, surrounded by tiny yellow half colonial knots using a single strand of thread.
- Leaves are each formed by three bullions in Silk Stitch, worked exactly as described for the first three bullions of the petals.

FLOWER SPRAY WITH BUTTERFLIES

EMBROIDERY CADDY WITH SAMPLER DESIGN COVER

HEART

ABSTRACT FLORAL DESIGN KNITTED VEST AND
JEWELLERY CADDY

FLANNEL FLOWER KNITTED VEST

NIGHTGOWN YOKE AND CUSHION WITH EMBROIDERED PANEL

AUSTRALIAN THEME CRAZY PATCHWORK BAG

CLOCK WITH BUTTERFLIES AND WILDFLOWERS

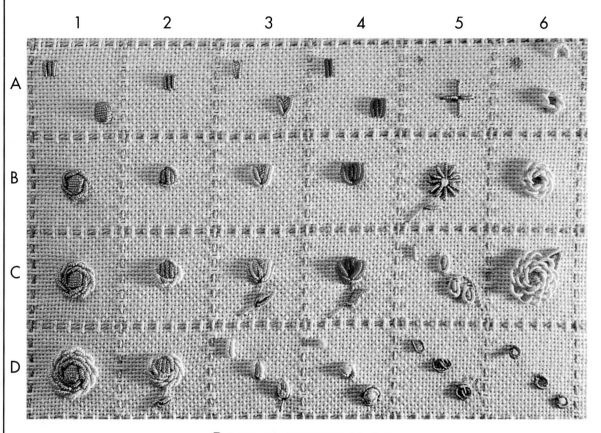

BULLION EMBROIDERY SAMPLER

FLORAL SPRAY IN BULLION STITCH

LAVENDER BROOCH, DAISY WREATH CRYSTAL POWDER BOWL AND OTHER GIFT IDEAS

KANGAROO PAW

Illustrated in colour on the clock face: 12 o'clock.

Stitches used:
    Bullion stitch — flowers, stems and leaves
    Back stitch — flowers

Threads:
    Kanagawa 1000 No 4 red
    Kanagawa 1000 and Silk Stitch No 161 green
    DMC stranded cotton No 817 red

- Using red Kanagawa 1000, work long stems, couching them into the curved shape as shown in the diagram. These stem sections may be joined and the joins hidden under the leaf stitches.

- Using green, work short 6-wrap bullions at the tip of the stem, graduating to 12- to 15-wrap bullions at the back of the flower head. Couch the longer stitches into a curve as necessary.

- Using three strands of stranded cotton, back stitch over the base of each green bullion stitch where it touches the stem of the flower.

- Work long spiky leaves in Silk Stitch, criss-crossing them over the red stems and couching them into curves.

STURT PEA

Illustrated in colour on the clock face: 9 o'clock.

Stitches used:
    Bullion stitch — flowers, stems and leaves
    Satin stitch — flowers

Threads:
    Kanagawa 1000 No 5 — flowers
    Kanagawa 1000 No 165 — leaves and stems
    DMC stranded cotton, black

To work a flower that has the appearance of curving round, rather than looking flat, the centre petals should be worked lower than the two outside sections. All petals are worked outwards from the centre.

- The centre top petal is symmetrical and is worked with a centre bullion of 6 wraps with a 10-wrap bullion on each side, both finishing at the same point just above the first stitch. One 14-wrap bullion on each side completes the petal. Couch the tops of the last two stitches to meet each other to form a slender point to the petal. (See diag. 1.)

1

- Side top petals, worked a little higher than the centre petal, consist of three bullion stitches of 6, 10, and 14 wraps, positioned in the same way as the blue bell petals (page 73), with the 14-wrap bullion next to the centre petal. A single strand of thread is couched down the outside edge of these petals to smooth the outline.

- Leave a small gap between the top and bottom petals and work the centre bottom petal next. Work one centre 10-wrap bullion with one 16-wrap stitch on either side. Couch the outer stitches to meet below the first bullion. Work two more short wing petals, from the outside towards the bottom of the first bullion, using 10 wraps. These stitches cross over the outside bullion stitches towards the centre of the petal (see diag. 3).

- The outside bottom petals are worked in the same way as the top outside petals, using 8, 12 and 16 wraps. Remember they should finish a little higher than the centre petal.

- Work small wing petals, using 10 wraps, from between the start of the second and third bullion to the tip of the first bullion and just outside the edge of the petal.

- Work horizontal satin stitches, using three strands of black cotton, to fill the gap between each petal. Satin stitch vertically over these stitches to form a raised centre between each set of petals.

- Work stems, in couched bullion, and leaves as shown in the pattern, using 8-wrap bullions.

GREVILLEA

Illustrated in colour on the clock face: 2 o'clock.

Stitches used:
Bullion stitch — flowers, leaves and stems
Pistil stitch — flowers

Threads:
Kanagawa 1000 No 169 — flowers
Kanagawa 1000 No 114 — leaves
Kanagawa 1000 No 54 — stems

- Work woody stems using brown in bullion stitch, joining where necessary and couching in place.

Each flower consists of six to eight bullions fanning out from a common base point, some couched firmly in place while others are left to stand away from the fabric.

- Using pink, work four to six 25- to 30-wrap bullions, couching them into a tight curve at the top. Add two to four extra bullions, allowing them to stand away from the fabric.

- Using the same thread, work a single pistil stitch from the top of each curved stitch that is firmly anchored to the fabric. Using very fine machine embroidery thread in yellow, work a colonial knot in the centre of the pistil stitch knot.

- Work short, spiky leaves along the length of the stem, using 8- to 10-wrap bullions and criss-crossing them over the stem.

GUM NUTS

Illustrated in colour on the clock face: 3 o'clock.

Stitches used:
Bullion and satin stitch

Threads:
Kanagawa 1000 No 52 for bullion stitch
DMC stranded cotton No 3021 for satin stitch

- Draw the shape of the nut lightly on the fabric.

- Fill in the top section with bullion stitches, along the length of the nut, of approximately 8 wraps each. A more symmetrical shape will result if the first bullion is worked down the centre of the area.

- Fill in the bottom shaded area with satin stitch.

- Work a 20- to 25-wrap bullion loop around the top of the nut and couch it carefully into place.

- Work a 8-wrap bullion stitch on either side of the satin stitch, couching in place as necessary.

GUM LEAVES

Illustrated in colour on the clock face: 3 o'clock.

Stitches used:
Bullion stitch

Threads:
Kanagawa 1000 No 114 for bullion stitch
DMC stranded cotton Nos 524 or 301 for couching

- Outline each leaf shape with long bullion stitches and couch into place.

HEATH

Illustrated in colour on the clock face: 5 o'clock.

Stitches used:
Bullion stitch — flowers and leaves
Satin stitch — flowers
Couching — stems

Threads:
Kanagawa 1000 No 7 — flowers
Kanagawa 1000 Nos 157 and 160 — leaves
Kanagawa Silk Stitch Nos 140 and 170 — flowers
DMC stranded cotton No 407 — stems

- Couch the stems in place.
- Work single 6-wrap bullions in pink at the top of each stem.
- Work single 8-wrap bullions in pink underneath.
- Work double 8-wrap bullions in pink below these, leaving room for leaves between each row of flowers.
- Each fully opened bell is worked as follows.
  - Work three 8-wrap bullions side by side (diag. 1).
  - Satin stitch a tiny circle in deep pink across the base of each set of three bullion stitches (diag. 2).
  - Using pale pink Silk Stitch, work five tiny 4-wrap bullions in a circle to outline the satin stitch (diag. 3).
  - Cluster the bells around the lower half of the stems.
- Add short, spiky leaves worked in between each row of flowers, using 8 to 10 wraps for each leaf. Use the lighter green at the top of the stem and the darker shade towards the bottom.

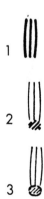

COLONIAL KNOTS

Stitch Glossary page 222.

BOTTLEBRUSH

Illustrated in colour on the clock face: 4 o'clock.

Stitches used:
    Bullion stitch — branches
    Colonial knot — nuts and flowers
    Straight stitch — leaves

Threads:
    Kanagawa 1000 No 54 brown — branches
    DMC stranded cotton:
    No 840 brown and 838 dark brown — nuts
    No 3347 green — flower clusters and leaves
    No 666 red — flowers

- Work the branches in bullion stitch, couching into place and joining where necessary (joins can be hidden under clusters of nuts).

- Using four strands of brown cotton and a size 3 or 4 milliner's needle, work colonial knots along the stem to form clusters of tiny nuts, allowing room towards the tip of the branches for the flower clusters and leaves.

- Using a single strand of dark brown and a size 8 or 9 milliner's needle, work a second colonial knot in the centre of each knot already worked.

- Using four strands of green and the large needle, work clusters of colonial knots towards the branches' tip.

- Using a single strand of red cotton double in the fine needle, work tiny tufts or loops in the centre of each knot to represent the flowers just breaking into bloom.

To work tufts, take the needle down through the centre of a knot, back stitch firmly in place, then bring the needle to the front of the work through the same knot and cut the thread. Leave the tufts longer than required, then trim when all have been completed.

To work loops, bring the needle up from the back of the work through the centre of a knot and return it to the back through the same knot, leaving a loop just visible in the centre of the knot. Back stitch firmly before repeating in the next knot.

Start with tufts at the base of the flowerhead, graduating to tiny loops toward the tip, depicting the gradual development of the flower head.

- Add straight stitch leaves, using four strands of cotton.

WATTLE

Illustrated in colour on the clock face: 1 o'clock.

Stitches used:
    Colonial knots — flowers
    Bullion lazy daisy — leaves
    Couching — stems

Threads: All stranded cotton
    DMC No 726 yellow — flowers
    DMC No 3053 green — leaves
    DMC No 840 brown — stems

- Work a network of single-strand couched stems, to give a main outline.

- Using two or three strands, work clusters of colonial knots down each stem for flowers.

- Work tiny bullion lazy daisy stitch leaves between the clusters of flowers.

PISTIL STITCH

Stitch Glossary page 235.

GUM BLOSSOM

Illustrated in colour on the clock face: 3 o'clock.

Gum blossom may be worked in any shade from creamy white to deep pink and bright red.

Stitches used:
    Pistil stitch — gum blossom
    Bullion stitch — branches

Threads:
    DMC stranded cotton Nos 712 and 726 cream — blossom
    Kanagawa 1000 No 54 — branches
    Machine embroidery thread — golden yellow.

- Work the branches using as many wraps for each stitch as you can handle. Joins in branches can be disguised by adding a side branch or leaf over the join.

- Mark the centre of each flower with a small circle.

- Using a single strand of cotton, work pistil stitch radiating in a circle from the outer edge of the marked centre.

To get an even distribution of stitches, work step-by-step as follows.

The flower is worked in three separate rows. The stitches in row 1 are equivalent in length to two-thirds of the distance from the outer edge of the centre of the flower to the extreme outside edge of the finished flower.

- First work four stitches to divide the circle into quarters then add three or four stitches in each section (diag. 1).

1

- For the second row, work a light scattering of longer stitches, taking them to the extreme outside edge (diag. 2).

- For the third row, work a light scattering of shorter stitches from the outer edge of the centre to finish short of the knots of the first row worked (diag. 3).

It is better to underestimate the number of stitches required in each row rather than overwork it. A few extra stitches can be added to complete the overall appearance but it is difficult to unpick if the first row is worked too heavily.

2

- To finish the flower, use fine machine embroidery thread and work a tiny half colonial knot over the end of the most of the pistil stitches. To work these stitches, bring the needle up just outside the knot of the pistil stitch and return it through the centre of the knot.

- Satin stitch the centre with fine green thread and work a long curved bullion stitch for the pistil.

3

BULLION LAZY DAISY STITCH

Stitch Glossary page 221.

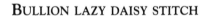

BANKSIA

Illustrated in colour on the clock face: 11 o'clock.

This is one of the more difficult flowers to work due to the shape of the cone and denseness of the stitching.

A hoop is recommended for working bullion lazy daisy.

Stitches used:
    Bullion lazy daisy, bullion and satin stitch

Threads:
    Kanagawa 1000 No 16 — cone
    Kanagawa 1000 No 52 — branch
    Kanagawa Silk Stitch No 19 — base of flower cone
    DMC stranded cotton No 502 — leaves

- Trace the outline of the cone given here and transfer to the fabric. Mark a vertical line down the centre of the cone to help line up the stitching symmetrically (diag. 1).

1

2

- Commence stitching at the centre top of the cone (point * on diag. 1) and work one bullion lazy daisy stitch. Keep the lower half of the stitch very small, picking up three or four threads only on the needle and using four wraps around the needle. Work one more stitch on each side of the first stitch.

Note that the bullion part of each stitch should be half the length of the whole stitch.

- Move down so that when the next row of stitches is completed, the bullion part of each stitch will fill the gap beside each lazy daisy section of the previous row.

Work two straight bullion lazy daisy stitches in the gaps between the first three stitches. Work two more stitches, one one each outer edge, sloping them in towards the top centre of the cone (diag. 2).

- Move down and work the stitches of each successive row between the stitches of the previous row. Overlap stitches as before, increasing each row and shaping the outside stitches in towards the centre line until the full width of the cone is established. Continue working straight rows, filling in the area.

- To finish the flower, cover the base of the cone with bullion stitch, using 20 to 30 wraps and allowing the stitches to vary in length and placement to give a slightly dishevelled appearance. Work a second row under the first row, overlapping the stitches on the first row and graduating down to the base of the flower.

- Stems are worked with long bullion stitch couched into place.

- Leaves are worked in satin stitch, using two strands of stranded silk or cotton. The outline of each leaf is back stitched with a single strand of the same thread. The centre vein is a single strand of thread, slightly paler than the leaf colour, couched in place.

WARATAH

Illustrated in colour on the clock face: 7 o'clock.

Stitches used:
   Bullion lazy daisy — cone
   Bullion stitch — base around cone and stems
   Satin stitch — leaves
Threads:
   Kanagawa 1000 No 4 — flowers
   Kanagawa 1000 No 52 — stem
   DMC stranded cotton No 367 for satin stitch

The cone of the waratah is worked in exactly the same way as the cone of the banksia (see page 81), varying only in the shape.

- Use the outline given to establish the shape of the cone and mark a line down the centre of the cone (this should help to keep the stitching symmetrical). Work according to the method given on page 81. Starting with five stitches in the first row, work one central vertical stitch and slope two on either side in towards it at the top. Fill the cone, increasing and decreasing as required. Note that all the outside stitches in the top half of the cone are sloped in towards the top centre of the cone to give a rounded appearance. You may find it easier to maintain a more symmetrical look to the cone if each row is worked from the centre outwards.

- The petals around the base of the cone are worked in the same way as the petals for the top half of the Sturt pea, shaping them with three or four bullions worked with 5, 10, 15 and 20 wraps.

- The stem, worked as a long bullion couched into place, and satin stitch leaves complete the design.

* The rest of the flowers in this chapter are depicted in the textured embroidery sampler on page C20.

DETACHED BUTTONHOLE STITCH

Stitch Glossary page 224.

The sampler depicting these flowers is reproduced to the original worked size, and gives a clear indication of the size variation that can be achieved using various threads. Coton Perle No 8 is a good thread to practise with for detached buttonhole stitch.

ROSES

Illustrated in colour on the sampler: 1A.

The step-by-step illustration is worked in two shades of Coton Perle No 8 using a milliner's needle.

- Work a 10-wrap detached buttonhole stitch picking up two or three threads of the fabric for the base stitch (diag. 1).

- Pull the base of the stitch close by stitching together with a tiny straight stitch before passing the needle to the back of the work between the anchor points (see page 225).

1   2   3

- Work four 12-wrap overlapping stitches around the centre stitch (diag. 2).
- Change to a paler shade of thread and work a circle of six 12-wrap overlapping stitches around the outer edge of the first circle (diag. 3).

The roses shown on the bottom row of 1A on the sampler are all worked with the same number of wraps on the needle, as detailed above. The variation in size results from the choice of thread and the size of needle.

Far left — 1 strand of Paternayan Persian wool
Centre — 1 strand of DMC Flower thread
Far right — single strand of Isafil machine embroidery thread.

HIBISCUS

Illustrated in colour on the sampler: 1B (top row).

- Draw a tiny circle as shown in diag. 1.
- Work five 15-wrap overlapping stitches around the edge of the circle (diags 2 to 5).
- Fill the centre with colonial knots worked with two strands of DMC stranded cotton in a contrasting colour (diag. 6).
- Add a small bead for the centre stamen. With a single strand of yellow thread in a fine needle, come up through the centre of the flower. Thread the bead onto the needle and back stitch through the bead, before returning the needle to the back of the work through the centre of the flower. Back stitch the thread carefully to finish off, taking care not to pull the loop too tightly.

1 2 3
4 5 6

BELL FLOWER SPRAY

Illustrated in colour on the sampler: 2B (lower right).

- Couch a stem into place.
- Work a single 15-wrap detached buttonhole stitch at the tip of the stem. Pull the edges together at the top to shape the petal.
- Work two 15-wrap overlapping stitches and stitch the edges together at the top to shape (diag. 1).
- Work four or five overlapping stitches of 15 wraps around a small circle. Fold over and stitch as for fuchsias (page 86).
- Work straight stitch in green across the top of the petals to join the flowers to the stem.

- The long straight leaf is worked with double-sided detached buttonhole stitch.

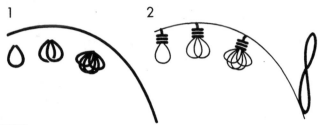

PANSY

Illustrated in colour on page C23.

Minnamurra Coton Perle No 8 in shade 10 is a perfect colour choice for these flowers. However, pansies can be worked in almost any colour, plain or shaded. A fine thread in black — Coton Perle No 12 — is required for the centre petals, while stranded cotton in cream and yellow is used for the centre line markings.

- Mark a small Y for the centre of the flower (these lines mark the centre line of petals 3, 4 and 5).

- Using Coton Perle No 8 and a size 4 needle, work the two top petals each with 25 wraps. The stitch base should be 5 mm (³/₁₆″). Position these petals as shown in diag. 2.

- Work side petals 3 and 4 using 20 wraps, picking up approximately 2.5 mm (¹/₈″) at the base of the stitch.

Note: The top marks should point directly up the centre line of each of these petals (diag. 3).

- Using black Coton Perle No 12 and a size 6 needle, work a 15-wrap stitch pulled into a circle to fill the centre petals 3 and 4 (diag. 4).

Work a tiny couching stitch at the centre point through the outer edge of the black stitch and the inner edge of the purple stitch, anchoring the petals together and to the background fabric.

- With Coton Perle No 8, work the fifth petal at the centre front with 28 wraps. Start the stitch level with the centre of the black filling stitches of the side petals (diag. 5). Using black, work an 18-wrap filling stitch in the centre of this petal, anchoring it to the outer petal and the fabric as before.

- Using a single strand of DMC (yellow for petal 5, cream for petals 3 and 4), work tiny straight stitches radiating from the centre into the black base of each of the three petals. Finish with a green colonial knot in the centre.

1

2

3

4

FUCHSIA AND LEAVES

Illustrated in colour on the sampler: 1B (bottom row).

- Work steps 1 and 2 as detailed for the hibiscus but with 25 wraps for each petal (diag. 1).
- Using a single strand of stranded cotton, work four or five pistil stitches hanging down from the centre (diag. 2).
- Fold the top petals down over the centre and stitch into a bell shape using matching thread, taking tiny stab stitches over the edges of the petals to shape the flower.
- With contrasting thread work a cluster of four or five straight stitches from the top of the bell towards the stem (diag. 3).
- Work three sepals in double-sided detached buttonhole stitch with 20 loops on the needle, from the top of the bell towards the stem (diag. 4).
- Using two strands of green thread, work a cluster of four straight stitches from the top of the pink cluster in the direction of the main stem (about half the length of the pink cluster). Complete by joining the flower to the main stem with a single straight stitch.
- Add buttonhole stitch leaves as follows:
  — Work two detached buttonhole stitches with 6 wraps on each side by side. Sew the tips of these stitches together at the outer end.
  — Work two more stitches of 10 wraps around the outside of the 6-wrap stitches. Sew the stitches together to form a point at the outer tip of the leaf.

DAISIES

Illustrated in colour on the sampler: 2A.

Minnamurra Perle No 8 (20) — large blue daisy
DMC Flower thread — cream daisy

- Mark a small circle for the centre, approximately 2 mm ($^1/_{16}$") in diameter (diag. 1).
- Stitches are about 7 mm (just over $^1/_4$") in length with 12 wraps.
- Work four stitches starting at the outer edge of the marked circle at 12, 3, 6 and 9 o'clock (diag. 2).

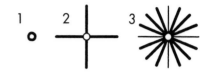

- Fill each gap with three stitches to complete the daisy (diag. 3).
- Fill the centre with colonial knots worked with one strand of Flower thread or two of stranded cotton.

To create a small daisy, use a finer thread and start with a smaller centre (a single dot). Work the marker stitches, about 5 mm ($^3/_{16}$") long and 10 wraps, and finish with a single colonial knot for the centre. The tiny daisy spray is worked with two strands of Minnamurra Threads stranded cotton.

- Work a spray of uneven feather stitching in a single strand of green.
- Picking up one or two threads for the base stitch, work 12 wraps on the needle and pull through firmly to form a circle. Pass the needle to the back of the work to close the circle.
- Work a tiny holding stitch across the edge of the stitch on the opposite side of the circle.
- Finish with a colonial knot in the centre of each flower worked in a single strand of stranded cotton.

SWEET PEAS

Illustrated in colour on the sampler: 2B.

Minnamurra stranded cotton (four strands) No 20, or Coton Perle

- Work two detached buttonhole stitches with 8 wraps for the centre. Stitch these two stitches together at both ends to make them stand up (diag. 1).
- Work a 24-wrap stitch around the first two stitches, taking care not to pull the stitch too tight (diag. 2).
- Work a stitch of 32 wraps around the edge of the previous stitches, adjusting the tension carefully so that the stitches just overlap.

- Stitch the last two stitches down on the fabric at the centre top of the flower (diag. 3).
- Shape the base of the flower by pulling the petals together towards the centre with a tiny holding stitch (as shown on page 226, diags 5, 6, and 7).

BUD

Illustrated in colour on the sampler: 2B (top row, far right).

- Work two stitches of 10 wraps side by side and stitch the tip of the bud together (diag. 1).
- Work three stitches of 6 wraps in green, one on either side of the bud and one in between the first two stitches (diag. 2).
- Stitch the outer green stitches together at the base of the bud to improve the shape.

DAHLIA

Illustrated in colour on the sampler: 3A.
Coton Perle No 8

These flowers work well in wool or thread. The stitch must be worked inwards from the outside and it is very important to judge the size of the circle to allow sufficient room for the required number of rows. Work in a hoop.

- Draw a circle approximately 8 mm ($^5/_{16}$'') in diameter (diag. 1).
- Work a row of knotted loop stitch around the outer edge of the circle (diag. 2).
- Work a second row just inside the first row, working the knots very close to the outer row and making the loops equal in size to those of the first row. The top of each loop will lie just inside the top of the loops on the previous row (diag. 3).
- Continue working in circles until the centre is filled. The rows must be packed closely to make a dense flower.

SMALL OR LARGE BLOSSOM

Illustrated in colour on the sampler: 3A (top right).
Coton Perle No 12

This is worked in the same way as the dahlia for the first two or three rows and the centre is then filled with colonial knots.

SINGLE PALESTRINA STITCH

Stitch Glossary page 234.

BUD SPRAYS

Illustrated in colour on the sampler: 4A.

- Couch stems into place.
- Scatter single palestrina stitches among the stems.
- Join the buds to the stems by working a fly stitch around the base of each knot in a single strand of green.
- Add leaves in bullion lazy daisy stitch.

LONG-LEGGED TWISTED CHAIN

Stitch Glossary page 240.

FANTASY FLOWERS

Illustrated in colour on the sampler: 4B.

Coton Perle No 8
Mohair wool (brushed to give a puff ball effect)

This flower is a little difficult to judge accurately at first but one or two practice runs should sort out any problems.

- Mark a small circle about 5 mm (³/₁₆") diameter and mark the centre of that circle (*not* shown actual size in diagram).
- Commence stitching about 5 mm outside the edge of the circle. Work a twisted chain stitch starting at A on the outer ring.
- Take the needle down at B and out again at C on the inner circle. Anchor the stitch by passing the needle to the back through the centre of the circles (diag. 2).
- Bring the needle up at D, down at A and out at E. Anchor this stitch in the centre (diag. 3).
- Repeat for F, D and G, then H, F and I etc.

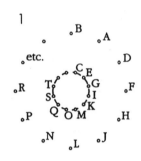

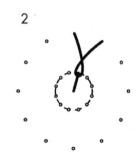

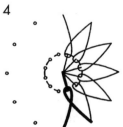

CHAPTER 12

TEXTURED EMBROIDERY DESIGNS

FLORAL SPRAY IN BULLION STITCH

This design, featured in colour on page C15, is also suitable for a cushion, a box top or for clothing.

- Prepare the fabric as directed on page 9.
- Photocopy or trace the main design lines from the pattern on page 91. Transfer to the prepared fabric as detailed on page 210.
- Work the main design lines in feather stitch, as shown in the diagram, using a single strand of Kanagawa 1000 No 114.
- Place a copy of the design over the stitching and pinpoint the centres of the five largest flowers and any others you think necessary. Once the large flowers are worked you may feel confident enough to build the design from that point, translating it in your own way. All flowers used in this design are worked from the instructions given in Chapter 11.

The following is a key to the design. The design is worked in Kanagawa 1000 and the colour numbers quoted are for that range of threads.

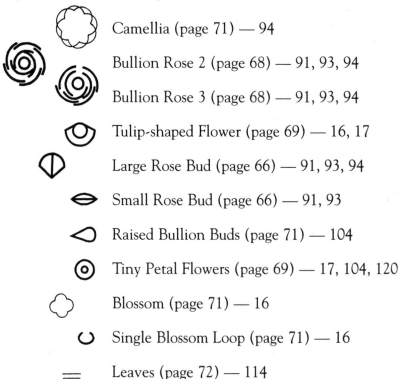

Camellia (page 71) — 94

Bullion Rose 2 (page 68) — 91, 93, 94

Bullion Rose 3 (page 68) — 91, 93, 94

Tulip-shaped Flower (page 69) — 16, 17

Large Rose Bud (page 66) — 91, 93, 94

Small Rose Bud (page 66) — 91, 93

Raised Bullion Buds (page 71) — 104

Tiny Petal Flowers (page 69) — 17, 104, 120

Blossom (page 71) — 16

Single Blossom Loop (page 71) — 16

Leaves (page 72) — 114

- Press embroidery face down on a towel when finished.

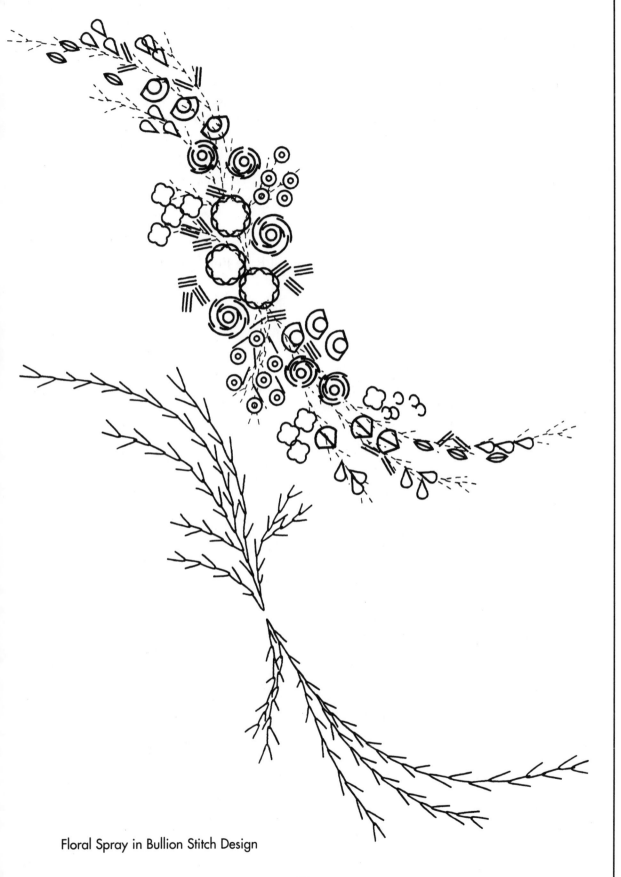

Floral Spray in Bullion Stitch Design

DAISY WREATH

This design, featured in colour on the crystal powder bowl on page C16, is suitable for box tops, pockets on bags, clothing and towels. It is made up of bullion daisies in Silk Stitch white and No 12 pink, the bullions are wrapped 8 times. Stems of lavender and small rose buds are worked with 10 and 9 wraps, using Silk Stitch Nos 170 and 140, tiny hanging flowers are worked in Silk Stitch white and No 17, and greenery in Silk Stitch No 161.

The following is a key to the design:

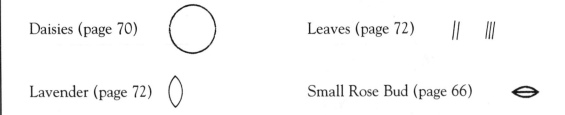

Daisies (page 70)

Leaves (page 72)

Lavender (page 72)

Small Rose Bud (page 66)

Tiny Hanging Flowers (page 70)

- Work a foundation of feather stitch around the design circle, then add some small side branches in feather stitch. Work the flowers, positioning the largest flowers around the circle first. Fill in with the smaller flowers to complete the design.

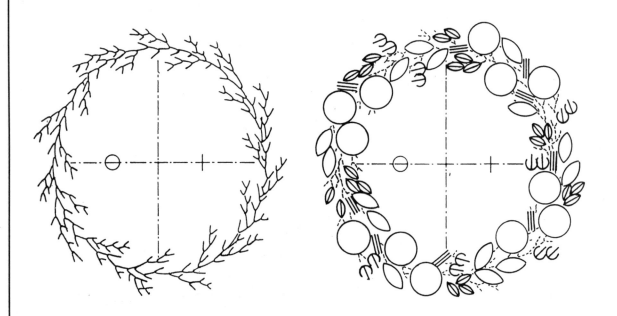

Daisy Wreath Design

TINY FLOWER SPRAYS

Lavender _____

The design for the lavender brooch, shown in colour on page C16, is given here.

- Couch the stems in place.
- Work lavender (see page 72).
- Make a tiny bow by couching looped bullion stitches in place.

Spot Decorations _____

The following flower sprays could be used to decorate the teddy bears pictured on pages C8 and C24 in the colour section. See page 162 for instructions on how to make a bear.

Lavender Design

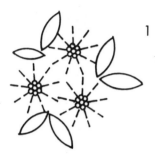

1

3

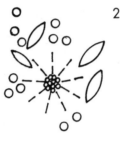

2

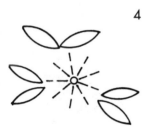

4

5

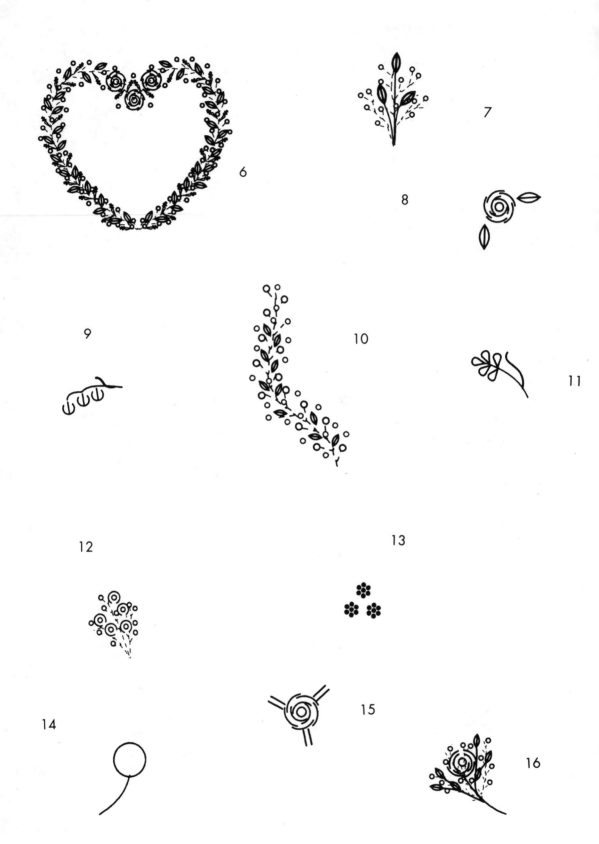

Pansy Spray

The pansy spray detailed can be used for a variety of projects such as a very special card, a needle case or on the pocket of a garment.

To work pansy spray:

- Position flowers and buds as shown. Couch stems in place using six strands of DMC for the stem and one strand for the couching.
- Work pansies as described on page 85.
- Lightly mark in leaf outlines. Work leaves in satin stitch using two strands of DMC, working from the tip to the base as shown in the diagrams.

To work buds:

- Work two stitches for each bud, positioning them as shown, using 14 wraps for the base and 12 wraps for the top stitch.
- Using a single strand of green DMC, work three 10-wrap or 12-wrap stitches at the base of the bud for the calyx.

To work butterfly

- Using Coton Perle No 8 or three strands of stranded cotton, work front wings with 20 wraps and back wings with 15 wraps.
- Work a bullion stitch across the middle in brown for the body.

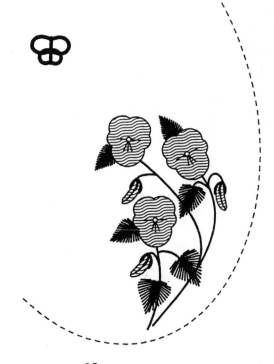

CHRISTMAS SPRAYS

These tiny sprays, shown in colour on page C17, can be used for decorations, cards or crackers as illustrated.

Candles

Bell

Poinsettia

Candles

- Using Kanagawa 1000 No 4 or 5, work three long bullion stitches (25 to 30 wraps) and couch into place.
- Finish with green leaves (page 72) and tiny gold beads at the base.
- Work three 10- to 15-wrap bullions in gold-coloured thread (Kanagawa 1000 No 79) for the flame.

Bell

- Draw the bell shape onto the fabric.
- Outline with long couched bullion stitches in Kanagawa 1000 No 79.
- Work a colonial knot for the clapper.
- Using red Kanagawa 1000 No 4 or 5, couch looped and straight bullion stitches in place to form a bow at the top of each bell.
- Add green leaves and gold beads as desired.

Poinsettia

- Draw a circle for the centre of the flower.
- Use couched bullion stitch in Kanagawa 1000 No 4 or 5 to form five petals around the centre.
- Work five more petals in the spaces between these petals.
- Fill the centre with colonial knots, working the centre knots with two strands of yellow thread and the outside ring with one strand each of yellow and green.
- Add green leaves and beads as desired.

SHORT CUTS FOR QUICK RESULTS

The design used on the front of the 'brag book' (page C17) illustrates how ribbon leaves and lace flowers can be used to supplement a few bullion flowers to achieve quick results.

The brag book was made from a cardboard template kit, and this type of design is suitable for many items based on these kits, including photo frames, box tops, book covers and greeting cards.

MATERIALS REQUIRED

Embroidery threads
Guipure lace flowers (sold by the metre)
Fine narrow lace
2 or 3 mm satin or silk ribbon

METHOD

- Work a grounding of feather stitch for the design.
- Make a large lace flower by gathering a strip of fine narrow lace into a circle. Position this flower in the bouquet, but do not sew at this stage (or the embroidery threads will catch around it as you work the bullion flowers).
- Mark the position for the remaining flowers, remove the lace flower and work the bullion stitch flowers.
- Make some ribbon leaves by cutting 1 cm (³/₈'') lengths of ribbon and folding as shown. Sew the leaves firmly across the base to the fabric, trimming the ends of the ribbon as required. Attach the leaves as you work so that the lace flowers cover the base of each leaf.
- Sew guipure lace flowers into position, working a colonial knot for the centre of each one. Guipure lace flowers can be coloured as required by painting with fabric paints.
- Replace the gathered lace flower and work a centre of colonial knots.
- Finish the design with a scattering of colonial knots in the background.
- Add a folded ribbon bow held in place with two bullion stitches.
- A tiny heart charm hangs from the bow on the original design.

Brag Book Design

Folded ribbon bow

AUSTRALIAN WILDFLOWER DESIGNS FOR CLOCK FACE

More details on how to make the clock pictured in the colour section are given on page 170. The embroidery is worked sampler-style to display each of the Australian wild flowers. The background fabric is a raw silk known as noil silk and is available as a dress fabric. The actual size of each spray of flowers is given here, each one being worked as detailed in Chapter 11.

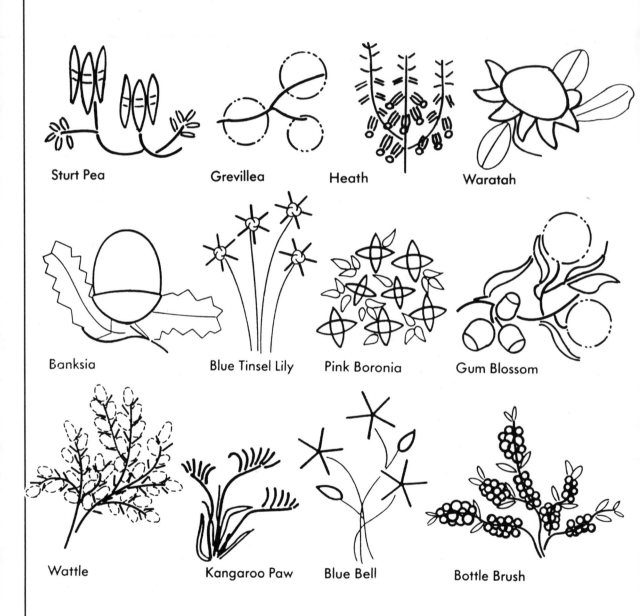

Sturt Pea Grevillea Heath Waratah

Banksia Blue Tinsel Lily Pink Boronia Gum Blossom

Wattle Kangaroo Paw Blue Bell Bottle Brush

FLORAL PICTURE

THREADS

Thread Description	Colour	No	Strands	Embroidery
DMC stranded cotton	green	523	6	main stems
DMC stranded cotton	brown	3790	6	main stems and frame
Coton Perle No 8	pale yellow	745		large and small dahlia
Coton Perle No 8	yellow	744		large and small dahlia
Coton Perle No 8	cream	712		hibiscus
DMC stranded cotton	pink/red	326	2	hibiscus centre
Minnamurra Thread	blue/pink	20		sweet pea and large and
Coton Perle No 8				small daisies
Leah's Over-dyed	pink	12		bell flowers,
Coton Perle No 8				fuchsia and
DMC Coton Perle No 8		776		small palestrina buds
DMC Flower thread	ecru			fuchsia and small blossom
DMC stranded cotton	pink/brown	3773	2	small blossom centres
DMC Flower thread	yellow	2745,		small roses,
		2743 and		large palestrina buds
or		2742		and flower centres
Leah's Over-dyed	yellow	10		
Coton Perle No 12				
Paternayan	pale pink	934	1	large roses
Persian Yarn	deep pink	932	1	rose buds
Appletons crewel	olive green	3403		fly stitch leaves (page 118)
Coton Perle No 8	green	3346		double leaves
DMC stranded cotton	green	3053	3	single leaves
Appletons tapestry	off-white	992		large blossom

- Mark the main stem lines and frame outline by machine onto a base fabric backed with Pellon.

- Couch the main stems into place.

- Starting with the largest flowers in the centre and working towards the outer small sprays, embroider the picture as detailed on page 101.

- Fill in the frame lines in coral stitch.

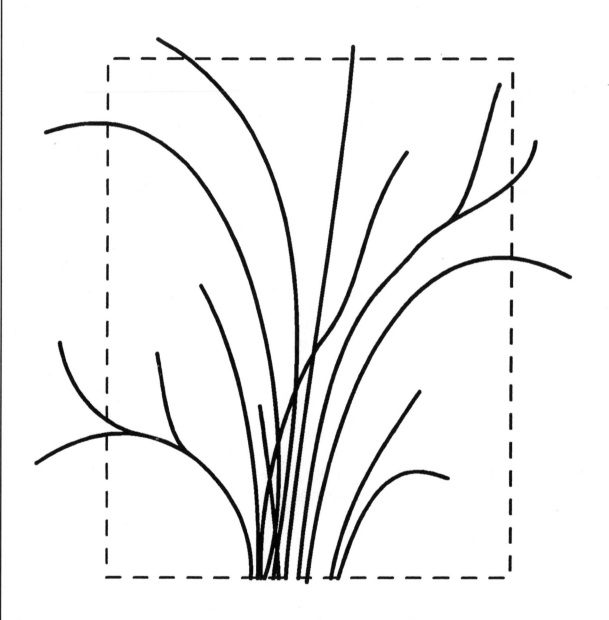

Floral Picture — main stem lines

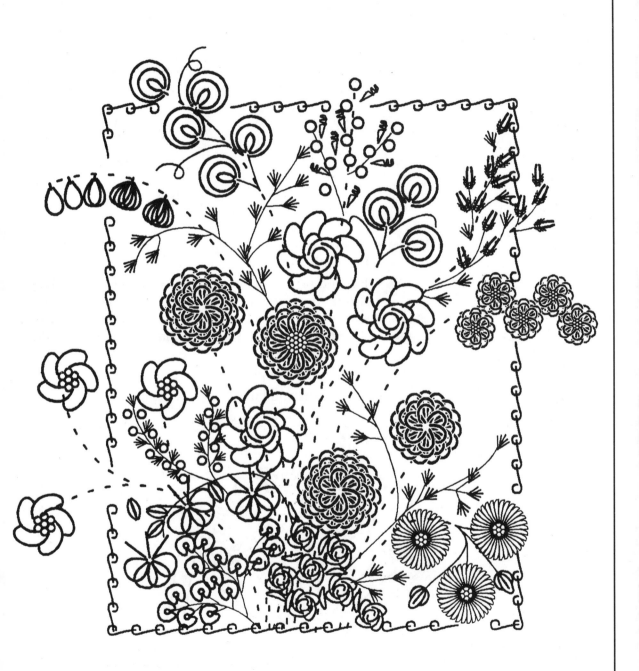

Floral Picture

POSY — BOX TOP DESIGN

This design is featured on the box top, shown in colour on page C22. It is suitable for enlargement and could be used on a cushion, blanket, or across the front of a sweater or 'sloppy joe'.

THREADS

Thread Description	Colour	No	Strands	Embroidery
DMC stranded cotton	dark green	3052	6	stems
			3	buds
Minnamurra Coton Perle No 8	yellow/pink	50		roses and buds
Jyava Ra Rame metallic thread	gold	22		bow outlining
taffeta ribbon 5 mm (³/₁₆'') wide	green			bow

- From the diagram below, mark the design lines (and box top) by machine (page 210).
- Pin and tack the ribbon to cover the bow shape. Edge stitch in place by hand before working Portuguese stem stitch in metallic thread along the edges. Alternatively edge stitch by machine using metallic thread if desired.
- Couch stems in place.
- Work roses and buds.

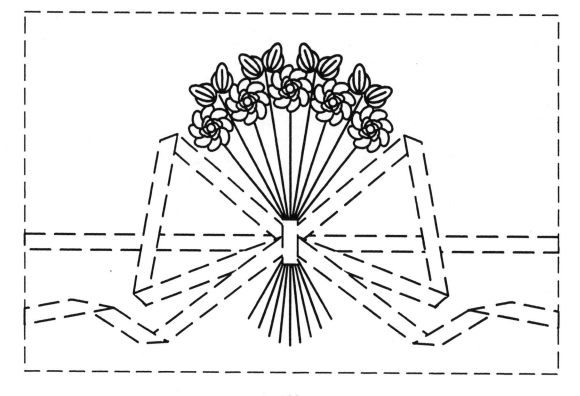

HEART — BOX TOP DESIGN

This design can be seen on the box top, shown in colour on page C22. It can be enlarged and worked in heavier threads on a cushion, or in wool on a blanket. Dahlias, daisies, blossom or hibiscus can all be substituted for the roses.

THREADS

Thread Description	Colour	No	Strands	Embroidery
Kreinik Balger Cord	silver	001C	1	feather stitching
DMC stranded cotton	green	3364	1	feather stitching
Coton Perle No 8	green	3346		leaves
Coton Perle No 8	pale pink	818		roses
	and pink	776		
DMC stranded cotton	white		2	baby's breath
Kreinik Balger Medium (No 16) Braid	silver	001		silver ribbons

- From the diagram on page 104, mark the design lines and lid outline by machine (page 210).
- Outline the heart shape with silver feather stitching overlaid with a second row of green feather stitch.
- Work roses and leaves.
- Work baby's breath in colonial knots.
- Work silver ribbons in long-legged bullion stitch.

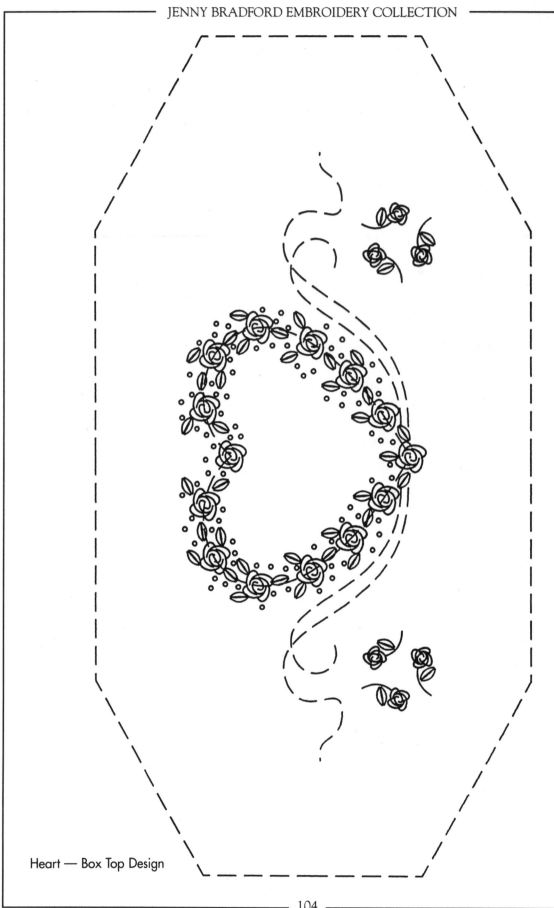

Heart — Box Top Design

RANDOM LINES AND FLOWERS

Needle Box Top Design _____

This design can be seen in colour on page C22.

THREADS

Thread Description	Colour	No	Strands	Embroidery
Coton Perle No 8	apricot	353		line work
DMC Flower thread	ecru			daisies
Minnamurra				
Coton Perle No 8	green	120		leaves
or stranded cotton	green	993	3	

gold beads and tiny gold charms as desired

- Photocopy the design and transfer as detailed (page 210).
- Work the curved line in palestrina stitch.
- Work daisies in the Flower thread, finishing the centre with a gold bead.
- Work leaves with two stitches in detached buttonhole stitch.
- Construct the box as instructed on page 155.
- Sew on tiny charms as an extra embellishment.

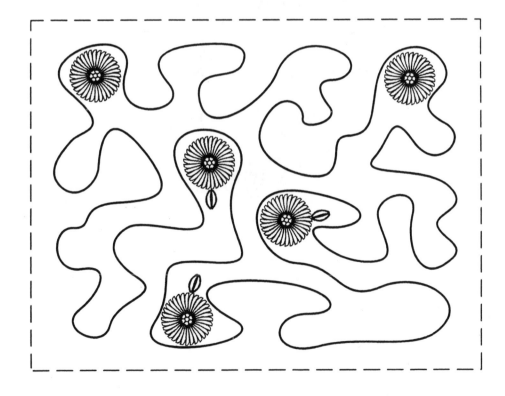

Scissor Holder Design _____

This design is featured in colour on page C22. It is very similar to the needle box design except that it has been worked in finer threads and roses have been substituted for the daisies. It would be suitable for collars or cuffs on blouses or lingerie. It can also be enlarged and worked in heavier threads for a bag. See page 180 for instructions on how to construct the scissor holder.

THREADS

Thread Description	Colour	No	Strands	Embroidery
Coton Perle No 12	cream	712		line work
Coton Perle No 8	green	120		leaves
or				
stranded cotton	green	993		
Leah's Coton Perle No 12	variegated	207		roses
or				
DMC Flower thread	ecru			

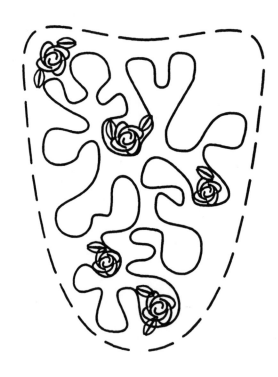

EASY-TO-MAKE TABLEMATS AND CHRISTMAS CRACKERS

QUICK DESIGNS FOR STRIKING RESULTS

HAND-TURNED CLOCK OF AUSTRALIAN WILDFLOWERS

RABBIT DESIGN FOR BABY'S THINGS

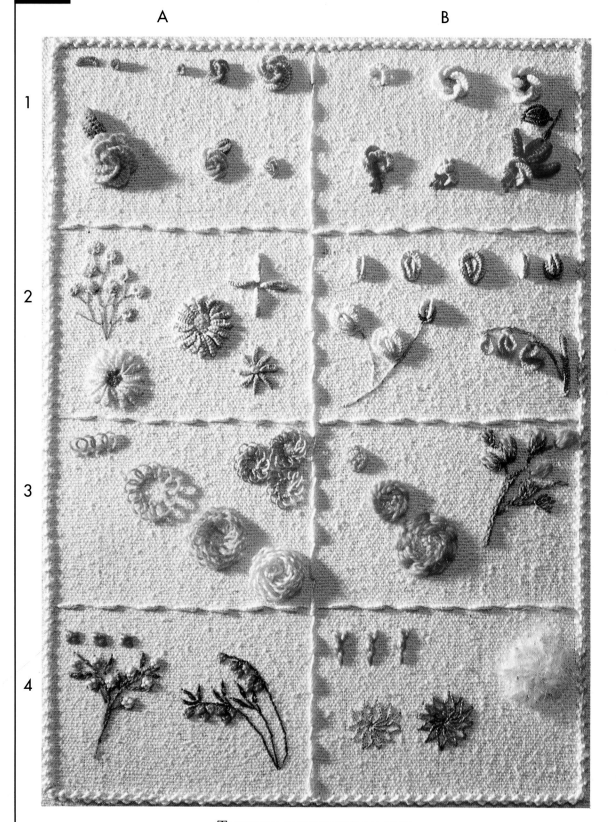

TEXTURED EMBROIDERY SAMPLER

FLORAL PICTURE

POSY AND HEART EMBROIDERED JEWEL BOXES

NEEDLE BOX AND SCISSOR HOLDER

DETAIL OF PANSIES (INSET) AND PANSY SPRAY
NEEDLE CASE AND CARD

FUCHSIA BAG

ROSY, THE EMBROIDERED HEIRLOOM TEDDY BEAR

Fuchsias

This design is featured on the bag on page C23. These fuchsias are very colourful and attractive but should not be used on any article that will require ironing as they are easily pushed out of shape. They are most suitable for picture work or articles such as the evening bag, padded hair bands and slides, or jewellery pieces.

THREADS

Thread Description	Colour	No	Strands	Embroidery
Minnamurra	blue/pink	10		bell
Coton Perle No 8	or			
or	shaded pink	30		
stranded cotton			3	
Coton Perle No 8	bright pink	602 or 603		back petals
	green	3346 or 3347		leaves
DMC stranded cotton	bright pink	602 or 603	1	stamens
	brown	919	6	stems
	green	471	2	flower stems

- Couch main stems into place to give a general shape to the design.
- Work clusters of flowers and leaves hanging from these stems. (See page 86 for detailed instructions.)

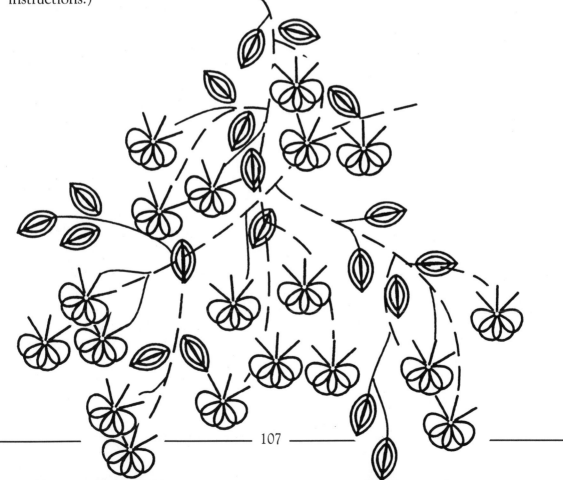

CHAPTER 13

WOOL EMBROIDERY MATERIALS

FABRICS

Wool embroidery can be worked on almost any fabric, as long as it is heavy enough to support the weight of the embroidery. However, the most popular types of fabrics for this work are pure wool blanketing and knitted woollen garments. It is possible to buy wool blanketing by the metre from many needlecraft shops. This can be used for baby blankets, knee rugs, garments (such as sweaters, jackets and dressing gowns), soft toys, pin cushions and hot water bottle covers. A lighter weight wool such as doctor's flannel is also ideal, particularly if working with the finer wool threads.

THREADS

WOOLS

There are many wools on the market providing a wide choice of thickness and colour. Do not ignore the fact that knitting wools can be used. These may stand up to repeated washing more successfully than tapestry wools, which are primarily designed for canvas work and not washable clothing.

DMC Medici _____

A very fine, smooth 2 ply wool excellent for very fine delicate work. A number of strands may be used together.

Appletons Crewel Wool _____

A fine 2 ply wool in a beautiful range of colours. Slightly fluffier than Medici. A number of strands may be used together.

Paternayan Persian Yarn _____

A 3 ply stranded tapestry wool in an excellent colour range. A single strand is approximately equivalent to a 3 ply knitting yarn.

Tapestry Wools _____

Available in a wide range of colours. A firm 4 ply twist, approximately equivalent to 8 ply knitting wool. DMC and Appletons both have excellent colour ranges.

Knitting Wools _____

Rowan 4 ply 'Botany' and 8 ply double knitting wools are those used by Kaffe Fassert for his beautiful knitting and tapestry designs. These are available in a lovely range of shaded colours not always obtainable in the more commonly used brands of knitting wools. A beautifully shaded range of hand-dyed knitting wools called Marta's Yarns is available in Australia. I have used wools from this range for many of the wildflowers.

Specialty wool shops dealing in more exotic knitting yarns can be inspirational. The hearts on the cream blanket on the colour pages are outlined with a silk and viscose knitting yarn purchased from one such shop.

Hand-dyed Embroidery Wools _____

Many hand-dyed variegated wools are now available. Those used in this book are by Mary Hart-Davies who dyes a range of wool threads in various weights and twists that are marketed under the trade name of Kacoonda. Heather Smith also makes a range of 2 ply wools with the brand name Torokina. I have used many of these wools in conjunction with Marta's Yarn for the wildflowers.

Hand-dyed wools are often available from spinners' and weavers' groups or from shops specialising in fibre arts. There are also ranges of over-dyed wools, equivalent in weight to Appletons crewel or DMC Medici, available from some specialty shops.

OTHER THREADS

Working with wool on wool fabric can result in a rather dull effect. To enliven the designs I like to use shiny threads such as Coton Perle No 8, silk or silk ribbon, and beads.

CHAPTER 14

WOOL EMBROIDERY FLOWERS

The construction of Australian wildflowers and wool roses is described in this chapter. In the accompanying stitch placement diagrams, bold lines are used to illustrate the stitch placement being described, whereas lighter lines and broken lines show previously completed steps.

The colour numbers quoted for the flowers in this section are for the 4 ply Marta's Yarn (MY) and the 2 ply Torokina Yarn (TY) that were used on the original cushion on page C28.

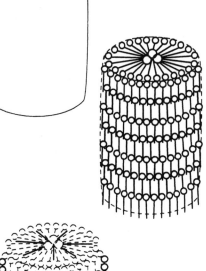

BANKSIA

2 ply dark olive green TY253— leaves
2 ply light olive green TY251— veins
4 ply gold — MY301 flowers
4 ply mid-brown MY203— woody stems

- Draw the leaf shapes with a marker pen and outline them with straight stitch.
- Mark the centre vein.
- Fill leaf shapes with straight stitch.
- Work from the centre vein to the outer edge, slanting the stitches as illustrated.
- Work the centre vein in stem stitch and side veins in straight stitch.
- Draw the banksia shape with a marker pen.
- Fill the top circle with pistil stitch as shown.
- Work three colonial knots in brown for the centre of this section and finish with six or seven straight stitches between the pistil stitches radiating from the knot cluster.
- Starting from the top of the flower, work overlapping rows of pistil stitch to fill the shape and cover the background fabric.
- Add a few extra colonial knots down each side edge of the cone and around the base.

BLUE BELL

4 ply blue MY415— petals
4 ply white — flower centres

- Mark a large centre dot for each flower.
- To achieve even spacing for a five petal flower, see page 10.
- Work three stitches for the centre of each petal as described for the flannel flower (page 113).
- These petals may be finished in either of the following ways:
  1 Work two more straight stitches around the centre cluster, each about 9 mm ($^3/_8$") in length.
  2 Work a bullion lazy daisy stitch around each base cluster with three wraps around the point of the needle for the bullion section.
- Work a colonial knot in white for the centre of each flower.

BORONIA — BROWN

2 ply light brown TY272— stem
4 ply red-brown MY205— petals
2 ply yellow TY244— tip of centre petal
2 ply dark olive green TY253— leaves

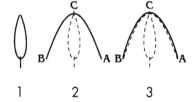

- Outline stem with stem stitch in brown 2 ply.
- Using 4 ply red-brown, work one 4 mm ($^1/_6$") lazy daisy stitch for each centre petal, starting just below the point at which the flower joins the stem (diag. 1).
- Come up at A and work a fly stitch around the base of the lazy daisy stitch anchoring at C (diag. 2).
- Come back up at A, pass the needle under the holding stitch at C and return the needle to the back of the work at point B (diag. 3).
- Highlight the tip of the centre petal with a small fly stitch in 2 ply yellow.
- Work spiky leaves along the upper part of the stem in fly stitch and straight stitch using 2 ply green. Work a few leaves between the flowers along the lower stem.

BORONIA — PINK

2 ply mid-pink TY213— petals
DMC stranded yellow 727— flower centres
4 ply light green — MY371 leaves

- Mark a small centre.
- Using 2 ply pink, work three close straight stitches for the centre of each petal, making the outer two stitches about 4 mm ($^1/_6$") long and the centre stitch 5 mm ($^3/_{16}$") long.
- Work a straight stitch on each side of the centre stitches. Start each stitch at the base of the petal and very close to the centre cluster and finish both stitches in the same hole 1 mm past the end of the centre stitch.
- Work four petals for each flower and fill the centre with colonial knots worked with a single strand of yellow DMC.
- Add leaves in lazy daisy stitch worked in 4 ply light green.

BOTTLEBRUSH

2 ply dark brown TY273— stem
4 ply mid-brown MY203— nuts
4 ply medium green MY221— flower clusters and leaves
DMC stranded red 666— flowers

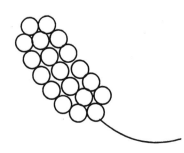

- Stem stitch the stem with 2 ply wool.
- Using brown 4 ply, work clusters of colonial knots for the nut clusters at the lower end of the stems.
- Using green 4 ply, work groups of colonial knots in the same arrangement towards the top of the stems for the flowering clusters.
- Add straight stitch leaves at the tip of each stem and between the clusters.
- Using two strands of DMC thread in a fine milliner's needle, work tiny loops and tufts in the centre of each green knot to represent the flowers just breaking into bloom.

To work tufts, take the needle down through the centre of a knot, back stitch firmly in place, then bring the needle to the front through the same knot and cut the thread. Leave the tufts longer than required, then trim when all have been completed.

To work loops, bring the needle up from the back of the work through the centre of a knot and return it to the back through the same knot, leaving a loop just visible in the centre of the knot. Back stitch firmly before repeating in the next knot.

Start with tufts at the base of the flower head, graduating to tiny loops towards the tip, depicting the gradual development of the flower head.

FLANNEL FLOWER

2 ply cream — petals
2 ply light olive green TY251— petal tips and centres

- Mark the centre of the flower as shown in diag. 1.

- For each petal, using 2 ply cream, work three close straight stitches for the centre, making the outer two stitches approximately 5 mm ($^3/_{16}$") long and the centre stitch 7 mm ($^5/_{16}$") long (diag. 2).

- Work a straight stitch on each side of the centre stitches, starting each stitch at the base of the petal and very close to the centre cluster and finishing both stitches in the same hole approximately 2 mm ($^1/_{16}$") past the end of the centre stitch (diag. 3).

- Repeat the previous step twice more, extending the centre point by 2 mm each time and working the stitches close together at the base of the petal (diag. 4).

- Work seven or eight petals for each full flower.

- Tip each petal with straight stitches in green wool by bringing the needle up at A (2 mm, or $^1/_{16}$", from the tip of the cream stitching) and down at B. Come out again at A and pass the needle through the wool of the outer stitch at point C (diag. 5). Repeat for the other side.

- Fill the centre with colonial knots.

GUM BLOSSOM

2 ply cream
DMC stranded yellow 727
2 ply dark olive green TY253
DMC stranded green 522

- Mark the centre of each flower with a small circle.

- Using a single strand of cream wool, work pistil stitch radiating in a circle from the outer edge of the marked centre.

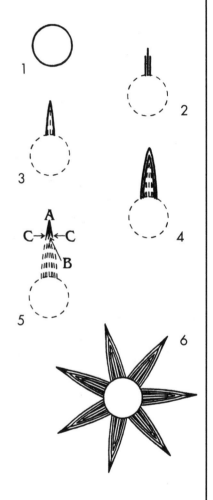

1

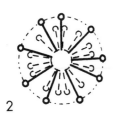

2

3

To get an even distribution of stitches, work step-by-step as follows.

The flower is worked in three separate rows. The stitches in row 1 are equivalent in length to two-thirds of the distance from the outer edge of the centre to the flower to the extreme outside edge of the finished flower.

- First work four stitches to divide the circle into quarters then add three or four stitches in each section (diag. 1).

- For the second row, work a light scattering of longer stitches, taking them to the extreme outside edge (diag. 2).

- For the third row, work a light scattering of shorter stitches from the outer edge of the centre to finish short of the knots of the first row worked (diag. 3).

It is better to underestimate the number of stitches required in each row rather than overwork it. A few extra stitches can be added to complete the overall appearance but it is difficult to unpick if the first row is worked too heavily.

- To finish the flower, use a single strand of yellow DMC and work a colonial knot in the centre of most of the pistil stitches.

- Fill the centre with straight stitch in green wool and work a long curved bullion stitch in green DMC for the pistil.

- Work hanging flowers in the same way, filling in a fan shape with pistil stitch and finishing the base of the flower with straight stitch in green.

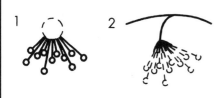

1   2

GUM NUTS

2 ply light brown TY272— nuts
2 ply dark brown TY273— shading

- Draw the outline for each nut as shown and outline with stem stitch in light brown (diag. 1).

- Pad the top section with horizontal straight stitches working over the edge of the outline (diag. 2).

- Work vertical straight stitches to cover the padding, keeping the stitches close and smooth (diag. 3).

- Fill the small oval with dark brown horizontal straight stitches working inside the stem stitch outline.

- Finish by outlining the division between the vertical and horizontal sections with a row of stem stitch.

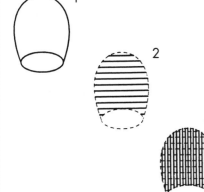

1

2

3

HEATH

2 ply dark brown TY273— stems
2 ply dark pink TY211— flowers
2 ply dark olive green TY253— leaves
2 ply pale pink TY214— flowers
DMC stranded brown 841

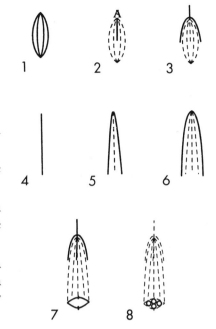

- Work stem in stem stitch in 2 ply brown.

- Small buds at the top of the stems are worked in straight stitch in dark pink.

- Work three or four stitches 6 mm ($^1/_4$″) long using the same hole to start and finish all stitches (diag. 1).

- Using green, bring the needle up at A and work a single straight stitch halfway down the centre of the bud (diag. 2).

- Starting on the left side of the bud, work a fly stitch around the end of the bud. Attach the bud to the stem by adjusting the length of the anchor stitch of the fly stitch (diag. 3).

- Work each bell with five straight stitches starting with the centre stitch approximately 8 mm ($^5/_{16}$″) long (diag. 4).

- Work a second and third stitch on each side of each of the centre stitches using the same hole at the base to create a slight fan shape (diag. 5).

- Work fourth and fifth stitches alongside the previous stitches (diag. 6).

- Finish the top of each bell flower with a straight stitch and a fly stitch in green as for the bud (diag. 7).

- Using pale pink wool, work two tiny fly stitches at the base of the pink cluster.

- Fill the centre of this outlined area with French knots using a single strand of DMC brown.

- Add stem stitch or straight stitch leaves between the flowers and at the top of the stalk.

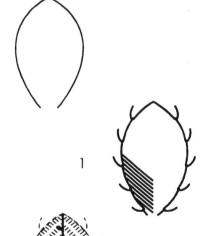

STURT PEA

4 ply bright red MY106— flower
2 ply mid-green TY255— leaves
4 mm black beads

The shape of the flower will look better if care is taken to work the petals as shown in the diagrams with the centre petals lower than the outer petals.

- Each petal is worked in red as described for the flannel flower, using the measurements shown here.

- Stitch two beads between each set of petals.

- Leaves are worked in pairs along a stem using 2 ply mid-green. Work the stem in stem stitch. Work the leaves using the same stitch placement described for the flannel flower but *working the first five stitches only*.

WARATAH

2 ply olive green TY255— leaves
2 ply light olive green TY251— veins
4 ply red MY107/2— flower
4 ply dark red MY67— flower

- Draw the outline of the leaves and cover the outline with one-sided feather stitching in 2 ply olive green. Work from the point of the leaf down each side to create a serrated edge.

- Fill in each leaf with slanting straight stitch in olive green, working from the centre out to the edge.

- Stem stitch the centre vein in light olive green, adding a few straight stitch veins between the other stitches.

- Draw the outline of the waratah as shown.

- Fill the top of the cone area with colonial knots in red then work two rows of pistil stitch around the base of the cone (diag. 2).

- Outline the base petals with stem stitch then fill in each petal with rows of stem stitch (diag. 3).

- To create the turned-up effect on the centre front petal, fill in the back of the petal with the dark red wool using straight stitch.

- Using red, work over the base stitching in straight stitch as shown in diag. 4

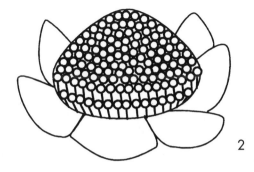

2

3

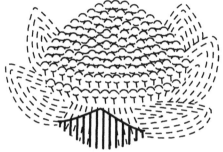

4

WATTLE

2 ply dark brown TY273— stems
4 ply light green MTY371 leaves
4 ply yellow MY401 — flowers
Yellow seed beads if desired

- Work stems in uneven feather stitching in brown.
- Scatter leaves along the stem working lazy daisy stitch. Start each stitch at the tip of the leaf and attach it to the stem with the holding stitch.
- Work clusters of French knots for the flowers, starting with a single knot for the centre and surrounding it with six or seven closely packed knots.

Note: Matching yellow beads may be used instead of some of the knots to add a lift.

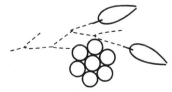

WOOL ROSES

Illustrated in colour on the textured embroidery sampler: 3B.

Kacoonda variegated wool and Coton Perle No 8

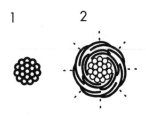

- Using Coton Perle, work a single colonial knot for the centre.
- Work six or seven colonial knots in a tight circle around the centre knot (diag. 1).
- Work a second circle around the outside of the centre cluster. It is important to pull the knots of this row in towards the centre of the flower by working the needle at an angle, sliding it in and out under the edge of the previous row. This helps to push the centre of the flower up, giving the finished flower a more rounded look.

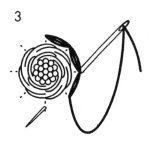

- With the wool, work two circles of stem stitch around the circle of knots, working with the thread above the needle and leaving the stitches slightly looped. Adjust the distance between the rows according to the thickness of the thread used. Do not cramp the stitches too much.
- Divide the outer edge into 8 as shown in diag. 2.
- Work two or three back stitches between each mark to complete the flower.

WOOL ROSE BUDS

Illustrated in colour on the textured embroidery sampler: 3B.

- Couch stems with fine wool or thread.
- Work the rose buds with four or five straight stitches using the same hole to start and finish all stitches (diag. 1).

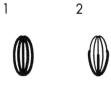

- Using fine green wool, work one or two straight stitches halfway up the centre of the bud.
- Starting on the left side of the bud, work a fly stitch around the base of the bud (diag. 2).
- Work a second fly stitch directly over the first one if required.

- Work fly stitch leaves. Start with a straight stitch for the top half of the leaf. Continue down the leaf working three or four fly stitches.

CHAPTER 15

WOOL EMBROIDERY DESIGNS

HEARTS AND FLOWERS

This design has been worked as a knee rug 100 cm x 80 cm (43" x 31½"), and is shown in colour on page C25.

THREADS

Thread Description	Colour	No	Strands	Embroidery
Kacoonda wool thick	orange/pink	6F		heart outline and roses
Kacoonda wool fine	green	8E		leaves and stems
Coton Perle No 8	yellow	742		flower centres
Kanagawa				
silk ribbon 4 mm	cream	156		buds
silk ribbon 2 mm	green	31		buds and colonial knots

- Using the diagrams on this page and the next, transfer the design to the blanket as described on page 210.
- Outline hearts using palestrina stitch and feather stitch as shown in the pattern.
- Work the wool roses, rose buds and fly stitch leaves as shown on page 118.
- Work cream silk ribbon buds using single bullion lazy daisy stitches.

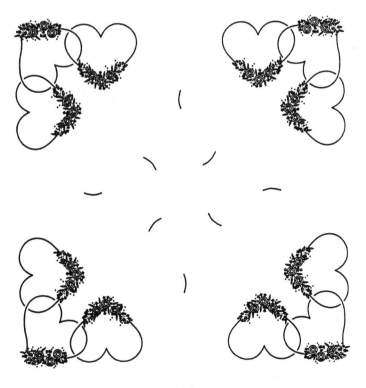

- Work two small straight stitches over the base of each bud in 2 mm green ribbon.
- Work French knots in green ribbon to complete the spray.
- Scatter single rose buds in wool over the centre of the blanket.

Hearts and Flowers Design — outline

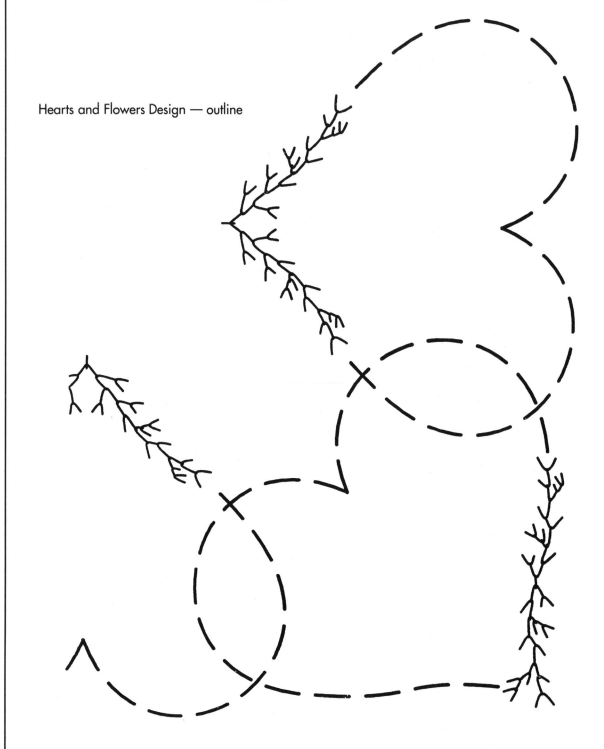

Hearts and Flowers Design

CIRCLE OF HEARTS

This design has been worked on a 110 cm x 80 cm [43" x 31½"] blanket. It can be seen in colour on page C25.

THREADS

Thread Description	Colour	No	Strands	Embroidery
Pengouin Talisman silk/viscose knitting yarn	cream	001		heart outline and colonial knots
Paternayan Persian yarn	pink	931, 932 and 933	1 1 1	roses
	green	A604		
Rowan Botany 4 ply wool	blue	123		colonial knots
Kacoonda thin wool or	green	8C	1	stems and leaves
Appletons crewel	green	3505	1	
Coton Perle No 8	yellow	742		flower centres

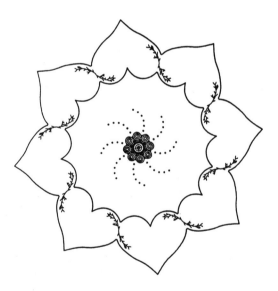

- Using diagrams above and on page 123, transfer the pattern to the blanket as described on page 210.
- Outline the hearts in Talisman knitting yarn with palestrina stitch.
- Work a spray of feather stitching in thin green wool for each rose spray.
- Work wool rose and rose buds using a single strand of Paternayan wool.
- Add colonial knots in blue and white.

Circle of Hearts Design — section

For the centre posy:

- Work a single rose for the centre.
- Using a single strand of green Paternayan wool, surround the rose with leaves worked in a single detached buttonhole stitch with 8 wraps for each leaf.
- Work three colonial knots in cream between the leaves.
- Work eight roses around the outer edge and complete the posy by working colonial knots in cream along the outer design lines.
- Small rose sprays can be worked across the outer corners if desired.

Circle of Hearts Design — centre posy

REPEATING FLOWER SPRAY DESIGN

This design, as shown in colour on page C26, consists of repetitive sprays of flowers scattered evenly over a blanket. It can therefore be adapted for use on any size fabric, increasing or decreasing the number of sprays worked according to the area to be covered.

The sprays in rows 2 and 4 are all the same but those in rows 1 and 3 decrease in size from the centre out to the top and bottom as detailed in the pattern given on page 126.

THREADS

Thread Description	Colour	No	Strands	Embroidery
Appletons crewel wool	gold		1	flower petals
	tan		1	flower centres
DMC stranded	green		1	feather stitching
	green		2	stems and small bud calyxes
	yellow		2	daisy centres
Paternayan wool	green		1	stems, large bud calyxes and leaves
	deep apricot		1	rose buds and rose centres
	pale apricot		1	rose petals
4 ply knitting wool	blue		1	daisies
2mm silk ribbon	cream			baby's breath

Row 1

- Work each spray of flowers in lazy daisy stitch using a single strand of Appletons crewel wool in gold.

- Work five petals for the inner flower, three for the middle one and two for the outer flower. Finish each flower with a tan colonial knot.

- Work these sprays in the 3, 2 and 1 formation shown in the pattern.

Row 2

- Using a single strand of green DMC cotton, work the feather stitch stems as shown.

- Using a single strand of Paternayan wool, work three rose buds as detailed on page 118. Use DMC Medici wool or stranded cotton for the green calyx and stems.

- Using 2 mm cream silk ribbon, work colonial knots on the feather stitch stems for baby's breath.

- Tie a half bow by folding a short length of ribbon in half, forming a loop and passing the folded end through the loop. Tighten and adjust to size, then trim the cut ends as desired. Sew in place.

Row 3

- Work 12 petal bullion stitch daisies in 4 ply knitting wool (see page 70 for instructions).
- Position and work small leaves with two bullion stitches as shown, together with a spray of daisies as detailed for row 1.

Note: Each spray has a different arrangement of the daisies as shown in the pattern.

Row 4

This is a larger version of the spray detailed for row 2 and includes three wool roses as detailed on page 118.

- Work feather stitch stems.
- Position and work roses between the stems.
- Add rose bud sprays.
- Finish feather stitch stems with silk ribbon colonial knots and a silk ribbon bow.
- Fold the ribbon into a bow shape and attach to the spray by straight stitching across the centre with ribbon.

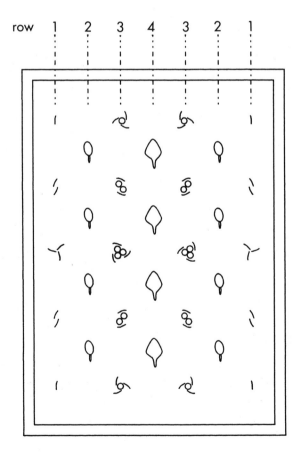

row 3

row 1

row 2

row 4

Coat hanger designs

Blue Hanger _____

Use mohair wool in off-white and Jyava Ra Rame metallic gold thread No 22.

- Fantasy flowers (page 89) in mohair are scattered over the surface, interspersed with smaller gold flowers in the same stitch worked with two strands of gold thread.

- Use two strands of gold thread to work stems in Portuguese stem stitch and leaves in double lazy daisy stitch.

- Single twisted chain stitches in mohair are scattered between the flowers.

Apricot Hanger _____

Use 4 ply (or similar) wool in off-white and 2 ply or Appletons crewel wool in very pale green. You will also need pale green tiny beads (Mill Hill No 2217).

- Work flower stems in stem stitch with pale green wool, using the spray design shown in the photograph on page C27, or single flowers scattered as depicted on the blue hanger.

- Work flannel flowers (see page 113), using small green beads in place of the colonial knots worked for the centre of each flower.

AUSTRALIAN WILDFLOWERS DESIGN

There are four different sections in this design, each of which can be used separately for smaller projects. Any one section can be omitted from the design to create a crescent or horseshoe shape. Each section could be worked across the corner of a rectangle for a blanket or knee rug with tiny sprays of pink boronia or wattle scattered across the centre of the blanket.

To work the design as illustrated on page C29, proceed as follows.

* Prepare the fabric by tacking the voile lining to the back of the wool piece.
* To mark a 26 cm (10$\frac{1}{4}$") diameter circle (dinner plate size) on the fabric, use one of the methods detailed on page 210.
* Mark the circle into four quarters at 12, 3, 6 and 9 o'clock.

Section 1 — worked between 3 and 6 o'clock _____

* Trace onto paper the shape of the banksia and leaves from the chart and cut out carefully.
* Position the pattern on the right side of the wool fabric and trace around the shape with a fadeable marker pen or tack around the shape with tiny stitches in cream sewing cotton.
* Work according to the detailed instructions for working the flowers in Chapter 14.
* Work heath and then fill in spaces with wattle sprays.

Section 2 — worked between 12 and 3 o'clock _____

* Position and mark the circles for the centres of the flannel flowers and work as described.
* Work brown boronia, pink boronia and wattle sprays as shown on the chart.

Section 3 — worked between 9 and 12 o'clock _____

* Trace the waratah and leaves as described in section 1. Mark the shaded leaf outlines carefully. Cut the leaves away from the paper pattern and replace the remaining shape to mark the waratah outline.
* Work the leaves as described, then the flower head and petals.
* Mark in the stems of the wattle sprays and stitch in stem stitch.
* Mark the gum nuts from a traced pattern and work as described.
* Work blue bells then finish the section with sprays of wattle flowers and leaves.

Section 4 — worked between 6 and 9 o'clock _____

* Work the main stem with dark brown, stem stitching directly over the marked circle.
* Mark the Sturt pea position, using a template if desired. Work the flower starting with the centre petals.
* Work the bottlebrush then the gum blossom.
* Finish with wattle sprays.

Press the finished work face down over a towel using a steam iron. If the lining puckers in the centre, trim away close to the embroidery and re-press.

Section 1

Section 2

Section 3

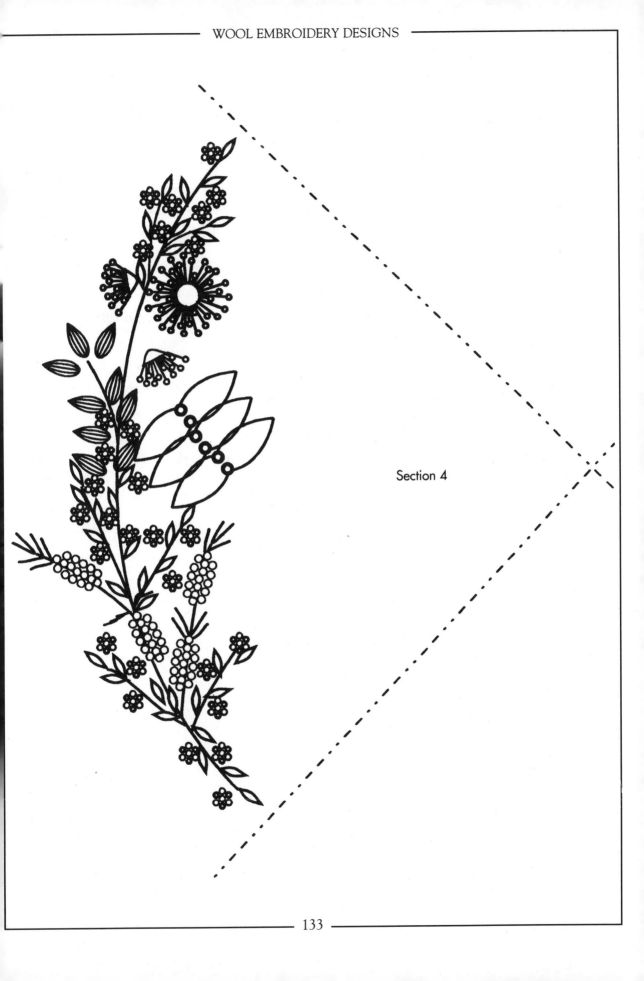

Section 4

CHAPTER 16

CANVAS WORK MATERIALS

CANVAS

The projects detailed in this section are all worked on 18 to 22 count canvas. To prepare the work, bind the edges with masking tape to prevent snagging of the working threads.

THREADS

All of the threads listed for textured and wool embroidery are suitable for canvas work.

NEEDLES

A size 24 tapestry needle should be used for all stitching unless otherwise directed.

FRAME

A small tapestry frame should be used for all of the canvas work in this section. It will help to hold the shape of the work, and it will enable you to work stitches more evenly. Lace the canvas into the frame as tightly as possible using strong thread.

Chapter 17

CANVAS WORK DESIGNS

Pin cushion

This is a simple little pin cushion worked on canvas, using a mixture of continental stitch, colonial knots and jacquard stitch on the back. The work will be more even if a small frame is used.

MATERIALS REQUIRED

Canvas: 18 cm square (7") (20 or 22 threads per inch)
Variegated thread 'Watercolours' by Caron for the centre
(No 59), or Paternayan yarn
Paternayan yarn colour Nos 716, 845 and A604 for
colonial knots and A604 for the outer triangles

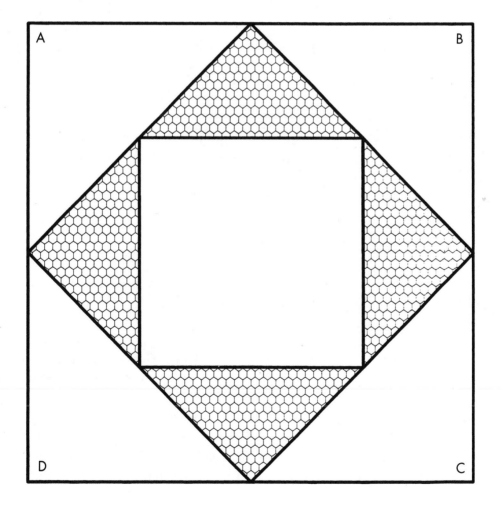

METHOD

- Mark a square 12 cm x 12 cm (4³/₄") in the centre of the canvas. Find the mid-point of each side and mark a second square as shown below. Find the mid-point again and mark a third square in the middle.
- Fill the centre square with continental stitch using a single strand of variegated thread or Paternayan yarn.
- Fill in the marked area with colonial knots. Pack them very tightly, working with one strand and using a variety of the Paternayan threads.
- Fill in the remaining areas with jacquard stitch in a single strand of Paternayan Yarn.
- Trim canvas, leaving a 5 mm (³/₈") seam allowance. Finger press the seam allowance to the wrong side.
- Bring points A, B, C and D together at the centre back with the right sides facing out.
- Oversew the edges together along the folded turnings.
- Stuff before completely closing the final seam.

HEART SCISSORS PILLOW AND PIN CUSHION DESIGN

MATERIALS REQUIRED

18 count canvas: 25 cm x 25 cm (10") is sufficient for both hearts
Minnamurra, Torokina and DMC threads
Ribbon: 1 metre (39") x 2 or 3 mm wide
Tapestry needle size 24
Tiny gold heart charm
25 tiny pearls
Small pair of embroidery scissors

METHOD

- Bind the edges of the canvas with masking tape before you begin.
- There are three different ways of working the basic heart for this design:
  1 Place the canvas directly over the pattern (diag. 1) and trace the heart outline onto the canvas with a marker pen.
  2 Work the outline of the heart in back stitch using thread that will match the filling stitches (diag. 2).
  3 Follow the chart (page 138) stitch by stitch.
  Note: 2 or 3 or a combination, e.g. 2 for the back and 3 for the front, will give the most accurate results.

- The continental stitch is worked with four strands of variegated stranded cotton. In order to keep the thread variegation as even as possible, cut the full skein at the knot, pull two six-strand lengths from the skein then pull two single threads from each bundle of six and smooth them together. If you are careful to take the threads from the same end every time, the variegations will match when the threads from two separate bundles are put together. Always strip stranded threads before using (see page 63).

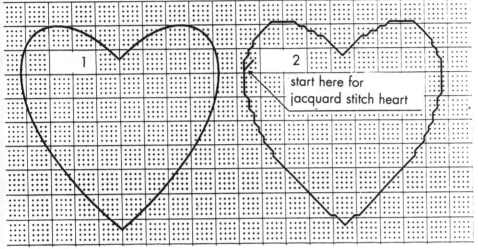

Pansy Heart Design

Threads used for the background stitching are Torokina wool No 254, Minnamurra No 120 and DMC stranded cotton No 712. Threads used for the pansies are Minnamurra stranded cotton No 10 (single strand for the outer petals), Isafil machine embroidery thread (for the inner black petals), Isafil machine embroidery thread in yellow and cream (for the petal markings) and DMC stranded cotton No 522 (for the leaves).

- Prepare the canvas for the back of the pillow by outlining the heart shape in back stitch (diag. 2).

- With a single strand of wool, work the first row of the Jacquard stitch pattern (see stitch diagrams) diagonally down and across the heart. Start stitching at the point shown on diag. 2 and continue repeating the pattern shown in the first stitch diagram until you reach the lower right side of the heart. *Be sure to count very carefully for this foundation row as the rest of the pattern is built on this row.*

- Using four strands of Minnamurra thread, work the second row of the pattern as shown in the second stitch diagram, above and below the foundation row.

- Repeat these patterns rows to fill the heart shape.
- Work the front heart using continental stitch, filling one side with green and the other side with cream. Leave a line of threads unstitched through the centre as shown in the diagram.
- Work the gusset in one long piece in green, using the same stitch as selected for the front heart. Leave one thread unworked at the centre mark. Each half of the gusset is worked over 75 threads by 5 threads. Allowing for the unworked centre thread, the total thread count for the gusset piece is 151 x 5.
- Decorate the cream side of the front heart with a spray of pansies, or any other flowers you fancy, and the heart charm, or simply use the charm for decoration.

To work pansies, see page 85. For Coton Perle No 8 substitute two strands of stranded cotton. For Coton Perle No 12 substitute Isafil machine embroidery thread.

- Sew pearls firmly down the centre of the heart.

Heart with Charted Bud Design _____

Threads used are Minnamurra No 10, Torokina No 224 and DMC green and cream.

- Work one heart for the back as described for the Pansy Heart using the Minnamurra 10 and the Torokina 224.
- Work the front from the chart on page 000 using Minnamurra and DMC stranded cotton.
- Work the gusset as described for the Pansy Heart.
- Sew pearls down the centre of the heart.

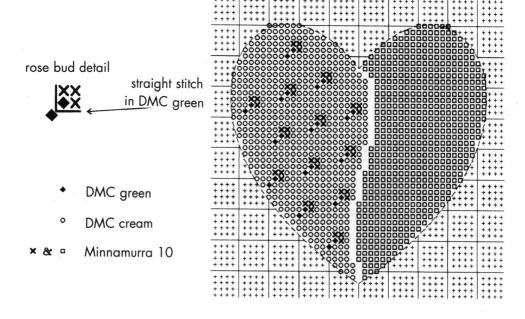

rose bud detail

straight stitch in DMC green

◆ DMC green

○ DMC cream

✕ & ▫ Minnamurra 10

BLANKET AND KNEE RUG IN WOOL

CREAM BLANKET

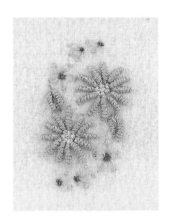

DETAILS OF FLOWER SPRAYS ON CREAM BLANKET

BLUE AND APRICOT HANGERS

AUSTRALIAN WILDFLOWERS DESIGN CUSHION

DETAIL OF AUSTRALIAN WILDFLOWERS DESIGN

PIN CUSHION

HEART SCISSORS PILLOW AND PIN CUSHION

COTTAGE GARDEN PICTURE

COTTAGE GARDEN PICTURE

The finished size of the original embroidery is 10.5 cm x 15.5 cm (4" x 6"). It is worked on canvas, nine threads to the centimetre or 22 threads to the inch. All stitching is done in stranded cotton, except for the bullion stitch flowers, which are worked in silk.

Shaded effects are obtained by mixing strands of threads of different colours. Alternatively there are various hand-dyed shaded embroidery threads available which can be used.

- Use four strands for all straight stitch areas, three for all colonial knots unless otherwise stated and single strands of silk thread for bullion stitches. Stranded cotton colour numbers quoted are for DMC brand.

- To work the picture, copy the design lines directly onto the canvas from the pattern on page 141. To make stitching easier, take care to line up as accurately as possible the vertical and horizontal lines on the pattern with the threads of the canvas.

- Place the canvas into a small tapestry frame for working.

Remember to spread the threads when working all straight stitches. Always 'strip the thread' for embroidery (see page 63). Pull one strand at a time and then smooth them back together before threading the needle.

1 Work the sky, blending strands of mixed blues. Take the stitching across the tree area in the top right-hand corner.

2 Work the thatch, mixing and blending the threads and using long and short stitch in section 2 and satin stitch in 2A. Vary the mixture of threads as you work.

3 Pad the chimney area with vertical straight stitch before working in horizontal straight stitch over three or four threads to form a brick pattern, blending the three colours. Fill in brick work on the right-hand side of the front door.

4 Work stonework in vertical straight stitch, blending the threads.

5 Work long straight stitch to fill in wooden beams, working an 'X' stitch where they intersect under the window on the right-hand side.

6 Work vertical straight stitch for the windows in 317, leaving one row of holes down the centre of each window. Using one strand of 762, work a diagonal criss-cross pattern, over the top of the straight stitch, into alternate holes of the canvas around the outside edge of each section of straight stitch. Straight stitch the window frames in 762. Straight stitch with 317 above the right-hand windows.

7 Use vertical straight stitch, mixing 646 and 647, for the door. Work horizontal bands in 645 for hinges and handle. Work a bullion stitch to complete the handle. Outline the door with 646.

Diagram Number	Detail	Thread Numbers
1	Sky	827, 828
2 + 2A	Thatch	646, 612, 782
3	Brickwork	355, 356, 758
4	Stonework	841, 842, 543
5	Wood beams	646
6	Windows and window frames	317, 762
7	Door and door frame	645, 646, 647
8	Front steps	647, 543
9	Paving stones	762, 543
10	Stonework	841, 842, 543
11	Tree	3345, 3348
12	Shrub	3051, 3364, 341, 333
13	Bush	3051, 3365
14	Rose bush — flowers	Silk Stitch No 17
	— greenery	367, 368
15	Bush	319, 367
16	Hollyhocks — flowers	602, 604, 605
	— leaves	502, 319
17	Delphiniums — flowers	793, 794, 554 (blended)
	— leaves	502, 319
18	Window box — flowers	Kanagawa 1000 No 4
	— greenery	3012
19	Shrub	772, 445 (blended)
20	Bullion — flowers	Kanagawa 1000 No 169
	— greenery	3012, 3013
21	Daisy bush	white, 3072, 972
22	Purple flowers	208, 3012, 3013
23	Pink bush	893, 891, 367
24	Blue bush	793, 794, 368
25	Yellow daisy bush	743, 922, 895
26	Pink bullion flowers	368, Kanagawa 1000 No 93
27	Bullion loop flowers	Silk Stitch white, 161
28	Iceland poppies — background	3072
	— flowers	Silk Stitch Nos 16, 17, 113, 175
	— centres	green embroidery thread
29	Rose bush — flowers	Kanagawa 1000 No 4
	— greenery	3345, 3347
30	Border	603, 605, 320

Cottage Garden Picture

8   Work front steps, alternating single horizontal straight stitches in 543 with 647.

9   Paving stones are worked in 762, using a diagonal straight stitch and alternating the direction of the stitch for each paver. Outline each stone with a single strand of 543.

10 Stonework is worked in small long and short stitches over two to four threads, blending the colours.

11 Cover this area sparsely with colonial knots worked in two strands of 3345 or 3348 or one of each.

12 Fill the area with colonial knots, using two strands each of 341 and 333 for flowers and mixing 3051 and 3364 for greenery.

13 Work colonial knots using two strands and mixing the colours.

14 Work tiny bullion roses, using a colonial knot for the centre and three 5-wrap bullion stitches for the petals of each flower. Note that when working bullion stitch on canvas it will be necessary to 'stab stitch' the bullion. Referring to the diagram on page 219, take the needle right through to the back of the work at point 2 (keep the thread on the surface), return the needle halfway through the canvas at point 1, wrap the needle and finish as usual. Work some colonial knots as buds and cover the remaining area with green knots.

15 Fill with colonial knots, mixing the colours.

16 Cover the area with horizontal straight stitch in 319 before working variegated
17 flowers of colonial knots in pink or blue. Work long vertical stitches in 502 below the flowers for leaves.

18 Using red, work a row of bullion stitches along the base of the window. Cover the lower area with straight stitch leaves over the base of the bullions.

19 Fill with colonial knots, mixing 772 with 445.

20 Scatter bullion stitches over the area. Cover the canvas with straight stitch leaves.

21 Fill the area with colonial knots worked with three strands of 3072. Scatter white knots, using four strands, over the green, and finish each white flower with a gold centre worked with a single strand of thread.

22 Cover the area with random straight stitches in 3012. Add flowers in colonial knots.

23 Work variegated flowers with four strands in colonial knots. Fill the area with green
24 knots, using three strands.

25 Work as for 21, using 895 for greenery, 743 for flowers and 922 for centres.

26 Work as for 20, using Kanagawa 1000 No 93 for flowers, No 368 for greenery.

27 Work looped bullion stitch, bell-shaped flowers in white and cover the remainder of the area with bullion stitch leaves.

28 Cover the area with horizontal straight stitch in 3072. Work bullion loop flowers with green colonial knot centres. Add bullion stitch stems and leaves to cover the area.

29 Work tiny bullion roses with red, starting each with a colonial knot. Fill the remainder of the area with colonial knots in green.

30 Fill the area with colonial knots in pinks and green.

CHAPTER 18

PROJECTS

BAGS

Depending on the look you are trying to achieve, you may prefer to construct your own bag using your own patterns, or to purchase one of the many commercial patterns available.

CONSTRUCTION METHODS

There are numerous and varied ways of making bags and purses and in many cases one way is as good as another. I was, however, intrigued by the neatness and simplicity of a method devised by Jean Wilson of the ACT Embroiderers' Guild. I am indebted to Jean for allowing me to print her method here and also for making up the sample bag shown on the colour pages (C16).

This construction method can be used for any size envelope bag, glasses case or tissue pack holder. It is neat because it is seamed together in a single process and has no stitching showing on the inside or outside.

Envelope Style Bag ⎯⎯⎯⎯⎯⎯⎯⎯⎯⎯⎯⎯⎯⎯⎯⎯

MATERIALS REQUIRED

Finished size: 20 cm x 14 cm (8" x 5½")
Silk dupion or similar fabric for outside:
25 cm x 50 cm (10" x 20")
Silk dupion or other lining fabric: 25 cm x 50 cm
Pellon fleece: 25 cm x 50 cm
Piping: 75 cm (30") of ready made or 75 cm piping cord
and bias strips to cover

METHOD

- Back the outer bag fabric with Pellon fleece, tacking the two layers together smoothly.

- Prepare a paper pattern for the size of the bag required. Fold the pattern to give the desired finished result and mark points A, B, C, D, E, F and G, as shown for the bag pattern on page 145. Note that it is much easier to work with rounded corners on the front flap.

- Mark the cutting line onto the outer fabric.

- Work any decoration that is required.

- Check the design position carefully and cut the outer fabric to the exact size required. Cut a lining piece to match.

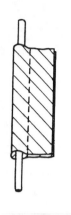

piping

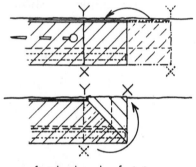

finished ends of piping

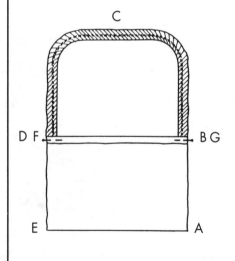

- Prepare the piping. Join bias strips as required, fold the strip over the piping cord and tack or machine to keep the cord in place (Note: Always use a zipper foot when sewing piping). Trim the raw edges of the strip to equal the seam allowance of the bag.

- On the right side of the outer bag, mark points A, B, C, D, E, F and G with pins.

- Starting from point A, pin the piping through B, C, D to E, easing it around the curves and keeping all the raw edges level.

- Unpick the ends of the piping and very carefully cut the cord to the exact length. Fold the excess bias covering at right angles out to the raw edges (fold back at correct length, then fold at 45 degrees towards the raw edges).

- Tack or machine A to E slightly closer to the cord than the first row of stitching.

- At the lower end, trim away 1 cm ($^3/_8$") from the interlining and press the remaining 1 cm fabric seam allowance to the wrong side, over the edge of the interlining.

- Match points F and G to D and B respectively and pin with the heads of the pins clearly visible outside the edge of the bag.

- Take the lining and press the seam allowance along the straight edge F-G to the wrong side.

- Match this fold, *wrong sides together* to points BG and DF on the main bag, replacing the holding pins through all thicknesses.

- Fold the curved end of the lining up to meet the curved end of the cover, but make the lining fractionally shorter than the cover at AE. Pin the lower folds AE and AE and smooth the lining fabric towards point C; any excess fabric at C will be trimmed off later. Pin all layers together, placing pins inside the shape.

- Turn the piece over and machine, following the previous stitching line from A through B, C, D to E.

- Remove all pins and turn inside out. You now have a good looking flap but two outside pockets.

- Turn the outside pocket right way out over the lining pocket.

- Check the finish of the bag before turning it inside out again to make any minor adjustments and trimming the turnings, in layers, so that they do not form a bulky edge.

- Turn the bag right side out, pin the upper edges of the pocket together and slip stitch in place.
- Press lightly if necessary.

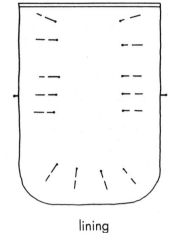

lining

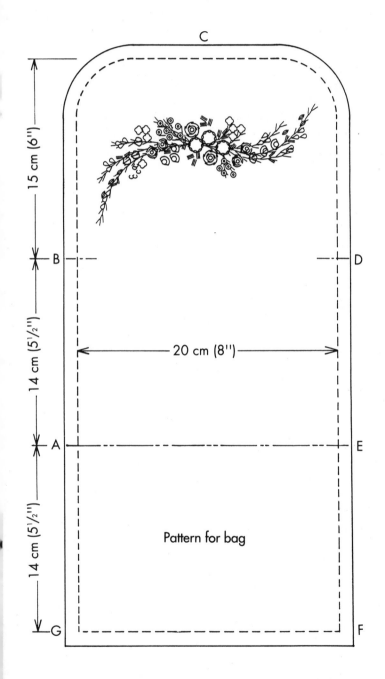

15 cm (6")

14 cm (5½")

14 cm (5½")

C

B

D

20 cm (8")

A

E

Pattern for bag

G

F

COMMERCIAL PATTERNS

For a more professional look you may prefer to use a commercial pattern. A full range of handbag patterns, together with the necessary frame parts, is available under the brand name 'Ghee's'. These patterns are multi sized, and come complete with full-sized patterns and detailed instructions. Metal frames, magnetic snaps and chains are available to use in conjunction with the patterns.

The bag with beaded panel pictured on page C2 is made from pattern style 951, using a 10" tubular aluminium frame. The panel carrying the embroidery is backed with quilt batting, the remainder of the bag fabric is quilted to give more body and hold the bag shape. The fabric used for this project was a medium-weight polyester linen-type fabric.

The Australian theme crazy patchwork bag (page C13) is made from pattern style 3801, using an 8" straight hex frame.

It may be possible to use a ready-made handbag for embroidery, as was the case with the fuchsia bag shown on page C23. The bag, made of black linen with a thin padding under the area embroidered, was not difficult to work using detached buttonhole stitch.

When working on this type of project, a slightly padded surface will be easier to handle and a careful choice of stitches is recommended. For example, colonial knots are not easy to work in this situation. Starting threads must be buried in the fabric some distance from where you wish to start. A tiny back stitch can be used for added security where it is hidden under the embroidery.

BOXES

COMMERCIAL PRODUCTS

There are a number of commercially produced boxes available for mounting embroidery. These are generally obtainable from specialist embroidery and craft shops. The Framecraft company produces a wide variety of porcelain, glass and metal boxes designed specifically to display handwork. The crystal powder bowl shown in colour on page C16 and the metal music box featured on page C2 are both from Framecraft. The following instructions are for the crystal powder bowl, but would be applicable to any work to be mounted in this way. It is essential to work on fine fabrics, otherwise mounting is too difficult.

- To prepare the fabric, draw two circles on a sheet of paper, the larger one being the same size as the inside of the lid rim and the smaller one being the circumference of the design.

- Choose a fine fabric for the embroidery (the original is worked on silk dupion) and back it with thin Pellon fleece or cotton fabric.

- Lay the paper pattern on the fabric and tack or machine around the inside circle first, then machine around the outer edge.

- Tear away the paper.

- Work the embroidery.

- Press the work face down on a towel.

I prefer to pull the fabric around the metal mounting disc provided, rather than cut it to the exact size of the lid as suggested in the Framecraft instructions. This removes all creases from the fabric and ensures that the fabric is firmly mounted, particularly as the perspex cover provided cannot be fitted over this type of embroidery.

- Trim the lining fabric right back against the outer ring of machine stitching, taking extreme care not to cut the outer fabric.

- Trim the outer fabric into a circle, allowing approximately 2 cm ($^3/_4$'') outside the machine stitching.

- Using a very strong thread, dental floss is good, run a gathering thread 1 cm ($^3/_8$'') from the edge.

- Centre over the metal disc, pull up firmly and tie off securely.

- If you wish to use a fabric protector, apply at this time in accordance with the manufacturer's instructions and allow to dry.

- Push embroidery firmly into the lid and glue the covering disc to the back.

BOXES WITH RECESSED LIDS

An alternative to using a commercial product is to find a wood turner who is willing to make boxes with recessed lids to accommodate the embroidery. The wooden box pictured in the colour section on page C2 was made for me by my husband and the embroidery is mounted on a plywood disc cut to fit the recess.

- Cut a template in plywood or heavy card to fit the recess, allowing a small gap to accommodate the fabric. This allowance will depend on the thickness of the fabric used.

- Centre the template on the fabric. Cut out, leaving ample turning allowance to permit correct centring of the design.

- Spray the template lightly with spray glue and place sticky side down onto a piece of batting. Cut out carefully.

- For oval or round templates, using strong thread, run gathering stitches around the edge of the fabric cover. Pull up firmly around the padded template, adjusting to centre the design correctly. Tie off firmly.

- For square-sided shapes, glue the seam allowance into place on the wrong side of the template, working alternately on opposite sides and pulling the fabric firmly to remove all creases.

- Glue the template firmly into the box top using a suitable adhesive.

FABRIC-COVERED BOXES — USING PLASTIC TEMPLATES

Often, however, the most convenient and inexpensive way is to make your own fabric-covered boxes which is not a difficult process. They can be made by hand or using a sewing machine.

No glue is required during construction and plastic templates are used for stiffening, making the boxes washable, provided the fabric chosen for the box can be laundered.

A variety of shapes and sizes can be made using the basic method. Inserts such as partitioned trays add interest to jewellery or sewing boxes.

For large boxes, extra strength can be obtained by using the plastic sheet double for the templates and choosing a firm fabric, such as furnishing cotton, to work with.

The method of constructing the box is exactly the same whatever the shape or size. The basic principle is to make a strip of pockets into which the templates are fitted for the sides of the boxes and single pockets for the top and bottom of the box. All these pockets are constructed on the sewing machine with the final construction of the box being worked by hand.

The following points should be kept in mind:

- Care must be taken to cut the templates accurately and label them to avoid confusion during construction.

- Lay out the templates very carefully to mark the pocket sizes. A firm snug fit is essential for good results. Each pocket should be about 3 mm ($^1/_8$") wider than the template to allow for the padding of the template.

- Firmly woven cotton fabrics are easiest for a beginner to work with. Once the technique has been mastered, silks, satins and synthetics are all suitable provided the weave is firm. Lighter weight fabrics are easier to handle for smaller boxes.

- When working embroidery on a box lid, back the fabric with Pellon and centre the design carefully. Always stitch the outline of the lid pocket when transferring the main design lines, as detailed on page 210. This outer line should include the extra pocket allowance mentioned above, as this stitching line is used when constructing the lid pocket after the embroidery is completed. *Note that all lid designs detailed in this book include the correct pocket allowance.*

- Trim the Pellon back to the seam line before turning the lid pocket.

- Trim all seams to approximately 9 mm ($^3/_8$") and always cut the fabric away across the corners before turning the pockets.

To construct box:

- Cut required templates carefully. Accuracy is essential.

- Cut or tear strips of fabric as specified.

- Fold side pocket strips in half, right sides together, and press.

- Lay out templates carefully across the strip with a 3 mm ($^1/_8$") gap between each one and 1.5 mm at each end. Mark the seam line at each end.

- Sew the side seams, trim the side seam allowance to 9 mm ($^3/_8$") and trim across the top corners, turn inside out and press.

- Re-position the templates along the folded edge of the pocket. Note that the spaces between each template should be even and the templates placed in the correct order if all the side panels are not identical in size.

- Draw a line between each template and mark the bottom of this line at the base of the template (see diagram on page 150).

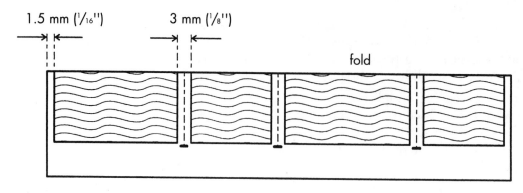

1.5 mm (¹⁄₁₆'')   3 mm (¹⁄₈'')

fold

(not to scale)

- Remove templates. Turn both raw edges in, in line with the bottom mark just made and pin, ready to sew down each vertical division between box sides. Note that one pin in line with each marked vertical line is sufficient.

- With matching thread and commencing at the bottom edge, sew up the marked line to the top fold. Stop the stitching at the fold with the needle in the down position. Turn the fabric and stitch down the seam covering the first stitching line. Note that double stitching in this way leaves all thread ends at the point where the boxes are sewn together and thus well hidden.

- All templates are covered with Pellon; usually one layer for the outside of the box and two for the inside. This must be sewn in place around the templates to prevent slipping when inserting them into the pockets. Stretch the wadding firmly around the templates, cutting it flush with the edges. Stitch the Pellon together working over the edges of the plastic. Do not allow the Pellon to bunch outside the edges of the templates. Extra layers of padding can be added if desired, but remember this may require extra fabric allowance for each pocket.

- Push covered templates into the fabric pockets. To make this process easier, the plastic can be rolled gently then flattened out inside the pocket, thus enabling irregular shapes to be inserted through small openings. Make sure all seam allowances are smoothed out and lying to the inside of the box.

- Tuck the bottom edges of the templates behind the seam allowance on the outside of the panel.

- Slip stitch the pockets closed. This seam should be on the inside when the box is constructed.

- Make a single pocket for the box base and complete in the same way.

- Cut a lining for the box top and match the right sides together. Stitch together along the stitching line already marked, leaving one side (preferably the back edge) open for turning. For a neater finish on all corners, carry the machine stitching around the back corners. Trim the fabric across the corners, turn and insert the template by rolling it to fit through the opening. Slip stitch the opening closed.

- Match the two ends of the side strip together and ladder stitch firmly together using strong thread (Coton Perle No 8 or linen thread is excellent).

- Fit the sides to the base and ladder stitch in place. (Note: Place the seamed edge next to the base with the handsewn corner to the back of the box.)

- Finish the lid and any tray inserts in the same way. Leave a small gap in the stitching at the centre back of the lid to allow for the decorative cord ends to be tucked in.

- Sew a decorative cord around the box top to hide the seam or work around the top with a row of palestrina knot stitch using a heavy thread.

Note that the lid of the box may be finished without side panels and hinged to the box by ladder stitching across the back edge. A button and loop can be used to hold the box closed.

Basic Rectangular Box _____

MATERIALS REQUIRED

Finished size: 15 cm x 10 cm x 7 cm (6" x 4" x 3")
Homespun or calico fabric: 30 cm x 112 cm (12" x 44")
Pellon or soft sew Vilene: 50 cm x 90 cm (20" x 36")
Sheet of template plastic: 45 cm x 31 cm (18" x 12")

For embroidery requirements and details refer to page 102.

METHOD

- Cut templates as detailed in diagrams on page 152.
- Cut fabric as follows:
  2 pieces 18 cm x 12 cm (7" x 5") for lid
  1 piece 20 cm x 17 cm (8" x 7") for base
  1 piece 16 cm x 50 cm (6½" x 20") for sides
  1 piece 9 cm x 50 cm (3½" x 20") for lid sides

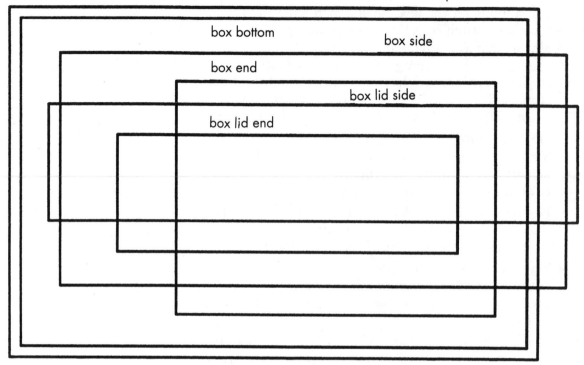

box top

box bottom

box side

box end

box lid side

box lid end

Template

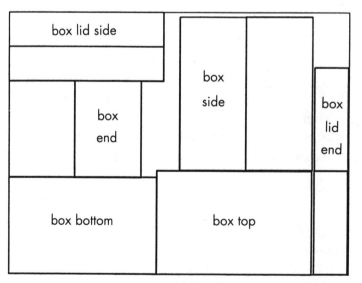

box lid side

box end

box side

box lid end

box bottom

box top

Layout for cutting templates from sheet plastic

Basic Rectangular Box

Elongated Octagonal Box with Tray Inserts _____

MATERIALS REQUIRED

Finished size: 22 cm x 12 cm x 9 cm deep (9" x 5" x 3½")
— includes one full tray and one 3-piece tray.
Plain fabric for outside of box and tray bases:
112 cm x 45 cm (45" x 18")
Patterned fabric for inside of box and sides of trays:
112 cm x 40 cm (45" x 16")
Pellon or soft sew Vilene: 1 m (39")
Template plastic: 77 cm x 30 cm (30" x 12")

For embroidery requirements and details refer to page 103.

METHOD

- Cut templates as detailed on pages 154 and 155.
- Cut fabric as follows:
  Plain fabric:
  one 63 cm x 11 cm (25" x 4½") box sides (outside)
  one 63 cm x 9 cm (25" x 3½") lid sides
  five 25 cm x 15 cm (10" x 6") top, base and tray bases
  one 26 cm x 13 cm (10½" x 5") tray base
  two 13 cm x 13 cm (5" x 5") tray base
  Patterned fabric:
  one 63 cm x 11 cm (25" x 4½") box sides (lining)
  one 25 cm x 15 cm (10" x 6") top lining
  one 60 cm x 11 cm (24" x 4½") tray sides
  one 40 cm x 10 cm (16" x 4") centre bottom tray sides
  two 30 cm x 10 cm (12" x 4") end tray sides
- Place the two box side pieces right sides together and mark a seam line 16 mm (⅝") from the top edge.
- Position templates along this line to establish side seam positions. Stitch along the side seams and the top of the pocket before continuing as before.

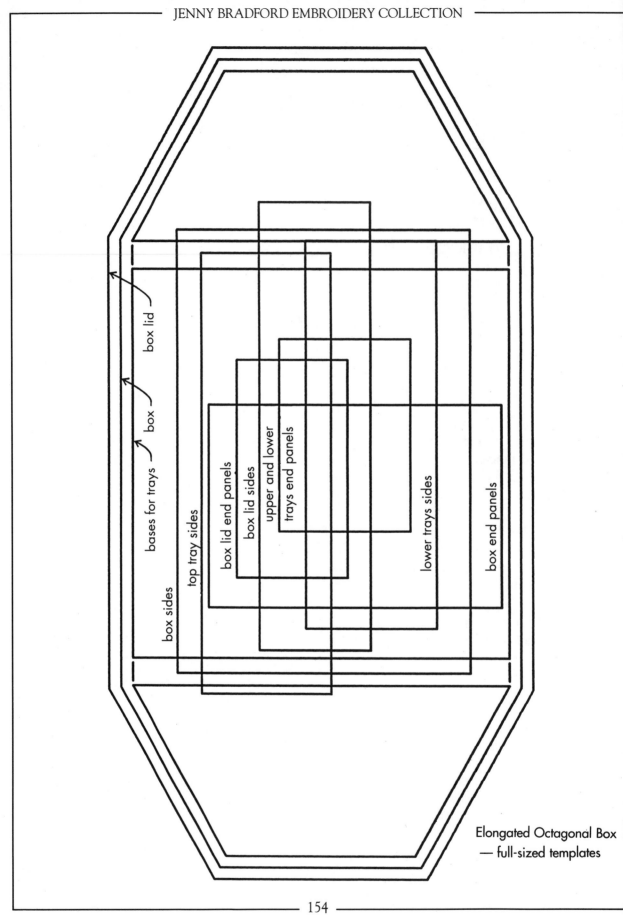

box lid

bases for trays — box

box sides

top tray sides

box lid end panels

box lid sides

upper and lower

trays end panels

lower trays sides

box end panels

Elongated Octagonal Box
— full-sized templates

Layout on plastic sheet 770 mm x 300 mm (30½" x 11¾")

1 box lid top 2 box base 3 top tray base
4 lower end tray base 5 lower middle tray base
6 box side 7 box end panel 8 box lid side
9 box lid end panel 10 top tray side
11 lower trays side 12 upper and lower trays end panel

Elongated Octagonal Box

Needle Box

This needle box is constructed in the same way as the boxes described earlier. Pockets are used along the folding section to hold packets of needles or cards of thread etc. Refer to the instructions for the basic box for more detail.

MATERIALS REQUIRED

Outer fabric: 115 cm x 30 cm (45" x 12")
Contrast pockets fabric: 62 cm x 13 cm (24½" x 5")
Pellon or soft sew Vilene: 30 cm (12")
Template plastic: 42.5 cm x 25 cm (17" x 10")

For embroidery requirements and details refer to page 105.

METHOD

- Cut out templates as detailed on page 156.
- Cut fabric as follows:
  Main colour:
  one 62 cm x 26 cm (24½" x 10½")
  one 38 cm x 24 cm (15" x 9½")
  one 14 cm x 14 cm (5½" x 5½")
  Contrast Colour:
  one 62 cm x 13 cm (24½" x 5")

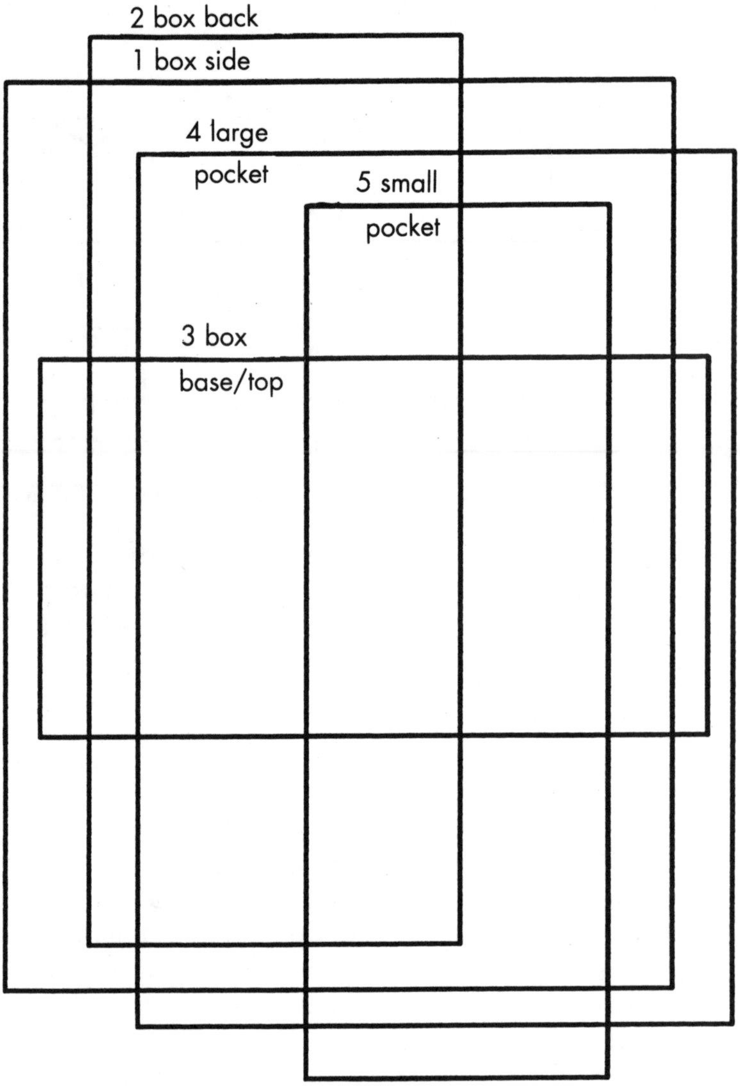

2 box back

1 box side

4 large
pocket

5 small
pocket

3 box
base/top

Full-sized template

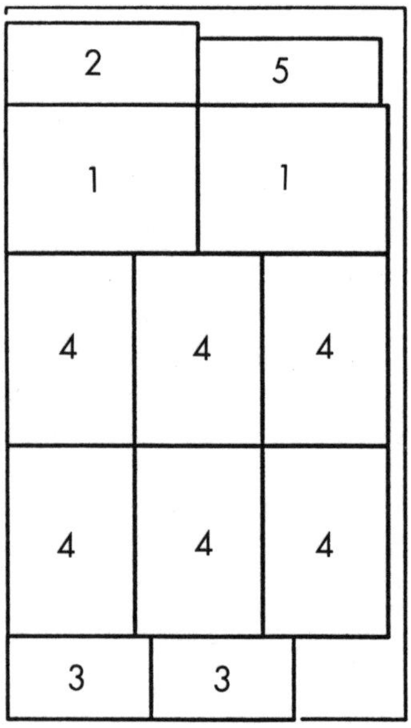

2	5
1	1
4	4	4
4	4	4
3	3	

1 box side   4 large pocket
2 box back   5 small pocket
3 box base/top

Layout on sheet size 250 mm x 425 mm (10" x 17")

Needle Box

Contrast Pocket Strip

- Fold the fabric in half and sew the long edges together allowing a 5 mm ($^3/_{16}$") seam allowance.
- Press seam open, turn right side out and press, centring the seam down the centre back of the piece.
- Place the pocket section along the 62 cm length of the fabric, 2 cm ($^3/_4$") up from the bottom of the strip. Sew in place across the bottom edge.
- Fold the strip in half, right sides together, and press. Lay the templates along the strip, carefully dividing it as shown below. Note that the gaps between the templates have been carefully calculated to allow the strip to fold correctly when finished.
- Continue construction as detailed for basic box side panel.

Outer Box

- Transfer the embroidery design to the lower right-hand corner of the 38 cm x 24 cm fabric strip and complete the embroidery.
- Construct box as detailed for the basic box.

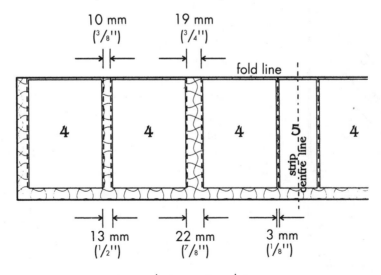

space between stitching

10 mm ($^3/_8$") 19 mm ($^3/_4$")

fold line

4 4 4 5 4

strip centre line

13 mm ($^1/_2$") 22 mm ($^7/_8$") 3 mm ($^1/_8$")

space between templates

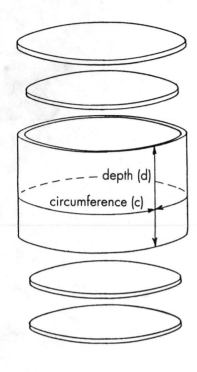

depth (d)

circumference (c)

FABRIC-COVERED BOXES —

USING CARDBOARD TEMPLATES

Cardboard templates can be purchased in kit form and normally come with assembly instructions. Boxes made using these templates will not be washable, but certain shapes such as round boxes are easier to work.

It is possible to cut your own templates for round boxes. Use a heavy duty tube (Postpak tubes are excellent) for the side and round discs of firm card for the base and top.

Cut three discs to fit just inside the tube, one for the base and one each for lining the base and top. Cut a fourth disc for the lid slightly larger in diameter than the diameter of the tube.

Round Box

The following method for covering a round box gives a very neat finish and does not require the use of glue in the main construction.

MATERIALS REQUIRED

Fabric and batting: 50 cm x 35 cm (to cover a box approximately 7.5 cm (3") in diameter by 5 cm (2") deep)
Spray glue

METHOD

- Measure around the outside of the tube section
- Measure the depth of the side.
- Fold the fabric on the *bias* (this is essential to achieve a good fit on the inside of the box), and mark out a bias strip to fit around the box using the measurements taken and adding 2.5 cm (1") to the box circum-ference and 2 cm ($^3/_4$") to the depth.

The folded edge of the fabric will be on the top edge of the box side. Do not skimp on the bottom edge seam allowance as stretching the biased strip around the box decreases the finished width of the strip.

- Lay the four top and bottom templates on the remaining fabric and cut out circles allowing 2 cm ($^3/_4$") turnings. When using an embroidered design for the top allow plenty of extra turning to ensure correct centring of the design.

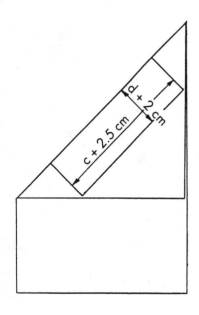

c + 2.5 cm

d + 2 cm

- To pad the box, lightly spray one side of all except the base disc with fabric glue and place them sticky side down on to the batting. Cut out each circle carefully. Cut a strip of batting to fit around the tube section covering both inside and outside surfaces. Spray the outside with glue and wrap with batting, lining up the bottom edge of the batting with the bottom edge of the template. Trim the batting so that the short edges just meet but do not overlap. Pull the batting over the top edge of the tube, stretching it firmly to remove as many creases as possible. Trim level with the base of the tube and whip stitch in place, stitching into the batting on the outside edge of the tube.

- Run a gathering thread using strong linen or buttonhole thread (dental floss makes an excellent substitute) around each circle of fabric. Centre templates, batting side down, on the wrong side of each circle. Pull up the gathering thread and fasten off securely, stretching the fabric firmly around each template.

- Mark the side seam position on the bias strip by stretching it firmly around the box side and pinning in place. Remove the strip and machine the side seam using a small stitch setting. Trim the seam allowance and press open. Press up the seam allowance on one long edge.

- Fit the strip carefully over the side of the box having the pressed hem on the inside and lined up with the base of the side.

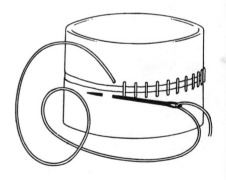

Pull the strip down over the outside of the box, pushing the raw edge to the inside under the pressed hem. Working the fabric to keep it crease free and a very firm fit, hem the edges together along the bottom edge.

- Ladder stitch the unpadded base circle into place. Apply glue to the base lining disc and push into place.

- Glue or ladder stitch the lid lining inside the lid and place on top of the box.

An alternative is to use ribbon or braid to decorate the box side, in which case the bias strip can be pulled around to position the edges to be joined on the outside of the box and the turnings trimmed back so that the fabric just meets. Ladder stitch the two edges together and cover the seam with ribbon or braid.

FABRIC-COVERED BOXES — USING PAPER

Origami Box

Based on the Origami method of paper folding, this small box is suitable for jewellery or tiny gifts.

MATERIALS REQUIRED

Finished size of box top: 5.5 cm (2¼") square
Heavy paper: 15 cm (6") square for box top and sides, and 14.5 cm (5¾") square for base
Fine cotton or silk dupion to cover the top
Spray adhesive

METHOD

- Lightly mark the diagonals on each square (diag. 1).
- Work the base of the box (smaller square) first.
- Fold the paper as shown in diags 2 to 4, pressing firmly along each crease. Open out flat (diag. 5).
- Repeat this folding process on the other diagonal lines. Open out flat again (see diags 6 to 7).
- Cut carefully along the heavy lines as shown in diag. 8.
- Re-fold the long sides, as shown in diag. 9, turning the cut end sections at right angles to overlap each other across the remaining sides.
- Fold the remaining side sections to the inside of the box, over the overlapping sections to hold them in place.
- Cut a square of paper to fit inside the base and glue in place to hold the box together.
- Fold the larger square as before (diags 1 to 5).
- Cut a piece of fabric the same size as this square. Position it over the paper (diag. 7) and carefully locate the centre square, which will be the box top, so that the embroidery can be accurately placed.
- Embroider a tiny spray of flowers within the lid area.
- Spray the paper square (ensuring that it is the correct way up to re-fold along the creased lines) with a *light* coating of spray adhesive.
- Attach the embroidered fabric square.
- Cut along the solid lines as before.
- Re-fold the box top as before, pressing the creases with a warm iron.
- Cut a fabric square to fit inside the lid and spray it lightly with adhesive. Press firmly into place.

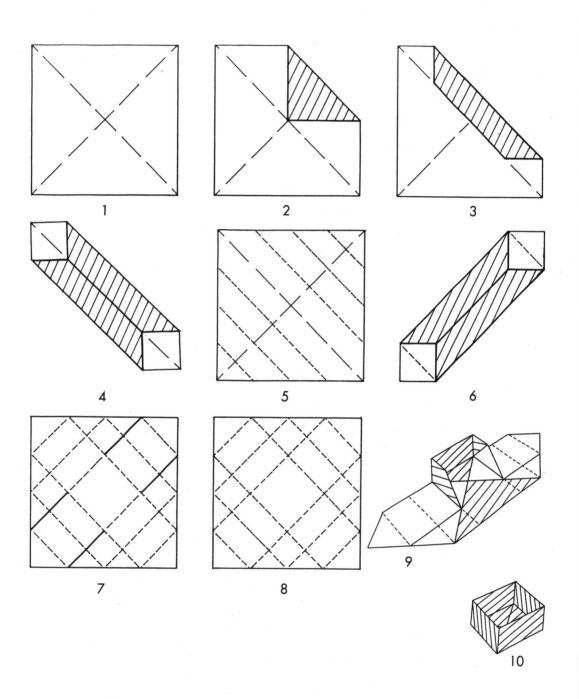

1

2

3

4

5

6

7

8

9

10

Origami Box Design

JOINTED TEDDY BEARS

There are two jointed teddy bears featured in colour on pages C8 and C24.

Woolly, made from wool blanketing, is cuddly, has wool-embroidered eyes and can be safely given to a young child.

Rosy, the heirloom bear, is made in homespun and is lavishly decorated with mock crazy patchwork including entredeux and other laces. Numerous tiny posies of flowers worked in textured embroidery add to her appeal. She would look equally as effective in velvet with touches of embroidery on the ears and paws and a pretty lace collar. Made in calico or homespun, without too much decoration, this bear can be used as a signature bear for a special occasion gift.

Both bears have button-jointed limbs but can be made with teddy bear joints if desired.

MATERIALS REQUIRED

Woolly:
Wool blanketing and Pellon fleece:
53 cm x 70 cm (21" x 27^1/$_2$")
Brown wool for features
— tapestry wool or 2 strands of Appletons crewel wool
Rosy:
Outer fabric and Pellon fleece:
57 cm x 70 cm (22^1/$_2$" x 27^1/$_2$")
Contrasting fabric for foot pads
Scraps of ribbon, lace and entredeux if desired
Threads for embroidery
Lace for collar: 50 cm x 5 cm wide (20" x 2")
2 snap-on eyes size 12 mm
For each bear:
Fibrefill stuffing: 500 g (18 oz)
4 good quality two-hole buttons
Extra-long doll making or upholstery needle
Very strong thread for attaching arms and legs — DMC Coton Perle No 3 or linen thread

METHOD

- Copy all pattern pieces onto paper, making right- and left-hand pieces as required. Do not cut out the pattern pieces. Lace placement lines as used on Rosy are shown on the pattern layout diagram (page 166).

- Back the chosen fabric with Pellon fleece and pin the pattern pieces to the fleece.

- Machine stitch the outline of each piece through the paper and fabric using a small stitch.

  Stitching the outline of each pattern piece through the paper pattern before cutting out prevents the pieces from stretching and distorting as the bear is constructed.

- Mark lace placement lines in the same way if required.

- Transfer the eye and limb placement marks to the right side of the fabric.
- Tear away the paper and cut the pattern pieces out carefully, just *outside* the machine stitching.
- Plan any lace placement carefully so that each strip covers the ends of the previous piece as it is sewn in place. Thread beading with ribbon as necessary as you work. See page 213 for more detail on mock crazy patchwork.
- Pin the lace and entredeux over placement lines and stitch in place, taking care not to pull the lace too tightly when sewing. Stretching the lace at this point may spoil the finished shape of the bear. Particular care should be taken when threading beading with satin ribbon as a tight strip of ribbon will not give as much as the fabric when stuffing the bear.
- Embroidery on either bear may be completed at this stage or, to gain more effective placement of the designs, when the individual pieces have been stuffed.
- Stitch all the darts in the side head panels.
- Place side head pieces right sides together and sew seam A-B.
- Match head gusset points C-A-C to side head sections C-A-C, tack into place and machine stitch carefully, using a small stitch.
- Join 'hand' pads to the inside arm pieces. Note that separate hand pads are not used in the pattern for Woolly.
- Stitch arms together, leaving open between X's for turning and stuffing.
- Stitch leg sections in the same way.
- Tack foot pads in place, right sides together, and stitch carefully.
- Stitch centre front body seam.
- Stitch centre back body seam, leaving open where the extra seam allowance is shown for turning and stuffing.
- Stitch front body to back body at side seams, matching the centre front and centre back seams at the base.
- Turn all pieces inside out.
- If using snap-on eyes, secure them in position.
- Stuff pieces firmly and ladder stitch openings together securely.

Successful stuffing is an art and if well done gives the work a professional finish.

Teddy's eyes

For the best results, always use good quality stuffing. Use a blunt tool, such as the handle end of a crochet hook or a screwdriver, to pack down small pieces of stuffing very firmly. You will be surprised how much can be packed into a small space. The use of an interlining when constructing the bear should make it easy to keep the surface of the bear smooth. A decorative bear should be stuffed firmly so that it holds its shape over a period of time. This is particularly important if the bear is to be used as a signature bear.

- If using embroidered eyes, work them in brown wool as shown in the diagram.
- Embroider the nose and mouth.

Using one strand of brown wool or two strands of stranded cotton, outline the nose area with a triangle of straight stitches. Fill in with satin stitch worked horizontally, and cover this with a second set of stitches worked vertically. Finally, outline the nose again with a straight stitch, and complete the mouth with straight stitch.

- Work any other embroidery necessary.
- Sew ears right sides together, turn and ladder stitch in place, from the head gusset seam down the dart stitching.
- Attach the arms and legs as follows:

If the long needle will not fit through the button holes, take a long double strand of strong thread and thread through the button, then thread the needle with one end of the thread and pass it through the limb and the body of the bear to the other side. Repeat with the other end of the thread. Leave threads untied while repeating the process to the attach the other limbs.

Pull the threads very firmly and tie off securely, each limb being tied off on the opposite side of the body between the body and the opposite limb.

- Tie a ribbon bow around the neck for Woolly, or make a lace collar for Rosy.

Sew short ends of collar lace into a circle and run a gathering thread around the straight edge. Slip over the bear's head, pull up, adjust gathers and tie off securely. Tie a ribbon around to cover the edge of the lace.

Note: The following pattern pieces can be used for both Woolly Bear and Rosy Bear. The seam line indicated is the seam line for Woolly Bear only. It is the cutting line for Rosy Bear, with a seam allowance of 2 to 3 mm ($^1/_{16}$" to $^1/_8$"). The hand pads are only required for Rosie.

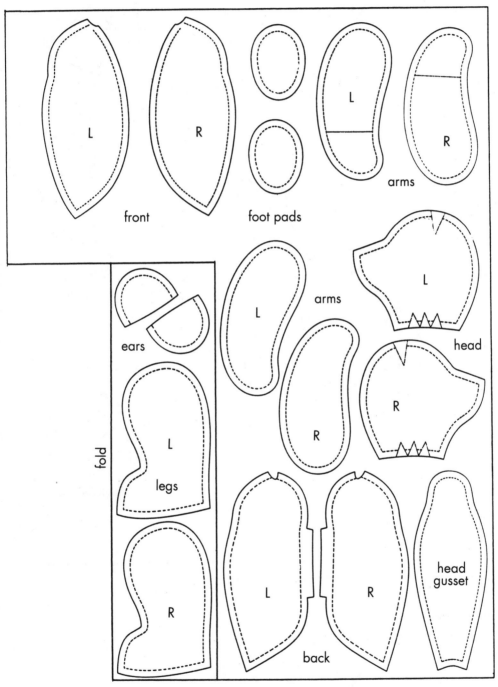

quarter scale layout for cutting from
53 cm x 70 cm (21" x 27$^1/_2$") material

Woolly Bear

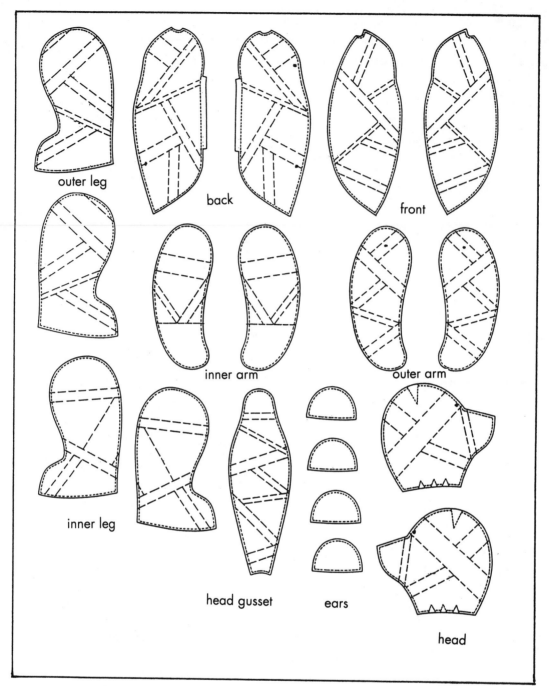

outer leg

back

front

inner arm

outer arm

inner leg

head gusset

ears

head

positioning of lace is indicated for the bear as illustrated

quarter scale lalyout for cutting from

57 cm x 70 cm (22½'' x 27½'') material

Rosy Bear

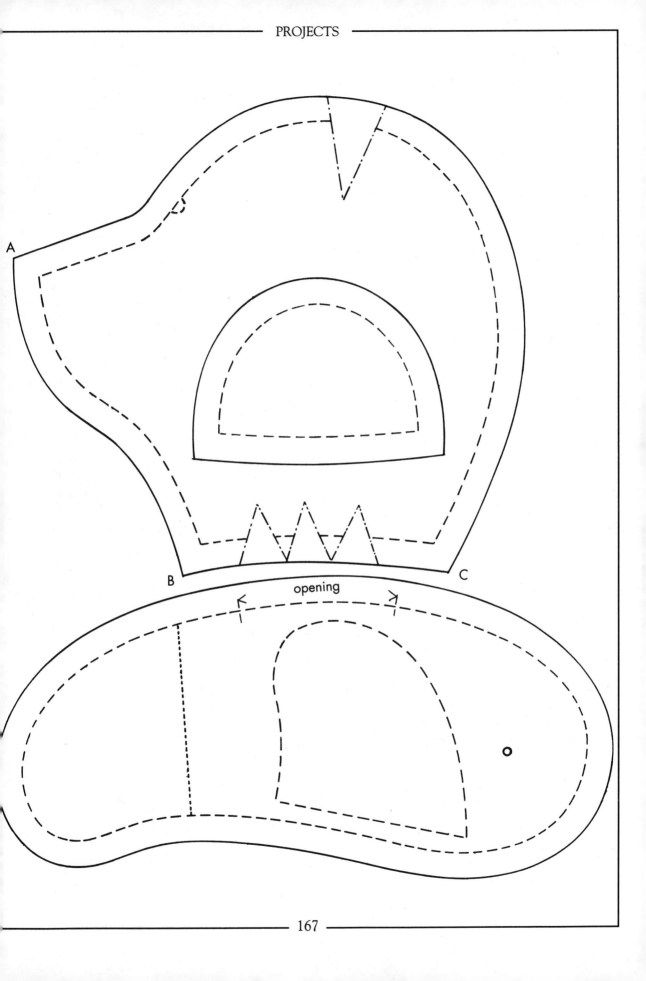

A

B   opening   C

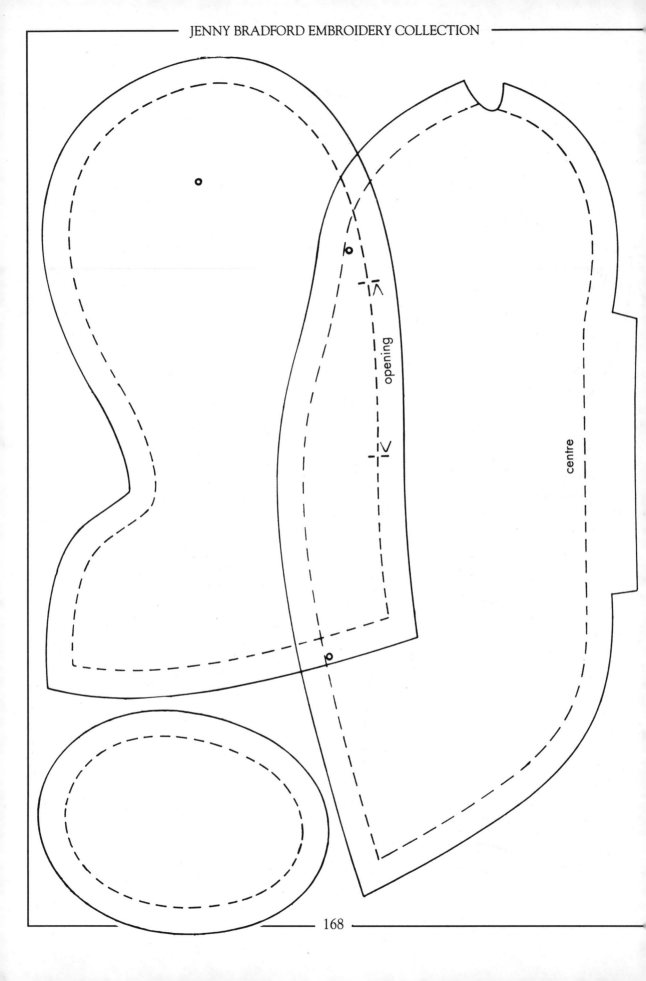

opening

centre

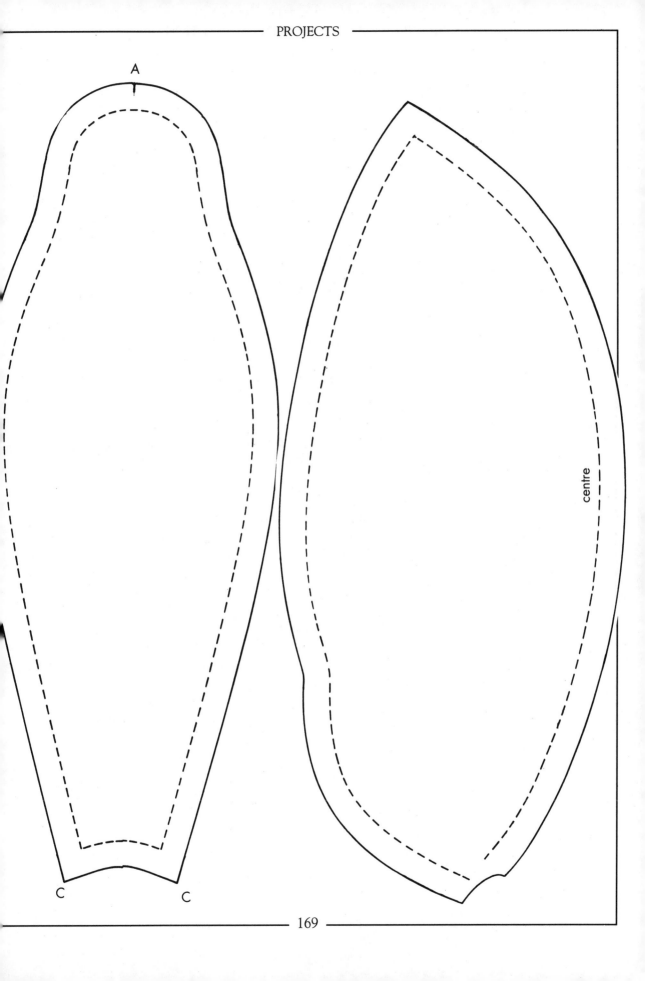

A

C   C

centre

CLOCKS

A clock kit, including a hand-turned Australian timber surround, was used to construct both clocks (featured in colour on pages C14 and C18). Made by my husband Don, it is available to order. Details for woodworkers are included on page 171.

Choose a firm fabric that is not too heavy for working the embroidery. The original designs were both worked on noil silk.

- To prepare the fabric, transfer the outlines of the disc and the required division lines by machine, as detailed on page 210, backing the fabric with Pellon fleece.

- Work the embroidery, taking care not to go too close to the machine-stitched guidelines, as the fabric will stretch a little when mounted.

- Trim away the Pellon backing close to the outer edge stitching. Trim the outer fabric to leave a 4 to 5 cm (2") turning *outside* this edge.

- Cut away the centre circle, leaving a similar turning allowance *inside* the inner marked circle.

- Cover the plywood template with a layer of thin wadding, cutting it flush with the edges of the disc.

- Run a strong thread around the outer edge of the fabric circle and pull to the back, centring over the disc. Tie firmly.

- Clip the inner turnings evenly around the circle to the machine-stitched circle.

- Using strong thread, lace the embroidery firmly in place, working across the back of the disc from the outer edge to the inner edge. Make sure the embroidery is correctly orientated in relation to the attaching screws or bolts and the 12 o'clock position.

- Protect with a fabric protector spray, if desired, before bolting into position on the clock.

  Mounting this way ensures that the fabric could be removed for dry cleaning if necessary.

- The divisions between each section are covered with a very fine craft braid, stretched across the front and sewn in at the back.

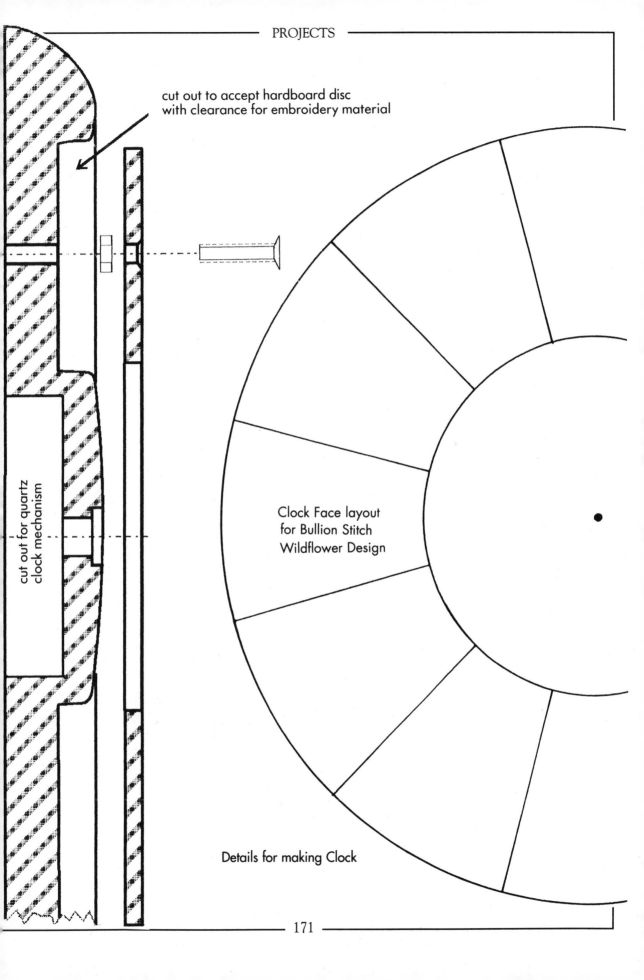

cut out to accept hardboard disc
with clearance for embroidery material

cut out for quartz
clock mechanism

Clock Face layout
for Bullion Stitch
Wildflower Design

Details for making Clock

EMBROIDERY AND JEWELLERY CADDIES

Armchair Caddy _____

A pretty gift for any needlewoman, designed to hang over the arm of your chair and keep your work things neat and tidy while working in front of the television. Two pockets holds scissors and thread, and a pin cushion protects your chair, and the rest of the family, from needles and pins.

MATERIALS REQUIRED

Fabric: 50 cm x 112 cm (20" x 45") is sufficient for one caddy, if cutting your own bias binding, or two if using purchased binding
Satin bias binding for the outside edges: 1.2 m (48")
1 piece firm batting: 60 cm x 25 cm (24" x 10")
Small quantity of stuffing for pin cushion
Ribbon for embroidery
Fancy cotton entredeux for simulating crazy patchwork: 115 cm (46")
Satin ribbon to weave through the beading: 115 cm

METHOD

- Trace pocket piece pattern (page 173), with all marked lines from page 174, onto paper twice. Prepare two pockets with all these guide lines marked. Tear away all paper.
- Prepare the pockets as directed on page 213 for mock crazy patchwork, and embroider with a selection of tiny flower designs.
- Quilt a piece of fabric 60 cm x 25 cm (24" x 10"), see page 212.
- Using the pattern on page 173, cut one backing piece from quilted fabric and one from the lining and pin wrong sides together.
- Cut two pocket linings. With right sides together match the top edges with the embroidered pockets and seam across. Turn pocket linings to inside, leaving a bound edge along the top.
- Position pockets at either end over the lining piece.

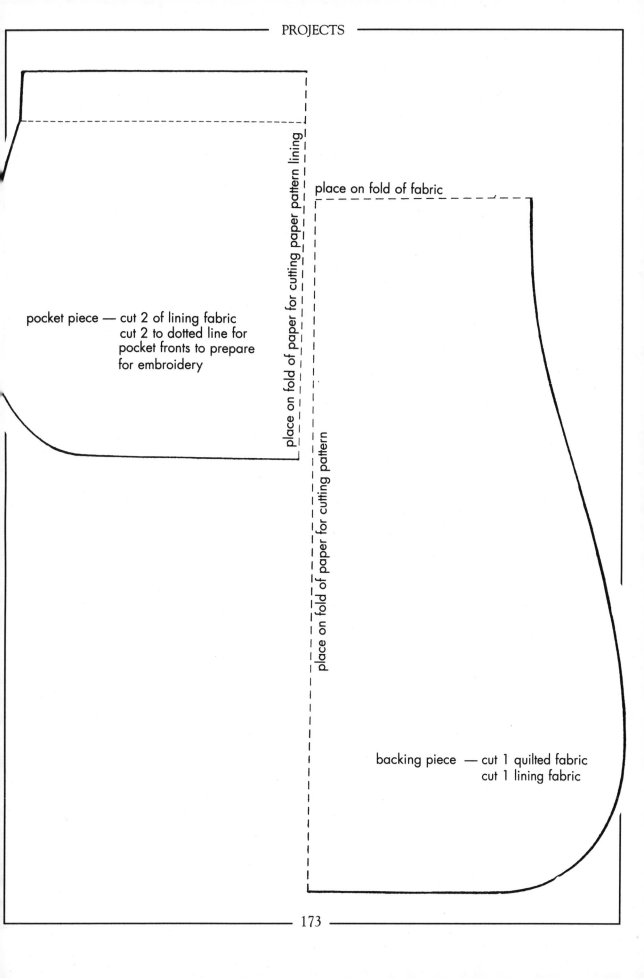

pocket piece — cut 2 of lining fabric
cut 2 to dotted line for
pocket fronts to prepare
for embroidery

place on fold of paper for cutting paper pattern lining

place on fold of paper for cutting pattern

place on fold of fabric

backing piece — cut 1 quilted fabric
cut 1 lining fabric

- For the pin cushion, cut a piece of quilted fabric 15 cm (6″) square and decorate as desired. Seam into a tube and turn right side out. Centre the seam at the back and seam across one end. Stuff, keeping filling towards the centre until the pin cushion is mounted. Measure against the centre of the backing piece, matching closed end with one edge. Trim open end to fit the width of the backing piece and sew across the end. Pin in place.

- Using a zigzag stitch, stitch right around the outside edge, taking care to hold the stuffing of the pin cushion away from the seam as far as possible.

- Bind the edge with a bias strip or purchased satin binding, stretching slightly around the curves.

- Work the pin cushion in the hands to distribute stuffing more evenly.

pocket front shows design area only,
not including bound edges

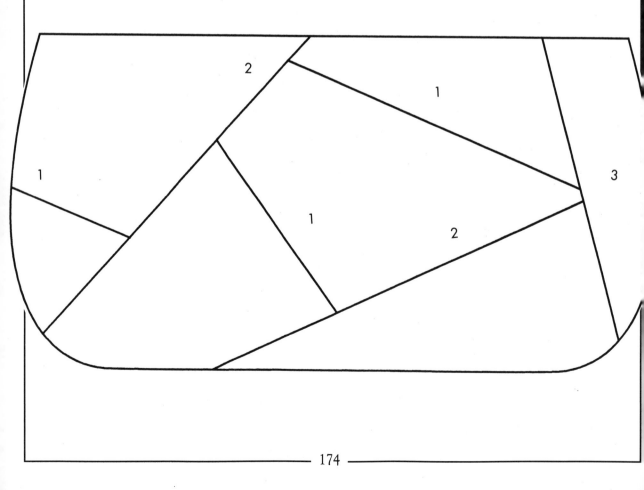

Embroidery caddy

This useful caddy is designed for the embroidery enthusiast to carry all the requirements needed for the latest project, or to keep packed ready for the next workshop or guild meeting.

It contains large pockets for a clipboard, design leaflet, notebook, etc. The spine is strengthened with a metal ruler, a useful piece of equipment, particularly at workshops, and there is ample room for threads, scissors, embroidery hoops, etc.

The finished size of the photographed front panel (page C10) is 39 cm x 28 cm (15$\frac{1}{2}$" x 11"). This allows for the easy storage of an A4 size clipboard or notebook and most embroidery design leaflets, as well as a 30 cm (12") ruler in the spine.

The size can be adjusted to suit your own needs. Start your calculations by selecting the length of the zip required for the pockets, which will determine the depth of the caddy. Then adjust the width in proportion to this.

MATERIALS REQUIRED

(For the caddy as pictured)
Fabric: 1.65 m x 115 cm wide (1$\frac{4}{5}$ yds x 45")
Pellon: 1.35 m x 90 cm wide (1$\frac{1}{2}$ yds x 36")
Cream aida band: 1.2 m x 5 cm wide (48" x 2")
Lace insertion: 1.6 m x 2 cm wide (63" x 1")
(braid or ribbon can be substituted for either of the above two items)
4 zips: 35 cm (14") long

METHOD

- Cut front panel 65 cm x 39 cm (25$\frac{1}{2}$" x 15$\frac{1}{2}$").

- Cut a Pellon backing piece, place the panel and backing together and transfer the required design to the front cover section. Make sure this is positioned correctly so that the folder opens from the right-hand side when finished.

- Work the embroidery (see page 51 for appropriate design).

- Quilt the following pieces:

(Note that the cut size is before quilting and the trimmed size is after quilting. Sizes are in centimetres with inches shown in brackets.)

Item	Cut Size	Trimmed Size
1 backing panel	42 x 68	39 x 65
	(16$\frac{1}{2}$" x 27")	(15$\frac{1}{2}$" x 25$\frac{1}{2}$")
1 large pocket piece	42 x 62	39 x 59
	(16$\frac{1}{2}$" x 24")	(15$\frac{1}{2}$" x 23$\frac{1}{4}$")
2 pocket pieces	42 x 23	39 x 21
	(16$\frac{1}{2}$" x 9")	(15$\frac{1}{2}$" x 8$\frac{1}{4}$")

- Cut lining fabric to match the three trimmed quilted pocket pieces.

- Place the lining right sides together with the three pocket pieces. Using a seam allowance of 5 mm ($\frac{3}{16}$"), sew along one long edge of each of the small pocket pieces and along both short edges of the large pocket piece.

- Turn right sides out and press along the machine stitching line.

- Place these finished edges along one side of each of the four zips and top stitch in place.

Make sure the zips will open from the left when the pockets are positioned as shown in the diagram on page 177.

- Cut two strips of fabric 8 cm x 39 cm (3" x 15^1/$_2$"). Fold each in half along its length and press firmly.

- Place the folded edge along the other side of the zips on the large pocket and sew in place. Decorate these strips with lace insertion.

- Place the smaller pocket pieces on the top of the large section, positioning the centre of the zips 6.5 cm (2^1/$_2$") away from the centre of the zips on the large pocket. Pin in place.

- Zigzag across the bottom edges of these two pockets.

- Embroider butterflies, using the charts on page 31, onto the aida band.

- Position a strip of the band to cover the zipper edge and top stitch in place. Top stitch the other edge across the top of the first pocket.

- Use the remaining aida band to make a pocket in the spine.
  — Cut a lining piece to match the remaining aida band and sew right sides together across the top of the band. Fold the lining to the wrong side and position across the middle of the caddy 2.5 cm (1") down from the top edge. (This edge must not get caught in the binding when finishing the caddy.) Trim the lower edge of the band to the lower edge of the caddy.

- Place the whole pocket section on top of the backing section, right sides up.

- Cover the edges of the spine pocket and the other larger pockets with lace insertion or ribbon. Top stitch in place through all thicknesses.

- Make two handles from quilted fabric. Cut two strips each 30 cm x 5 cm (12" x 2"). Sew into a tube, right sides together. Turn inside out and pin to the sides of the pocket section as indicated on the pattern.

- Place the cover section right sides together with the pocket section and sew across the side edges.

- Turn right sides out, match the top and bottom edges and trim if necessary. Stitch together.

- Cut two straight strips 67 cm x 7 cm (26^1/$_2$" x 2^3/$_4$"). Fold in half along the length, press firmly and use to bind the top and bottom edges (see page 211).

Embroidery Caddy Layout

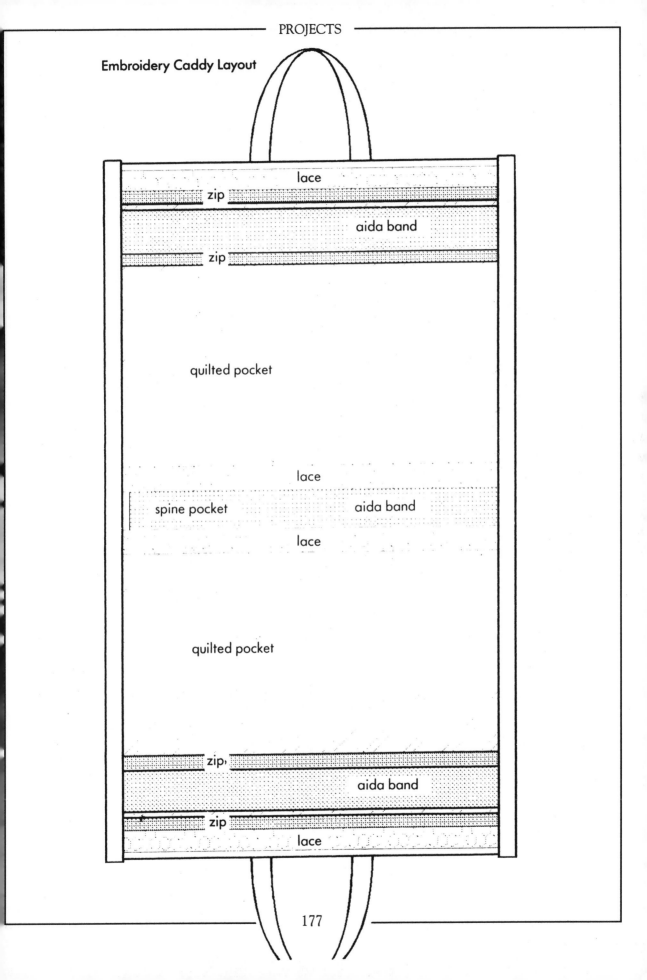

lace

zip

aida band

zip

quilted pocket

lace

spine pocket   aida band

lace

quilted pocket

zip

aida band

zip

lace

Jewellery caddy

The finished overall size of this caddy is 31 cm x 17 cm (12¹/₄" x 6³/₄"). There are two zip pockets, one open pocket and a quilted panel on which to pin brooches, etc. The caddy is made from silk dupion, both inside and out.

MATERIALS REQUIRED

Fabric: 35 cm x 80 cm (14" x 31¹/₂")
Pellon: 35 cm x 75 cm (14" x 29¹/₂")
2 zip fasteners: 15 cm (6") long
Ribbon or decorative braid: 35 cm (14") x approximately 1.5 cm (¹/₂")
Ribbon for ribbon ties: 50 cm (20") x 2 or 3 mm (¹/₈")
Decorative button for fastening
Silk ribbon for embroidery

METHOD

- Cut the outside panel 35 cm x 18 cm (14" x 7"). Back with Pellon and centre the design 8 cm (3") from one end of the panel. Transfer the design as detailed on page 210.

- Cut one lining panel 35 cm x 18 cm (14" x 7"). The backing of this panel will depend on the weight of the fabric selected for the caddy.

- Cut three pocket pieces and three Pellon pieces, each 15 cm x 18 cm (6" x 7"). Tack a Pellon piece to each pocket piece.

- Work all embroidery, including a flower on each pocket piece as shown in the diagram on page 179, using a section of the design detailed for the knitted vest.

- Fold the pockets in half, wrong sides together, and press along the folded edge.

- Lay the zips under the folded edges of two of the pockets, allowing the fold to completely cover the teeth of the zip. Pin each zip in place *to the lining section of the pocket only*. Open out the pocket and, with the wrong side of the zip uppermost, stitch the zip in place.

- Fold the pockets again and position on the lining panel.

- Use the ribbon or fancy braid to cover the free edge of the zip and the bottom of the next pocket. Top stitch neatly into place. Repeat for the second zip pocket and the base of the third open pocket.

- Cut a piece of fabric and Pellon 13 cm x 18 cm (5" x 7") and quilt (see page 212).

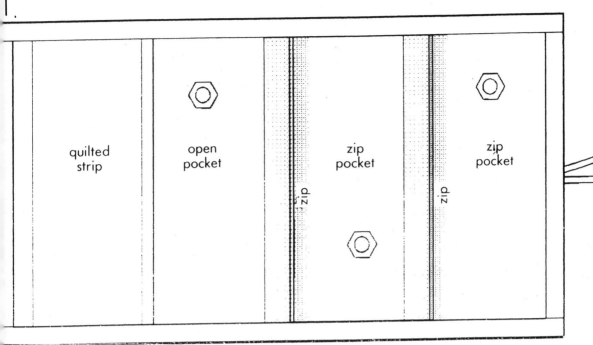

quilted
strip

open
pocket

zip
pocket

zip

zip
pocket

zip

Layout — half size

- Bring the long edges right sides together and sew into a tube.
- Turn inside out, centre the seam at the back and press firmly. Tack into place along the side edges.
- Measure the lining section carefully and trim to size of 31 cm x 18 cm (12" x 7"). Measure and trim the outer panel to 34 cm x 18 cm (13¹/₂" x 7"). Note that the outer panel is longer than the lining panel.
- Place the two panels right sides together, matching the short ends to each other. Sew across both ends, taking 5 mm (³/₁₆") turnings. Trim the Pellon in the seam allowance close to the stitching from the outer panel section only.
- Turn right side out. The extra fabric allowance on the front panel now forms the binding on the ends of the caddy.
- Bind the sides with a straight strip of matching fabric cut double. (See page 211.)
- Fold the ribbon tie in half and stitch in place, using two bullion lazy daisy stitches to hold the ribbon loop firmly. Sew a back shank button on the other end close to the fold. Tie the ribbon around the button.

SCISSOR HOLDER

The holder pictured on page C22 is decorated with knotted lace worked from the book *Knotted Lace* by Elena Dickson and published by Sally Milner Publishing. However, purchased lace edging and beading will look just as pretty if you do not have the time or inclination to make your own lace.

MATERIALS REQUIRED

Homespun or similar fabric: 35 cm x 15 cm (14" x 6")
Pellon or soft sew Vilene: 35 cm x 15 cm
Ribbon: 1 m x 2 cm wide (39" x $^3/_4$")
Entredeux: 2 m (78")
Beading for ribbon insertion: 1 m
Ribbon for insertion: 1 m
Lace edging for insertion and scissor holder: 3 m (117")
2 metal rings: one 45 mm ($1^1/_3$") inside diameter
                    one 25 mm (1") inside diameter
Template plastic: 15 cm x 15 cm (6")

METHOD

- Cut plastic templates from the pattern.
- Using the method given on page 210, mark the design on page 106, including the outline for the front of the scissor case, onto the homespun backed with Pellon.
- Work the line embroidery.
- From the diagram on page 181, trace the outline of the template for the back of the case onto the wrong side of the homespun.
- Back the front and back marked pieces with a second piece of fabric, right sides together, and sew around the edges. Stitch 1 mm ($^1/_{25}$") outside the marked lines but leave open between A and B for turning and insertion of the templates.
- Cut out both pieces. Trim the Pellon back to the seam line on the front section and turn right side out.
- Cover the templates with Pellon as described for the box construction on page 150.
- Slide the templates into the pockets and hem stitch the opening closed.
- Slip stitch lace along the top edge of the front pocket.
- Place the two pieces together and ladder stitch with strong thread. Slip stitch lace in place around the outer edge.

To make the strap:

- Join the entredeux down both edges of the beading and join lace edging to the other side of the entredeux.
- Thread ribbon through the beading and back the strip with the wide ribbon, sewing down the centre of the entredeux on both sides to join.
- Attach one end to the back of the scissor holder.

To make the thread holder:

- Bind the two rings with Coton Perle No 5 or 8, working buttonhole stitch over the ring. Pack the stitches very close to cover the metal completely and turn the ridged edge of the stitching to the inside of the ring.
- Fill in the small ring, working a crisscross of stitches across the ring and passing the needle through the ridged edge of the binding to hold them firmly in place. Pad the centre with a circle of Pellon or a small amount of wadding as you work.
- Gather a piece of narrow lace to fit around the edge of the smaller ring and sew in place.
- Work the flower embroidery, starting in the centre of the ring.
- With strong thread stitch the two rings together at the top and sew the other end of the strap to the back of the rings.

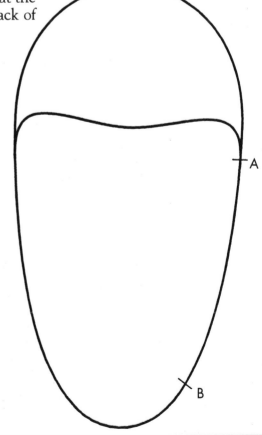

NEEDLE CASE

This needle case is made using the pocket method described in box making. Plastic templates are used to stiffen the front and back cover sections. It could be embroidered with the pansy spray design on page 95.

MATERIALS REQUIRED
Finished size (when closed):
8.5 cm x 10.5 cm (3³/₈" x 4¹/₈")
Homespun or similar fabric: 20 cm x 23 cm (8" x 9")
Doctor's flannel or felt: 16 cm x 10 cm (6¹/₂" x 4")
Plastic for templates
Pellon or soft sew Vilene
Minnamurra stranded cotton: 2 skeins of colour to match embroidery for tassels
Coton Perle 8 and gold thread for edging

METHOD
- Cut two plastic templates 10 cm x 8 cm (4" x 3¹/₄")
- Fold fabric in half (right sides together) to make a piece 20 cm (8") wide by 11.5 cm (4¹/₂") deep with the fold as the top edge.

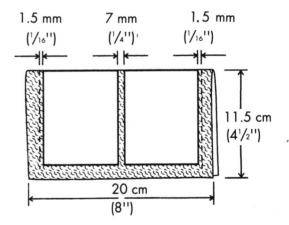

- As shown in the diagram, lay templates side by side on the fabric, short side to the fold and with a 7 mm (just over ¹/₄") gap between the long sides down the centre of the pocket. Mark the outer edges 1.5 mm (¹/₁₆") outside the plastic template edges.
- Finger press or iron the fabric into quarters to help position the embroidery accurately.

- Work the embroidery, positioning the design in the lower right section of the fabric.

- Fold the fabric right sides together and sew along the marked side edges of the pocket.

- Trim across the top corners and along the side edges. Turn the pocket right side out and press carefully.

- Replace the plastic templates flush with the folded edge and mark the lower edge of the templates and the inner edges, allowing a little room for padding the templates.

- Trim the lower edge to leave a turning about 1 cm ($^3/_8$") wide. Turn both raw edges of the pocket to the inside at the marked centre points. Pin in place.

- Using matching thread, sew along the marked two lines at the centre as described on page 150.

- Cover the templates with Pellon, sewing it in place (see page 150). Slide templates into the formed pockets. Turn in remainder of seam allowance and hem stitch in place.

- Overlock or hem the edges of the flannel and slip stitch in place between the machine stitching.

- Work palestrina stitch around the outer edges using two strands of Perle 8 and one of gold thread.

- Finish with a twisted cord (page 215) approximately 28 cm (11") long decorated with two tassels (page 214), all made from stranded cotton to match the embroidery.

SCISSORS PILLOW AND PIN CUSHION

The designs used for the hearts pictured are detailed in the canvas work section. To assemble the hearts, you will need a small quantity of Toy Fill or wool tops for stuffing.

- Cut out the worked pieces, allowing a 5 mm ($^1/_4$") turning all around each piece.

- Back stitch very firmly the short ends of the gusset together with matching thread. Stitch only across the five stitched rows; leave the turnings unstitched.

- Finger press the turnings to the back of each piece leaving one unstitched thread for joining. *Do not* clip any curves at this point.

- To sew the gusset to the base, work from the right side and use six strands of stranded cotton. Fold the gusset along the centre unstitched thread and match this to the bottom point of the back heart. Work long-legged cross stitch over the edge of the two pieces, picking up one thread from each side for each stitch and pulling the edges firmly together.

- Work around to the top point of the heart which should match up with the join in the gusset. As you get close to this point, clip into the top point of the heart turning to within two threads of the stitching. (This point can be strengthened with a spot of anti fray or fabric glue.)

- Continue stitching around the other side, leaving the last 2 cm ($^3/_4$") open for stuffing.

- Sew the gusset to the front section in the same way, starting at the bottom point and stitching right around the heart.

- Stuff the heart firmly and close the opening.

- Stitch ribbon loops on the front and back of the heart.

- Attach to your scissors by looping the ribbons over one handle of the scissors.

DECORATING READY-TO-WEAR CLOTHING

When choosing a purchased garment or pattern to make your own, bear in mind the following:

- The design should be simple, in order to focus on the embroidery. Other embellishments such as tucks or lace should complement the embroidery but not overshadow it by being too prominent.
- Careful placement of the design so that it does not conflict with darts, etc. that will be sewn later.
- Careful placement of the embroidery to focus attention on the wearer's good figure points, rather than attracting attention to the bad points.
- Embroidery usually looks better on a plain-coloured background; however, it can be used effectively to highlight and accentuate parts of a background design.
- Finally, give careful consideration to laundering, see page 215, when choosing the fabric for your project.

Daisy

Towelling Robe

Suitable items of clothing can be hard to find; however, one soon gets used to looking for key design detail that can be used to advantage. Occasionally this can involve a slight alteration to a garment. For example, the towelling robe pictured in the colour pages was originally a wrap-over style. By purchasing a size smaller than normally required and sewing in a heavy duty, open-ended zip, the front panelling became an ideal place for embroidery.

The bullion daisies are quick to work using San Remo five ply cotton knitting yarn, requiring just eight wraps for each petal. The quilted edging on the gown provides an ideal base for the embroidery. The actual size of each flower is shown here. They are scattered in groups of one, two or three flowers along the front panel and around the cuffs. The centre of each flower consists of colonial knots worked with two strands of stranded cotton in gold.

Collar and Cuffs

Patterns for detachable collars are generally featured in commercial pattern books under 'accessories' or are available from specialty shops selling supplies for heirloom sewing.

The child's collar pictured on page C4 is made using lace beading threaded with white satin ribbon to divide the basic yoke pattern into sections. The lace is applied over the collar fabric and the satin ribbon held in place with tiny colonial knots worked in 2 mm pink silk where the satin ribbon passes under the lace beading. The embroidered designs are worked in each panel in soft pinks and white.

The dress pictured on page C7 was rather dull until the silk ribbon rolled roses were used to decorate the large white collar. In this case the embroidery has been carried further to a touch on the sleeve, replacing the original button trim, and the plain buckle has been replaced with a fabric-covered porcelain disc (see page 194). The fabric used to cover the buckle came from the hemline when the dress was shortened.

Lady's Nightgown

Motifs such as the pink roses on this nightgown (page C13) can be added directly to a garment or embroidered onto a strip of fabric that can be used as an insertion into the collar or yoke. Heirloom sewing techniques are useful for adding insertion pieces. There are many publications on heirloom sewing, both by hand and machine, and your local sewing machine specialist should be able to assist you with setting up your machine for this beautiful specialised form of needlework.

Christening Gown or Petticoat Panel

The christening gown was made up from silk batiste, using a smocked bishop daygown pattern lengthened by the addition of lace bands and the embroidered panel.

Matinee Jacket

This little jacket, made from wool challis, is cut from a purchased layette pattern. The same idea could be used on the yoke of a dress, a sleeping bag, cot cover or the bib of a pinafore dress or dungarees.

The decorative quilting is worked with a twin needle and shiny machine embroidery thread.

A fine Pellon or one of the lightweight waddings designed especially for clothing makes an ideal backing for quilting. If you do not want such a thick padding, a layer of flannelette is quite satisfactory.

The embroidery design is detailed on page 49.

- Quilt the fabric and cut out the pattern pieces before working the embroidery.
- Lightly trace the main lines of the design on to the fabric by placing a copy of the design between the quilt batting and the design area.
- Neaten the edges of the cut pieces with a machine zigzag stitch to prevent fraying.
- Work the embroidery.
- Finish the garment according to the pattern you are using.

Black Vest

The vest was made from a commercial vest pattern. Choose a pattern carefully. The only shaping in the pattern I used was in the side seam and two tiny darts at the back neck edge. Heavy dart shaping should be avoided as it may interfere with the final positioning of the embroidery. Patterns designed for patchwork garments are usually ideal. The garment photographed is embroidered with three different styles: the heart on the centre back yoke area, the line design on the lower half of the front and back panels, and the mock crazy patchwork design on the front yokes. Each of these styles could be used individually on a garment with great effect.

Lines of whipped running stitch, pearl stitch and rosette chain are used to section the yoke, in place of the beading used on the sewing caddy. The positioning of the lines on the front yoke section are shown in the diagram, which has been reduced by 50 per cent.

The line treatment on the lower half of the garment is worked directly over some of the quilting lines.

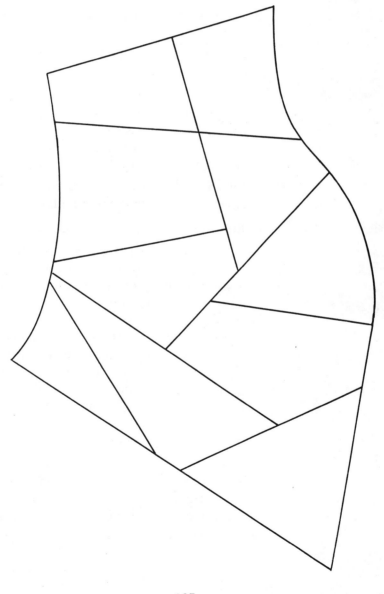

- To design your vest, cut out the pattern pieces in plain paper and draw the outlines of the design on the paper. Transfer design lines to the fabric pieces using the method given on page 210. All regular quilting can be done as described on page 212 without the use of this paper method.

- Tear away paper and complete any further quilting. In the case of the original vest the lower section is quilted with a twin needle in vertical unevenly spaced lines.

To make matching panels of unevenly spaced lines using the quilting guide, work on both fronts at the same time and complete the same line on each front before altering the position of the guide.

Work the back in the same way starting at the centre line.

- Work all embroidery. You could use designs from page 47.

- Re-position the original pattern carefully and cut away any excess fabric.

- Cut out the vest in the lining fabric.

- Construct the vest and the lining separately by joining the shoulder and side seams. Place them wrong sides facing and tack or edge stitch together around the armhole and outer edges.

- Bind all edges with matching bias, satin bias binding or double fold braid designed for the purpose.

Knitted Vests

The woollen garments chosen for the projects in this book are all fine knits, which tend to look better with fine stitch embroidery. However, if you choose to work with heavier embroidery threads, a chunkier knit would be more appropriate.

Knitted fabrics often have too loose a weave to hold silk ribbon securely. This problem can be overcome by backing the area to be embroidered with a very fine non-stretch fabric such as voile or silk organza.

To decorate a garment of the type illustrated on page C12, cut a facing to fit the neckline of the garment, neaten both edges by rolling and whipping or over-locking before tacking into place.

Note: By using a non-stretch fabric the stretch will be removed from that area of the garment. Do not use this method where it is necessary to stretch the neckline in order to put the garment on!

QUICK AND EASY PROJECTS

GREETING CARDS AND GIFT TAGS

It is possible to purchase the mounts for these in many craft shops, however, if you intend to make a number of them, it will cost less to cut your own.

Correspondence cards in various sizes, usually with fancy edges, can be purchased from stationers and can be used for place cards and gift tags.

To cut your own mounts you will need a sheet of heavy paper or thin card obtainable from art suppliers, a small craft knife and a template for the shape of cutout required. Either a picture frame matt board or the front section of a cardboard photo frame template, used for fabric-covered photo frames, will make an ideal template.

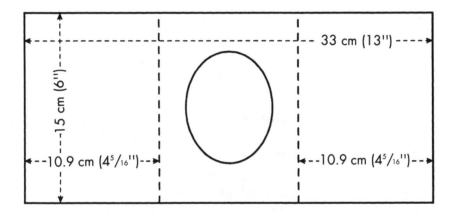

Cut the mount as shown in the diagram. Note that the third section is for folding behind the mounted embroidery. See page 43 for full-sized drawings of the cut-out shape.

Gift tags can be cut from the template given below.

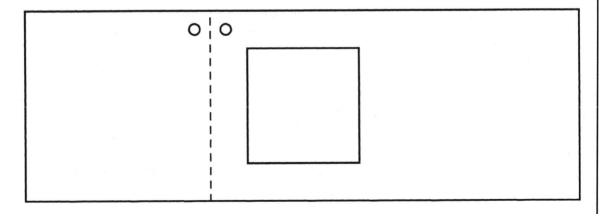

- Work your chosen design onto the fabric. As you work, position the card mount over the embroidery to check for size and positioning of the design.
- Cut the fabric to size, slightly smaller than the full size of the card front.
- Before mounting the fabric, cut a piece of thin batting to fit inside the window in the card.
- If you wish to cover the mount with fabric, proceed as follows using a suitable lightweight fabric:
  — Cut a piece of fabric the exact width of the front of the card but allowing 2 cm ($^3/_4$") for each of the turnings at the top and bottom of the card.
  — Glue the fabric into position on the reserve side along the top and bottom edge.
  — Cut away the centre opening, leaving a turning.
  — Clip the turnings around the curves to the edge of the opening and glue the turnings around the edge on the reverse side.
  — Finish the edges with fine braid.
- Position the embroidery and glue into place, stretching it as the glue dries to remove as many creases as possible.
- Spread glue sparingly over the backing sheet section of the card, making sure that you glue the correct one so that the design is the right way up when the card opens from the right side.
- Carefully position the thin batting behind the embroidery over the cut out area and fold over the glued section to cover. The insertion of the batting helps to smooth out any slight creases in the embroidery.

The designs used on the cards photographed are detailed in Chapter 9. However, I am sure readers will be able to add many more. If you have a flair for painting, try creating designs with fabric paint and adding just a touch of embroidery.

PRETTY PACKAGING

Attractive packaging can add the final personal touch to a special gift. The following ideas are quick and easy and certain to add that special touch.

Velvet Heart Jewellery Pouch _____

MATERIALS REQUIRED

Each piece requires a 10 cm (4") square of fabric
2 squares of velvet
2 squares of lining fabric (lightweight)
4 squares of interlining — voile or muslin
Fine braid: 40 cm (16")

Velvet Heart Jewellery Pouch

METHOD

- Copy the heart pattern four times.
- Place one piece of interlining fabric with each velvet piece (right sides together) and one piece of interlining with each lining piece (right sides together).
- Position the pattern on each piece and sew right around the outline of each heart.
- Cut out the hearts, leaving a small turning *outside* the stitching line. Clip all curves carefully.
- Make a cut in the centre of the interlining fabric and turn right sides out through the slit.
- Press carefully.
- Embroider a tiny spray of flowers on one heart.
- Slip stitch the hearts together in pairs — one velvet, one lining.
- Sew the two hearts together, leaving the top curves open.
- Trim the seams with a narrow braid. Beginning on the left side of the opening, sew the braid across the front curves, around the base of the heart and back across the back top curves, making a loop at the centre back for the fastening.
- Sew a decorative button on the centre front.

Christmas Crackers

(Designed for decoration or packaging, not pulling)

MATERIALS REQUIRED (FOR ONE CRACKER)

1 piece of fabric: 60 cm x 23 cm (23½" x 9")
1 piece of gold or silver fabric:
10 cm x 23 cm (4" x 9")
or 23 cm (9") of 8 cm (3") wide ribbon
Aida band: 5 cm wide x 23 cm (2" x 9")
1 card tube from a toilet roll
2 pieces of medium-weight iron-on Vilene:
7 cm x 23 cm (2¾" x 9")

METHOD

- Embroider a design in the centre of the aida band.
- Fold the short ends of the large fabric piece to meet in the centre, *wrong sides together*, and press firmly to crease. Open out flat.
- Position the iron-on Vilene strips along the folds, extending away from the centre panel, and press.
- Bring the ends back to meet in the centre again, but with *right sides together*.
- Machine down each side seam.
- Turn right side out through the opening and press. Press a 1 cm (⅜") turning along each long edge of the gold or silver fabric and centre it across the outside of the prepared piece.
- Place the cardboard roll on the inside at one edge of the fabric and roll into a tube. Tie together with cotton around the centre.
- Wrap the aida band around the centre of the roll and sew in place at the centre back, over the join.
- Tie the fabric firmly with narrow satin ribbons at the ends of the tube.

PLACE MATS AND NAPKINS

Made on an evenweave linen such as lugana, these are quick to work and easy to finish.

MATERIALS REQUIRED

Fabric
Place mats: 41 cm x 29 cm (16" x 11½") for 1 mat
Napkins: 29 cm x 29 cm for 1 napkin
Embroidery threads
Coton Perle No 5 for weaving

METHOD

Draw threads of the fabric to the required size before cutting to ensure straight edges and correct placement of the design.

Needleweaving has been used to add extra design detail to the plain fabric used for this project.

- Starting at the top left-hand corner, measure 8 cm (3") along the top edge. Remove one vertical thread from the fabric at this point. Skip two threads and remove the next one. Measure 8 cm down the side from the same corner and remove two horizontal threads in the same way.

- Using a tapestry needle and contrasting Coton Perle thread, replace these threads by weaving over and under the remaining threads two at a time.

To ensure the point where the threads cross looks even, the first row in each direction should be started at this intersection.

- Press work thoroughly and trim the coloured threads level with the edges of the fabric.

- To finish the edges, first remove the *ninth thread* in from each edge.

- Using matching thread and a close zigzag stitch on the machine, stitch round the edge of the fabric, working over two or three threads *inside* the line of the withdrawn threads. Removal of the single thread first makes stitching easier to keep accurate and in line with the threads.

- Remove all threads outside the machine stitching to form a fringe.

- Work the embroidery in the top left-hand corner. Designs from the clock are used on the original samples.

JEWELLERY

Specialty needlework shops usually stock a range of mounts suitable for jewellery pieces. Mounts originally designed to display photographs can often be found in antique shops and can be used for a very special piece.

- For ease of mounting embroidery in this type of frame, use fine fabric and stiffen it with iron-on Vilene.
- Mark the outline of the finished piece on the Vilene. Embroider the design, positioning it carefully within the marked outline. Cut out the stiffened disc and insert it into the frame.

The jewellery mounts in Framecraft's range are particularly attractive and easy to assemble. One of the designs used for these, shown on page C4, has been worked on hardanger 22 fabric. A second brooch shown on page C16 is worked on cotton voile.

- Cut a piece of fine iron-on Vilene to the size of the frame and iron it to the back of the fabric *before* working the embroidery.
- Centre the design carefully on the Vilene shape and work the embroidery. It is important when working small pieces such as this to keep the back of the work as flat as possible in order to achieve a smooth, flat finish when mounting the work.
- Frame in accordance with the manufacturer's instructions.

Less expensive jewellery and belt buckles can be made using porcelain china painting discs for a base.

- Work the design to fit the disc size.
- Cut out, allowing sufficient turning to run a strong gathering thread around the outer edge.
- Pull up around the disc and fasten securely.
- Cut a backing piece to fit from leather or felt.
- Attach a brooch pin if required to the backing piece before sticking it to the back of the disc.

Rose Earrings

Pretty earrings can be made by working single roses in bullion or detached buttonhole stitch, rolled roses or single carnations (page 36) onto fabric.

- Paint the back of the fabric with fabric glue and allow to dry.
- Cut out each flower with sharp scissors very close to the stitching.
- Glue the flowers to earring mounts with an epoxy or similar strong adhesive (such as Araldite).

Folded Rose Brooches _____

These are lovely little posy brooches, mounted on nothing more expensive than a brass ring!

MATERIALS REQUIRED

Small scraps of silk organza
Iron-on Vilene
Scrap of fine narrow cotton lace
Scrap of leather or felt for backing
Brass ring: 3 cm (1¼") diameter
Small brooch pin
7 mm silk ribbon for roses
2 mm silk ribbon for leaves

METHOD

- Draw around the brass ring onto the iron-on Vilene, cut out and iron on to a piece of silk organza. The silk organza should be large enough to fit into a small embroidery frame.

- Each brooch requires 10 to 12 roses, made as described on page 35. Leave the ribbon ends of each rose long enough to thread into a needle and sew through the Vilene-stiffened fabric.

- Arrange the roses into a tight posy. The ends of the ribbons can then be back stitched firmly or sewn to the fabric with thread if you find that easier.

- Add looped straight stitch leaves in 2 mm green ribbon between the flowers.

- Draw around the brass ring on to the leather or felt for the brooch backing and cut out the shape. Make two small slits the length of the brooch pin, and spaced the width of the brooch pin, just above the centre line.

- Cut a straight strip of the leather or felt to fit across the width of the brooch pin.

- Using a strong suitable adhesive, stick the pin to the backing piece. Thread the straight strip up through the top slit, across the pin and down through the bottom slit. Glue the ends of the strip firmly to the inside of the backing, clamp and put aside to dry.

- Cut out the brooch, allowing enough turning to gather and pull the fabric to the back of the brass ring.

- Gather the lace into a circle and fit around the outside of the flowers. Sew in place.

- Glue on the backing piece.

WEDDING HORSESHOE

MATERIALS REQUIRED

Fabric and thin batting:
20 cm x 40 cm (8" x 16")
Lace: 1.5 m (60")
Pearl edging: 75 cm (30")
Silk ribbon
Pearls
Fabric glue
Stiff card and paper

METHOD

- Cut two cardboard templates from the pattern on this page and trace the pattern onto paper twice.
- Sandwich the batting between the paper pattern and the fabric and machine around the outline using matching thread. Repeat with the second pattern.
- Tear away the paper.
- Embroider one horseshoe with design on page 44.
- Carefully cut away the batting along the stitching line. Trim the fabric away leaving a 2.5 cm (1") turning outside the machined line.
- Clip the curves to the machine stitching, position the card templates over batting and glue the seam allowance down securely.
- Gather lace and stitch or glue around the edge of the embroidered horseshoe together with the pearls.
- Cut three or four 35 cm (14") lengths of 7 mm silk ribbon and glue into position at the top.
- Glue the two sections firmly together.

BRIDESMAID'S ALICE BAND

The original band is worked on double georgette cut on the bias. Any fabric that would normally be used for a bridesmaid's dress would be suitable. Cutting on the bias gives a smoother finish to the band. You will also need batting and matching braid to neaten the inside of the band.

METHOD

- Carefully draw an accurate pattern of the band onto a sheet of paper. Cut out and double check against the band. Trace around this pattern onto a second sheet of paper.

- Cover the wrong side of the fabric with a layer of thin batting and lay the traced pattern on top *on the bias* and at least half the width of the Alice band plus 5 mm ($^3/_{16}$") from the edge. Sew around this outline on the machine using matching thread (see page 210). Tear away the paper.

- Embroider with chosen design.

- Very carefully cut the batting away along the machine stitching line.

- Trim around the stitching of the band, allowing enough turning to meet and be hemmed together down the centre on the underside of the band.

- Sew the edges neatly, stretching the fabric as you work and trimming any excess fabric as you stitch.

- Glue a band of braid over the seam line.

Purchased Alice bands can be embroidered if a careful choice of stitches is made.

- For ribbon embroidery, straight stitch and bullion lazy daisy are the easiest to work.

- For thread embroidery, bullion lazy daisy and detached buttonhole stitch are effective.

COAT HANGER COVERS

These soft padded hangers are easy to make and the covers can be removed for laundering.

MATERIALS REQUIRED

Blanketing: 46 cm x 26 cm (18" x 10")
Firm wadding and small amount of toy stuffing: 45 cm x 35 cm (18" x 14")
Satin bias binding to cover the hook: 15 cm (6")
Ribbon for decoration: 50 cm (20")
Lace edging: 2 m (2 yds) x 5 cm (2") wide
1 wooden coat hanger

METHOD

- Cut two strips of wadding 45 cm x 8 cm (18" x 3") and wind firmly around each end of the hanger.
- Cut out the wadding according to the pattern on page 199.
- Sew darts and side seams, turn right side out and fit over the hanger (hook removed).
- Add toy stuffing to pad area under the hanger and machine sew the lower edge closed using a zigzag stitch.
- Cover the hook with satin bias binding. Re-press the binding with one raw edge across until it almost touches the other folded edge and press. Fold in half again and stitch carefully with a zigzag stitch very close to the edge, folding in one end as you stitch. Slip over the hook, pull down tightly and trim to expose the screw end.
- Replace hook and sew base of covering firmly to the wadding.
- Cut outer cover from blanketing and embroider with chosen design.
- Sew darts and side seams.
- Gather lace and zigzag around the bottom edge.
- Pierce a hole for the hook, neaten with buttonhole stitch or seal with washable fabric glue.
- Slip cover over the hanger and tie decorative bow around the hook to finish.

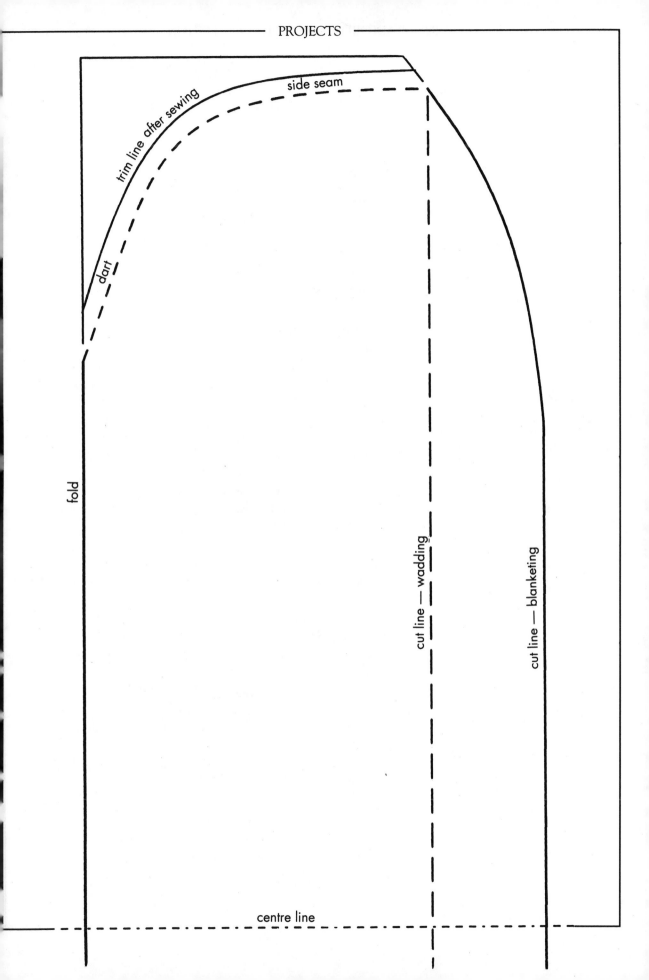

trim line after sewing

side seam

dart

fold

cut line — wadding

cut line — blanketing

centre line

GIFTS FOR BABY

Baby's Bear _____

MATERIALS REQUIRED
Wool blanketing: 21 cm x 42 cm (8¹/₄" x 16¹/₂")
Torokina wools for embroidery
Extra-long doll making needle
Milliner's (straw) needle
Fibrefill stuffing

METHOD

- Copy pattern pieces as detailed on pages 203 and 204 onto paper, but do not cut them out.

- Pin pattern sheet to the fabric. Using a light contrasting thread and a small straight stitch setting, sew around the outline of each of the four pattern pieces, working directly over the heavy outline.

This method of outlining the pattern pieces with machine stitching *before* they are cut out is used to prevent fraying and stretching of the seams during assembly. It also makes cutting out more accurate. If possible use a clear or open front foot on your machine to make it easier to follow the outline. Note also that it is easier to sew curves at slow speed. If your sewing machine has a speed reduction feature (as most machines do), use it to make construction of your bear easier.

- Tear away the paper pattern. Cut out the pieces carefully just outside the machine line. *Cut as close as you can to the stitching but take care not to cut into the stitching line.*

A more accurate seam line will be maintained if you whip the edges of the pieces together before stitching. Use large stitches as they should be removed after machining.

- Place fronts right sides together. Whip the centre front seam together. Machine carefully along the seam line. Remove tacking and press turnings open at the top and bottom.

- Repeat for backs, leaving the seam open as marked for turning and stuffing.

- Match front to back and whip together around the entire outline, taking care to match and tack the opened centre front and back seams. Machine carefully along the seam line.

- Carefully clip into the seam allowance along all inner

curves. Trim across the curve of the nose. Turn right side out.

- Using one strand of matching wool, stitch across the ear line using two rows of running stitch to form a single unbroken line of stitching.
- Stuff carefully with Fibrefill. Do not close the back seam until the embroidery is finished.
- Embroider eyes. Jean Greenhowe, designer and author of many craft books featuring wonderful knitted toys, uses these eyes for many of her designs. They are easy to make and very effective.

  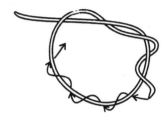

  — Take a length of wool, about 25 cm (18") long, make a loop in the centre and thread one end through the loop six times. Tighten the knot by pulling evenly on both ends of the thread.
  — Use pins to established the position of the eyes on the face of the bear. Thread one end of the knotted thread through the long needle and pass it through the face and out through the centre back of the bear. Thread the other end of the thread through the needle and anchor it in the same way. Pull the threads until the knot sits firmly in position. Tie the threads firmly together. Repeat for the other eye. Note that the expression on the face of the bear will vary according to the position of the eyes and the indentation achieved when tying off the threads.
- Embroider nose and mouth.
  — Using one strand of brown wool, outline the nose area with a triangle of straight stitches.
  — Fill in with satin stitch worked horizontally and cover this with a second set of stitches worked vertically.
  — Finally, outline the nose again with straight stitch and complete the mouth with straight stitch.

- Work embroidery design as desired.
- Cut small hearts from white felt and pin in place on the bear.
  — Working with a single strand of wool, satin stitch over the felt shape working from the centre out.
  — Outline the heart with a row of stem stitch in paler or darker wool.
- Work the floral designs.
  — The roses used on the bears photographed are the detached buttonhole stitch roses featured in the textured embroidery section of the book (page 83). Other flowers can be substituted such as bullion roses (page 67) and daisies (page 70).
  — Outline the shape required with feather stitching or a couched stem in green.
  — Position the largest flowers first then fill in the gaps with lazy daisy leaves and tiny colonial knots.
- Start and finish all ends through the back opening. You may find it easier to pass the needle from side to side or from front to back when working colonial knots on the head or neck area.
- Close back opening with ladder stitch using a single strand of matching wool.

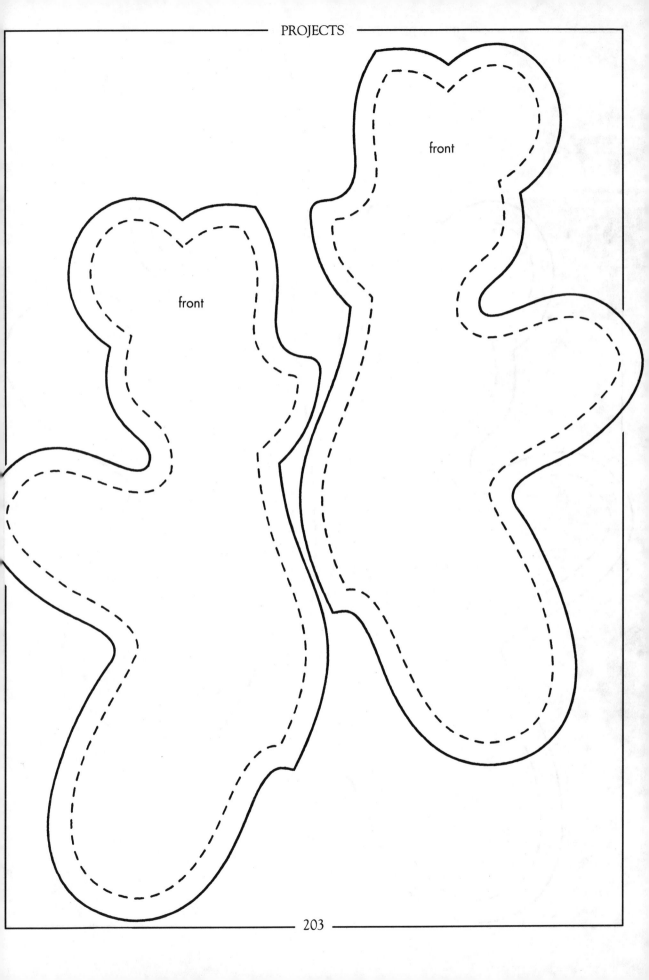

front

front

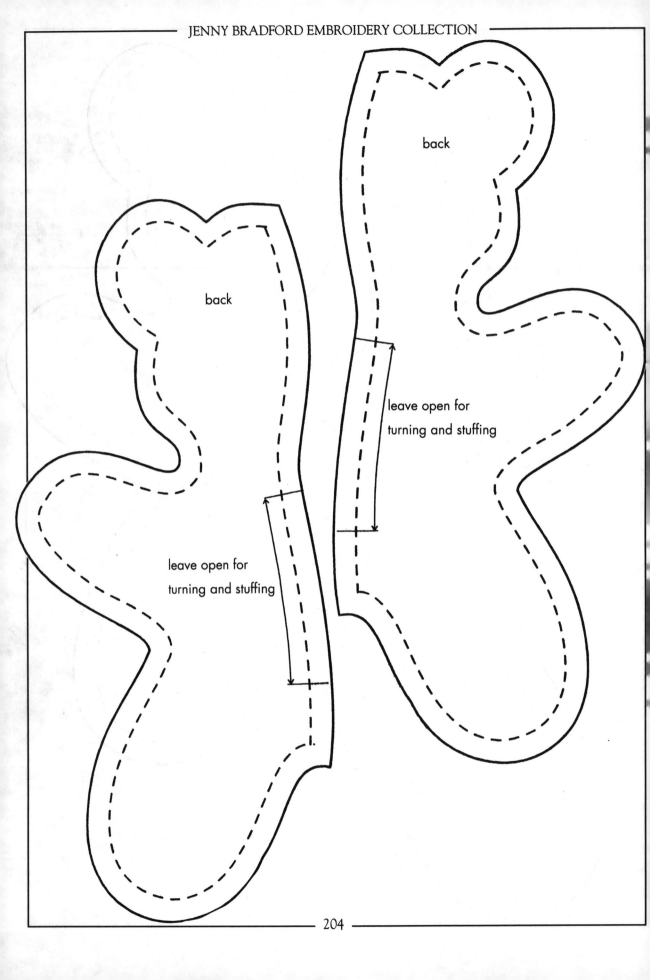

back

back

leave open for
turning and stuffing

leave open for
turning and stuffing

Baby Bibs _____

These easy-to-make bibs are very practical, with a snug-fitting rib-knit finish at the neckline.

Use a fingertip towel, fringed if possible, to make one bib; or a larger towel to make several. This will give a wider choice of colours and thicker, better quality towelling than can normally be purchased by the metre.

Note that it is possible to fringe the woven band across the end of a towel by removing the crosswise threads of the band.

MATERIALS REQUIRED

1 piece of towelling: 29 cm x 42 cm ($11\frac{1}{2}''$ x $16\frac{1}{2}''$)
Fabric for applique — flannelette or towelling scraps
1 piece of knit ribbing: 7 cm x 34 cm ($2\frac{3}{4}''$ x $13\frac{1}{2}''$)
Ribbon for ties: 60 cm (24'')
Threads for embroidery

METHOD

- Cut a panel 29 cm x 42 cm from the towel, positioning the bottom of the bib on the fringe or along the base of the woven band.

- Fringe the band if necessary.

- Strengthen the fringed edge with zigzag stitch in matching thread across the top of the band.

- Mark the neck cut-out with a marker pen. Slit the centre back from A to B.

Note that it is important to stitch the following seams in the order given to keep the corners neat and reduce bulk as much as possible.

The raw edge is turned to the back and a zigzag stitch used to hold the hem in place and neaten the edge in one process.

- Stitch both side edges from C to D.

- Turn over the corner E to F and stitch; then trim close to the stitching line.

- Turn over the corners B to F and stitch; then trim close to the stitching line.

Trimming after stitching, when working on the cross grain, gives a neater hem.

- Applique the rabbit (see page 210).

- Cut out the neckline, fold the neckline ribbing in half (right side together), insert the ribbon ties and stitch across the short ends.

- Turn the ribbing right side out and mark into quarters.

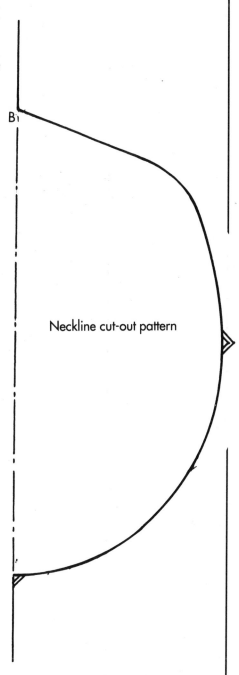

Neckline cut-out pattern

- Match these marks with the corresponding marks on the neck edge of the bib.
- Stretch the ribbing firmly and pin in place around the neck edge before stitching with an overlock stitch on your sewing machine or overlocker.
- Finish the bib with touches of embroidery as shown in the colour pages.

The original design is worked using the bullion roses and rose buds, a cluster of three at the base of one ear and a collar of buds around the neck.

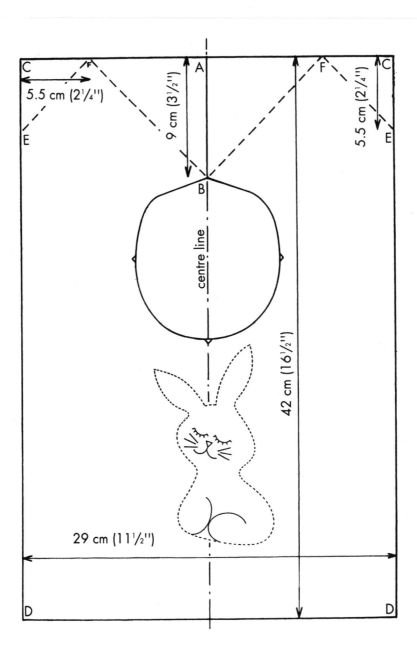

Toy Rabbit _____

Worked in felt, this tiny rabbit is quickly assembled.

MATERIALS REQUIRED

Brown, fawn or white good quality felt:
18 cm x 24 cm (7" x 9½")
Threads for embroidery
Small amount of Fibrefill

METHOD

- With the pattern transferred to paper, fold the felt in half and place the paper pattern on the back.
- Using matching thread, sew through paper and felt, leaving a small opening for stuffing at the base.
- Tear away paper and remove all remaining traces with a pin or needle.
- Cut out the rabbit, allowing a 2 mm (½6") seam allowance *outside* the machine stitching.
- Stuff firmly and close the opening with neat back stitching.
- Embroider features with stem stitch or couching and decorate one ear with bullion roses or daisies. Decorate the neck with a narrow ribbon held in place with an embroidered flower.

  Use as a gift-wrap decoration, sew a safety pin on the back to make a brooch or hang two or three together as a mobile or crib toy.

Cot Quilt _____

MATERIALS REQUIRED

Finished size: 76 cm x 61 cm (30" x 24")
Cotton fabric for front panel, edge binding and backing:
1.3 m x 114 cm (51" x 45")
Batiste in each of four contrasting colours: 15 cm (6")
Flannelette or similar for backing the front panel:
62 cm x 77 cm (24½" x 30½")
Quilt batting: 62 cm x 77 cm
Scraps of flannelette for rabbits
Embroidery threads, matching sewing thread

METHOD

- Cut a piece of flannelette or similar fabric as a base for the front section, making it the size of the finished quilt.
- Cover the bottom right-hand corner with a triangle of fabric (see diagram below).
- Cut or tear strips of fabric for the strip quilting; measurements are given on the diagram for the quilt shown in the photograph.
- Place the first strip over the edge of the triangular piece, right sides together, and seam in place.
- Press the strip away from the triangle section. Pin the next strip over the raw edge and sew.
- Repeat until the base fabric is covered.
- Trim all the edges even.

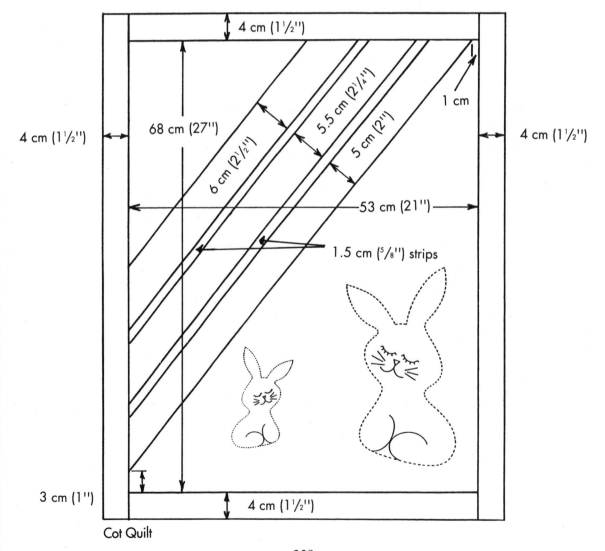

Cot Quilt

- Applique rabbits, as on page 210, enlarging the pattern to twice the size for the big rabbit. (Many modern photocopiers have the facility to enlarge or reduce.)
- Embroider sprays of bullion roses, daisies and tulip flowers along some of the diagonal strips, and the features on the rabbits, using stem stitch or couching in grey on white rabbits and fawn or brown on brown rabbits. Work a collar of flowers and a decoration of flowers around one ear on each rabbit.
- Cut one piece of backing fabric and quilt batting to fit the quilt front.
- Put all layers together, sandwiching the batting between the front and back sections.
- Starting from the centre of the quilt, pin and tack all layers together smoothly.
- Quilt by machine, using matching thread and working along the seam line of the strips and around the outline of the rabbits.
- Cut strips of border fabric 17 cm (7") wide. Fold wrong sides together to form an 8.5 cm (3¼") wide strip. Press carefully.
- Pin the raw edges of the strips to the right side of the quilt, 3.5 cm (1³⁄₈") in from the edge.
- Stitch 4 cm (1½") in from the quilt edge, the top and bottom edges first, then the side edges, folding in the ends at the corners where necessary.
- Hem the folded edges to the back of the quilt.

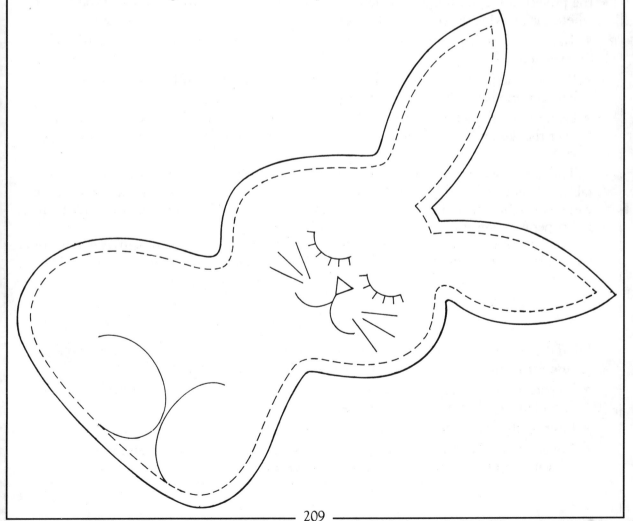

CHAPTER 19

USEFUL SEWING TECHNIQUES

TRANSFERRING A DESIGN TO THE FABRIC

This can be done in various ways, depending on the type of design you are working with. In most cases, transferring the main design lines, together with the position of the largest flowers, should be enough. Once these have been established, the remainder of the design should be easy to position by eye.

- The main lines can be traced off onto the fabric with a marker pen or pencil, if the design can be seen through the fabric. Try placing the fabric over the design print or tracing, and taping it onto a window so that the light shines through. This makes an excellent substitute for a light box. (This method can be used to reverse a design; simply tape the design face against the window and trace the design on the back of the paper.)

If the background fabric is too dark to use that method, or if you do not want to mark the project fabric, outlining by machine is an excellent alternative. This method is best where the marking of symmetrical shapes, such as ovals, hearts, etc. is required.

- Trace or photocopy the pattern onto a sheet of paper; reverse the design if it is asymmetrical.

- Position and pin the design to the back of the work, placing any backing fabric required between the base fabric and the paper.

- Using a fine thread that matches the surface fabric, sew directly (from the wrong side) over the design lines you wish to mark. Use a short length stitch when marking tight curves.

The advantage of stitching through the paper is that it prevents any stretch in the fabric as you work, so there is no distortion of the shapes as they are stitched. The fabric can be manipulated and turned smoothly and evenly around curves by gently rotating it; the paper will prevent any uneven stretch or pull.

Once marking is complete, the paper is torn away and the design is ready for embroidery. When embroidering over the sewn lines, work just to one side of the stitching.

APPLIQUE

I find this method — based on working from the back of the design — very easy, and ideal for use with embroidery, as it does not require the use of any adhesive bonding.

- Prepare a copy of the design on a sheet of paper, reversing the design if necessary. (See 'Transferring a Design to the Fabric'.)

- Position the traced design on the reverse side of the work and pin in place.

- Cover the applique area on the right side with the chosen fabric and pin in place, allowing ample coverage around the outer edges.

- With the wrong side of the work uppermost, and using a straight stitch, sew around the outline of the design through the paper and fabrics. Follow the outline of the design carefully, remembering that the smaller the stitch length used the easier it is to negotiate curves.
- Using a small pair of sharp embroidery scissors, trim away the excess applique fabric as close to the machine stitching as possible.
- Using a satin stitch setting on the machine, with the right side of the design uppermost, stitch carefully, working over the edge of the design. One of the many machine embroidery threads now available will give the best results for this stitching.
- Finally tear away the paper from the wrong side of the work. Working through the paper pattern keeps the fabric firm and wrinkle free and helps to keep the satin stitch even.

This method of applique also eliminates the use of bonding fabrics, which can result in stiff unpliable areas in the work.

ROLLING AND WHIPPING

This is an excellent way of finishing edges for attaching lace or entredeux. Although originally worked by hand, this process can be quickly completed on any sewing machine that will do a simple zigzag stitch.

To work successfully, fine pure cotton fabrics should be used, the edges must be cut and not torn and a fine sewing thread (No 60 cotton) will produce the best results. No 60 cotton can be obtained from specialist shops that handle heirloom and fine sewing supplies.

Use a stitch length just short of the satin stitch setting and a width setting of $1\frac{1}{2}$ to 2. (The needle should catch about 2 mm [$\frac{1}{16}$"] of the fabric and clear the raw edge as it swings from side to side.) Tighten the top thread tension and work with the fabric wrong side up.

As you stitch along the edge, the fabric should roll over to form a very fine hem. Practise adjusting your machine settings until this works smoothly and neatly.

Working from the right side, place the lace or entredeux edge to edge with the rolled hem and zigzag together, using the finest zigzag setting practicable.

BIAS OR STRAIGHT BINDING

When using lightweight fabrics, cut twice the required width and use the binding folded double.

Match the cut edges, press and sew in place, matching all raw edges. Turn and hem along the fold.

This method is neater, easier to sew and the double thickness gives a smooth finish and reinforces the edge where the most wear occurs.

Be sure to calculate the width required carefully, as there is no adjustment once the band is stitched in place.

MACHINE QUILTING

A small attachment known as a quilting guide is available and often supplied with many brands of sewing machine. This guide is essential for quilting and makes the process very quick and easy to do.

An attractive variation to plain quilting is to use a twin needle and one of the fancy line stitches that many machines have. The use of machine embroidery thread will add an extra sheen to the stitching.

I always work on the diagonal, making the first row across the bottom right-hand corner.

Never tack the fabrics together, as you need to be able to smooth the top fabric as you go, to prevent small wrinkles. If necessary, pin the fabric and remove the pins as you come to them.

Use a firm batting which will hold its shape and not catch on the feed teeth of the machine. Soft fluffy batting used for hand quilting is not suitable.

Always quilt a piece slightly larger than the size required and cut your pattern out afterwards. This will give a neat edge and any slight distortion that might occur in quilting will not be transferred to your project.

- Cut a piece of fabric and a piece of batting.
- Pin the pieces together, moving across the fabric from the bottom right-hand corner to the top left-hand corner.
- Set up the machine according to the manufacturer's instructions. Work a small test piece to check tension and spacing.
- Stitch across the bottom right-hand corner, starting and finishing 2 to 2.5 cm (1") from the corner.
- Line the stitched row up with the bar on the quilting guide and stitch a second row.
- Repeat across the fabric, removing the pins and smoothing the surface as you stitch.

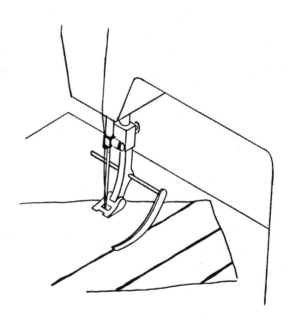

CRAZY PATCHWORK

True crazy patchwork is worked by laying down a variety of fabrics onto a backing piece of calico or similar fabric. Small pieces are generally started with a five-sided block of one of the darker fabrics placed close to the centre of the backing piece. Subsequent pieces are added, working around the five-sided block until the backing fabric is covered.

There are some excellent books available on the subject of crazy patchwork. Judith Montano is particularly well known for her many publications and inspiring workshops on the subject.

The following crazy patchwork layout has been used for the bag design on page 59. The numbers indicate the order in which the fabrics are assembled.

Crazy patchwork bag layout

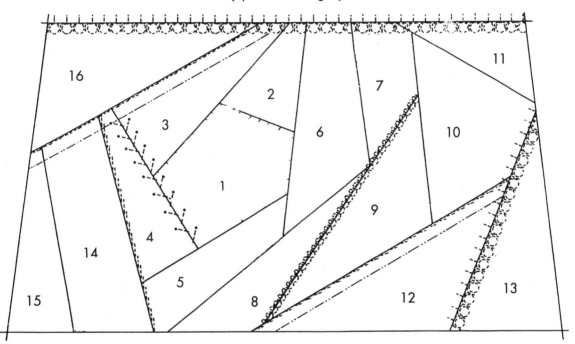

MOCK CRAZY PATCHWORK

This is a method of dividing a piece of fabric with lace or stitching to create interesting shapes of varying sizes in which to work tiny flower sprays.

Working on the principle that small designs are much easier to work than large pieces, this is an excellent way for beginners to create an interesting design.

Plan the design carefully if using lace and entredeux as it is necessary to cover the ends of the previous piece as each strip is sewn in place. Thread beading with ribbon as you go so that these ends are covered as well.

To prepare work for stitching as shown on the vest yoke:

• Draw the lines on a copy of the pattern piece, pin to the back of the fabric and transfer (as detailed on page 210) using matching thread.

• Tear away paper, work embroidery sprays and then cover the machine lines with your choice of decorative stitches.

To use lace for decoration, prepare the fabric as above. Before working the embroidery, cover the machine lines with the lace, sewing it in place with very small zigzag stitches.

TASSELS

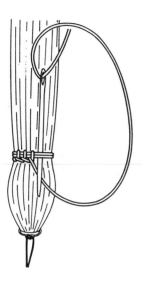

- If necessary, iron the thread to remove packaging folds.
- Using a plastic or cardboard template cut to size, wrap it the required number of times. Start and finish at the bottom edge of the template and keep the wraps as compact as possible at the top.
- For ease of working, tie the loops through the folds at both ends, leaving long ends on the tying threads.
- Remove from the template and tie the neck of the tassel firmly approximately one-quarter of the way down from the top tie.

When working with shiny, slippery threads, it is easier to use a matching dull finish thread (e.g. DMC stranded cotton) for tying. Alternatively, dampen the tying thread to prevent slipping.

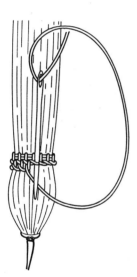

- To cover the top of the tassel, thread a fine tapestry needle with matching thread approximately 1.5 m (60") in length to avoid joining, pass the needle up through the centre of the tassel and out just above the neck tie. Holding the head of the tassel and working towards the top, make a row of buttonhole stitches around this tie, stitching carefully in order to avoid pulling the tassel threads back up through the tie. Space the stitches out, leaving a small gap between each stitch.

You will find it easier to work from this point if the tassel is anchored by means of the long thread used for tying the bottom of the tassel.

- Pin or tie the threads to a firm surface so that the tassel can be turned as you stitch.
- Work rows of detached buttonhole stitch (work into the top of the previous row without sewing into the tassel head). Continue stitching until the tassel head is covered.

A tight tension will produce a slender head, while a more relaxed tension will result in a more rounded head. A small amount of stuffing (or even a bead) can be inserted as you work to round out the head.

- To finish the tassel, thread the needle through the top of the last row and pull up firmly. Fasten the thread securely, then pass the needle down through the centre of the tassel.
- Cut the bottom loops and trim if necessary.

TWISTED CORDS

The thickness and texture of a twisted cord will vary according to the number and variety of threads used. Mixing shiny and dull threads or plain and metallic threads gives interesting and attractive alternatives to using a plain basic thread.

- Cut the required number of threads, each six times the finished length of the cord required.
- Fold the three strands in half and hook over a door handle or behind the lowered foot of your sewing machine.
- Knot the loose ends together and roll in a clockwise direction to twist the threads together. This can be done by rolling the knot between the fingers or slipping a pencil or crochet hook in the loop behind the knot.
- Continue rolling the threads, pulling away from the anchor point to prevent the threads from twisting back on themselves, until the threads are very firmly twisted.
- Take the knotted end in the left hand and, keeping the thread pulled tight, place the first finger of the right hand halfway along the thread. (If you are making a long cord it will be easier to get help with this.) Fold the knotted end to the anchored end and hold firmly while twisting the cord with the right finger in an *anti-clockwise* direction.
- Twist sufficiently to prevent the cord from twisting back on itself, then release the looped end and allow the cord to twist naturally.
- Knot the ends or wrap firmly to hold in place.

CARE OF EMBROIDERY

Always wash embroidery in accordance with the most delicate fibres used in the project. Preferably launder by hand, using a suitable washing agent, and avoid detergents on silk.

Some silk ribbon embroidery stitches do wash more successfully than others and the general guide is that the more firmly knotted or twisted the stitch, the better it will stand up to washing and wearing. It is therefore wise to choose stitches and flowers that fall into this category for garments and other projects that will have hard use. (See the Stitch Glossary for the stitches to use.)

Most of the ribbons are colourfast; however I have found some of the strong colours — deep reds, purple, blue and black — may colour-leak a little. I therefore recommend care when selecting colours for use on pale backgrounds if you do not wish to go to the expense of having the item dry cleaned. If you do have ribbon embroidery dry cleaned, I suggest that you ask that the dry cleaners do not press the item and always make sure that they are aware that silk has been used for the embroidery.

All textured embroidery in ribbon or thread will be spoilt if flattened by ironing, so take this into consideration when planning your project. Embroidery should be placed face down on a soft towel and pressed from the wrong side.

STITCH GLOSSARY

Instructions on how to work the following stitches are given in this chapter:

Basketweave stitch
Bullion stitch
Bullion lazy daisy stitch
Long-legged bullion stitch
Colonial knot or candlewicking knot
Continental stitch
Coral stitch
Couching
Detached buttonhole or cast-on stitch
Double-sided detached buttonhole stitch
Feather stitch
Fly Stitch
French knot or half colonial knot
Jacquard stitch
Knotted loop stitch
Ladder stitch
Lazy daisy stitch

Long and short stitch
Long-legged cross stitch
Palestrina or double knot stitch
Pearl stitch
Pistil stitch
Portuguese stem stitch
Ribbon stitch — flat
Ribbon stitch — looped
Rosette chain
Satin stitch
Stem or outline stitch
Straight stitch — flat
Straight stitch — looped
Twisted chain
Long-legged twisted chain
Whipped running stitch
Whipped stitch — single

The following information is included in key form with the stitch headings:

Washing information	Key reference	Needle recommendation	Key reference
Washable	W	Chenille	Ch
Wash with care	W/C	Crewel	Cr
Not washable	NW	Milliner's	M
Ironing no problem	I	Tapestry	T
Iron with care	I/C		
Not suitable for ironing	NI	Hoop essential	H
		Frame essential	F

On all the diagrams, the *odd* numbers refer to the needle passing *up* through the fabric from back to front, while the *even* numbers refer to the needle passing *down* through the fabric from front to back.

HELPFUL HINTS FOR LEFT-HANDED STUDENTS

There are more left-handed people around than there used to be and I think that teachers of embroidery can no longer ignore this so-called problem. It takes time and concentration for a right-handed teacher to be able to demonstrate for left-handed students.

Fortunately, I find students very patient and appreciative of efforts to understand their problems and it can be very worthwhile to try to master the techniques their way.

The following points may help both teachers and students to reverse the techniques described in the following pages.

- Remember that not only is the needle held in the opposite hand but the direction of the thread must be altered as well. For example, if a right-hander has the thread on the left of the needle, then the left-hander must put the thread on the right of the needle.

- If the right-handed worker is working from left to right, either in a straight line or a circle (clockwise), the left-hander will work from right to left in a line or a circle (anti-clockwise).

- Starting positions for left-handers are normally opposite to those for right-handers.

- Try using a mirror positioned as shown in the diagram to convert the diagrams to left-handed techniques.

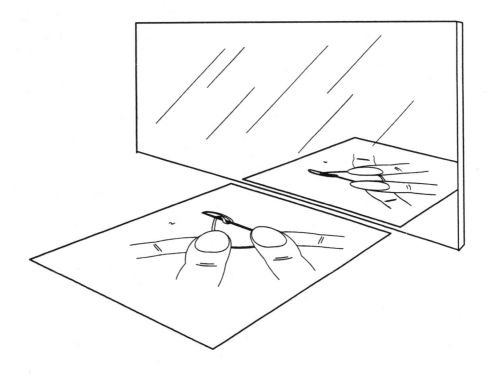

BASKETWEAVE STITCH — CANVAS WORK

T F

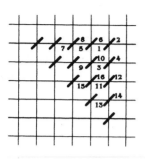

This stitch is often used in place of continental stitch. It is called basketweave because, when worked in the correct order, the stitches on the back of the work form a woven pattern. This helps to keep the canvas from distorting, and it also makes it hard wearing because the back of the work, as well as the front, is completely covered with stitching.

- Commence stitching in the top right-hand corner of the area to be covered, at 1.

- Continue working from the chart, working the needle from back to front on the uneven numbers and front to back on the even numbers. The rows of stitching are filled in on the diagonal.

BULLION STITCH — THREAD

W I/C M

When working bullion stitch it is important to understand how much the size of needle, thickness of thread and tension will govern the size of the stitch produced.

No two students will produce exactly the same results. It is therefore necessary to experiment and practise to establish your own tension and understand how to adjust your stitches to give the required results.

Refer to Chapter 10 for advice on threads and needles.

The way a thread is spun (i.e. in a clockwise or anticlockwise direction) can dictate which way the thread should be wound around the needle when wrapping a bullion stitch. The basic rule is to wrap the thread around the needle in the same direction as the twist of the thread; if the thread appears to unravel as you work, try wrapping in the opposite direction.

TO WORK A BULLION STITCH

Secure the thread with a small back stitch where it will be covered by the stitching. A knot can be used, but be careful not to pierce the knot with the needle when working the bullion stitch.

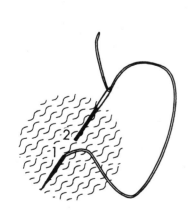

- Bring the needle up through the fabric at point 1.

- Take the needle down at point 2, about 5 mm (³/₁₆″) from point 1, and back up through point 1 (but not through the thread).

- Slide the needle forward, but *do not* pull the needle right through the fabric at this time (diag. 1).

- Position the first finger of the left hand under the fabric and the needle, and the left thumb on top of the fabric a short distance ahead of point 1.

- Place the second finger of the left hand firmly against the eye of the needle, forcing it against the first finger of the left hand, to make the point of the needle stand straight up (this is only possible if you are not using a hoop).

- Pick up the thread in the right hand and wrap the thread around the needle seven or eight times (diag. 2). See page 218 to establish the direction of the wrapping.

- Hold the wraps gently between the thumb and the first finger of the left hand and pull the needle through.

- Tighten the thread until the wraps are even by pulling the thread gently in line with the direction of the stitch back to point 2. Keep it parallel with and as close to the surface of the fabric as possible.

- The wraps may be moved gently along the core thread by using the thumb and forefinger of the left hand or the left thumb nail.

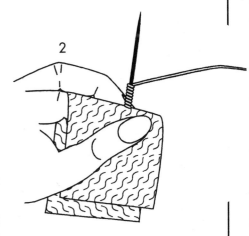

- When the stitch has been tightened the wraps should sit snugly against the fabric between points 1 and 2. Failure to tighten the core thread sufficiently at this point will result in untidy loops at one or both ends or, if using a slippery thread, the wraps may slacken as the stitch is anchored, resulting in an untidy stitch.

If the core thread is tightened too much, this may result in puckering of the base fabric.

- Once the stitch has been adjusted satisfactorily, anchor the bullion by passing the needle to the back of the work at point 2 (diag. 3).

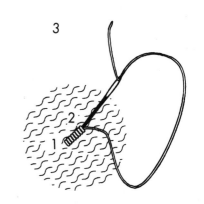

The core thread should be completely and evenly covered by the wrap thread. If the wraps are too tightly packed to lie flat, use fewer wraps; if the wraps do not cover the core thread, resulting in a 'strung out' skinny stitch, add more wraps around the needle.

The number of wraps required to give an even result depends on:

1 Thickness of thread used

2 The length of stitch required

3 How tightly the thread is pulled to finish the bullion stitch, which has a direct bearing on the thickness of the finished stitch. The tighter the tension, the thinner the bullion.

If the wraps do not tighten evenly, it may be possible to loosen the core thread gently and re-tighten the stitch, depending on the type of thread being used.

Rolling the stitch gently from right to left under the thumb may help to even the wraps, provided the thread is wrapped in a clockwise direction around the needle. Roll in the opposite direction if the bullion is worked with an anti-clockwise wrap.

STRAIGHT AND CURVED BULLION STITCHES

A straight bullion stitch requires just enough wraps to cover the thread smoothly as it spans the gap between points 1 and 2.

To create a curved stitch between points 1 and 2, the core thread will be left slightly longer to allow for a curve and therefore more wraps will be needed in order to cover it. For example, if seven wraps cover the straight stitch then 10 to 12 wraps will be required to cover the curved stitch.

To work a bullion loop stitch, the distance between 1 and 2 is reduced and the number of wraps is increased.

Success with bullion stitch does depend largely on accurate judgement and consistent tension. Many experienced workers do not need to count the number of wraps used; they work by eye, wrapping the needle until it 'looks right'! Working this way takes a great deal of practice and largely depends on how much and how often you work this type of embroidery.

BULLION LAZY DAISY STITCH — RIBBON

W I Ch H

This is a variation on the standard lazy daisy stitch. A small bullion stitch takes the place of the usual anchor stitch at the point of the stitch. The shape of the petal or leaf will depend on the length of the bullion stitch used and the anchor point of the bullion.

The secret of this stitch is to keep the ribbon taut at all times and not to be afraid to tighten it firmly before anchoring the bullion.

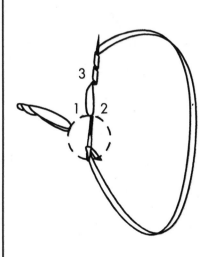

- Bring the needle up at 1, down at 2 (just to the right of 1) and out again at 3, remembering that the bullion part of the stitch will extend beyond this point. Care should be taken to keep the ribbon flat at all times.

- Holding the ribbon firmly against the needle between points 1 and 3, fold the ribbon at right angles as it is passed under the needle at 3.

- Wrap it around the point of the needle two or three times, keeping it smooth and flat and spiralling the wraps up the needle so that they do not overlap too much.

- Lay the ribbon firmly to the base of the petal and hold it in place gently by covering with the left thumb as you pull the needle through, keeping the ribbon close to the fabric and in line with the bullion stitch. Try to tighten the stitch firmly by 'stretching' the stitch away from the base of the petal, *not* by pushing the stitch down towards the base of the petal with the left thumb.

- Pull the bullion tip 'off line' to create in the selected position a more natural appearance, and anchor by passing the needle to the back of the work at the tip of the petal.

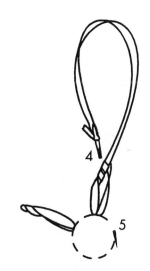

BULLION LAZY DAISY STITCH — THREAD

W I M or Ch

Work as described above, ensuring the bullion wraps are neatly wound onto the needle without overlapping.

LONG-LEGGED BULLION STITCH — THREAD

W I/C M

- Come up at 1, down at 2 and back out at 3. Do not pull the needle through at this time (diag. 1).

- Pick up the thread at 1 and wind it around the point of the needle until the wraps on the needle equal the length of the stitch between 1 and 2.

- Hold the wraps lightly between the thumb and finger of the left hand and gently pull the needle through. Tighten the thread until the wraps are snug against the fabric.

- Carry the needle forward to 3 and back stitch to 4. Note that 3 to 4 is equal to 1 to 2 in length with a short space between 2 and 4.

- Wrap the needle again using the thread from the end of the previous stitch.

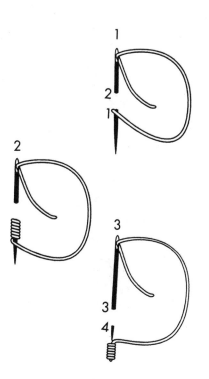

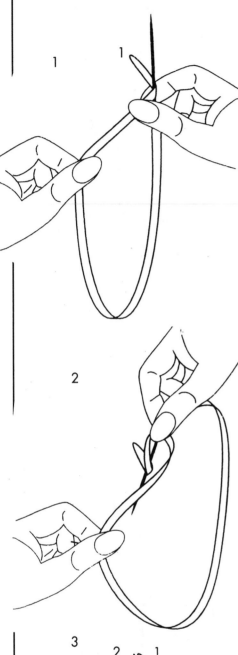

COLONIAL KNOT OR CANDLEWICKING KNOT — RIBBON

W   Ch or T

Varying the size of the needle can affect the look of a colonial knot considerably and I suggest you experiment with both the size of the needle and the width of ribbon used. Basically a fatter needle will produce a knot with a larger hole in the centre, which can look very pretty when used for the centre of a rose or as a miniature bud.

The knot will have a better shape if the ribbon is kept flat as it is picked up on the needle and not allowed to twist or fold.

Maintaining a flexible, relaxed wrist is the key to easy execution of colonial knots, allowing easy change of direction as the ribbon is picked up on the needle.

- Bring the needle up through the fabric and hold the ribbon between the thumb and first finger of the left hand, leaving a loop approximately 8 cm (3") in length.

- Slide the first finger of the right hand under this loop and 'sandwich' the ribbon between this finger and the needle, which should be pointing away from you, and hook the needle under the ribbon (diag. 1).

- Turn the needle anti-clockwise through 180 degrees and hook the needle under the ribbon again (diag. 2).

- Return the needle in a clockwise direction to the original position and pass the needle back through the fabric close to but not through the original exit hole (diag. 3).

To produce well-shaped, even knots always neaten the ribbon around the shaft of the needle, while the needle is held in a perpendicular position in the fabric, before completing the last step.

COLONIAL KNOT — THREAD

W   I   M   H

Work the knots exactly as detailed above.

CONTINENTAL STITCH — CANVAS WORK

T F

This stitch is worked in rows across the area to be covered. The stitches on the front of the work lie diagonally across the intersecting threads of the canvas, while those on the back of the work will be vertical.

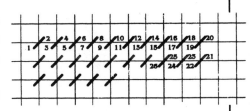

- Working from left to right, follow the numbers on the diagram for correct needle placement.

- Turn the work at the end of the row to work back along the next row.

CORAL STITCH — THREAD

W I Ch or Cr

- Working from right to left, pull the needle through at 1 and lay the thread over the line to be followed.

- Looping the thread below the line, make a small vertical stitch from 2 to 3, bringing the needle out over the top of the looped thread.

- Tighten the thread around the needle gently and pull the needle through.

- Repeat to form a line.

Note that spacing between stitches should be even and the distance between 2 and 3 will determine the size of the knot.

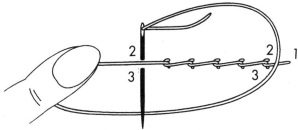

COUCHING — RIBBON

W I Ch H

Always spread the ribbon and gently tighten the stitch to the desired tension. Use matching embroidery thread to anchor the ribbon with a couching thread as you fold the ribbon to change direction.

- Come up at 1, leave the ribbon on the surface and work a holding stitch in thread from one side of the ribbon to the other before anchoring the ribbon in the required position.

Bent or twisted leaves can be worked as shown in the diagram.

COUCHING — THREAD

W I Cr or M F

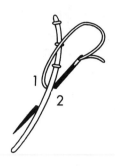

It is easy to work fine stems with a natural curve using couching.

Very short stems can be worked with a single needle, but for longer stems greater control is maintained by using two needles. The first needle carries a thread of suitable thickness for the required stem, usually one to four strands of embroidery thread. The second carries a single matching strand of thread.

- Using the first needle, come up at one end of the line to be covered and go down at the other. Anchor this needle out of the way.

- Bring the second needle up close to the starting point of the first thread and work tiny invisible straight holding stitches across the main thread, using the same hole for points 1 and 2, and curving the main thread as desired.

DETACHED BUTTONHOLE OR CAST-ON STITCH — THREAD

W NI M

This is a versatile stitch and has been used for six of the flowers shown on the textured embroidery sampler in the colour pages. Once you have mastered the technique of the stitch it is easier to work than bullion stitch and just as effective.

The thickness of the thread used and the size of the needle chosen will have a direct result on the size of the stitches. A milliner's needle will give the best results. Large-eyed needles will distort the stitches as they are pulled through the wraps.

I recommend Coton Perle No 8 as a good thread with which to practise, using a No 4 or 5 needle.

TO WORK A DETACHED BUTTONHOLE STITCH

Secure the thread with a small back stitch where it will be hidden under the flower centre.

- Bring the needle up through the fabric at point 1.

- Take a back stitch going down at 2 and back out at 1, taking care not to pierce the thread at point 1 or to pull the needle right through the fabric.

- Slip the first finger of your right hand into the thread loop (diag. 1).
- Hold the thread over the thumb nail and across the middle finger of the right hand to tension the thread as you twist the loop and slide it onto the needle (diag. 2).
- Pull the thread until the loop tightens around the needle, making sure the loop slides to fit snugly at the point where the needle emerges through the fabric (diag. 3). (The knot created is a half hitch.)
- Repeat until the required number of loops have been worked onto the needle, making sure that each one fits snugly beside the previous one. There should be no gaps and no overlapping loops (diag. 4).
- Pull the needle through the fabric gently holding the loops between the finger and thumb of the left hand. Tighten the thread until the loops fill the length of the core thread.
- Anchor the stitch by passing the needle to the back of the work at point 2. For loop stitches, used for petals, 1 and 2 are close together. To form the stitch into a cup shape, as required for some flowers, pull the base of the stitch in closer by stitching together the first and last knot, as shown in diags 5, 6 and 7.

POINTS TO REMEMBER

- The shape of the finished stitch will be governed by the length of the foundation back stitch and the number of loops worked onto the needle.
- Tighten the core thread carefully so that the loops fill the thread sufficiently. Too few loops worked for the size of stitch required will result in a loose floppy stitch that will not retain the shape of the flower.
- Care must be taken not to pull the back stitch too tight as you lay the stitch or the base fabric will pucker. This is most likely to happen if there are too few loops worked onto the needle.

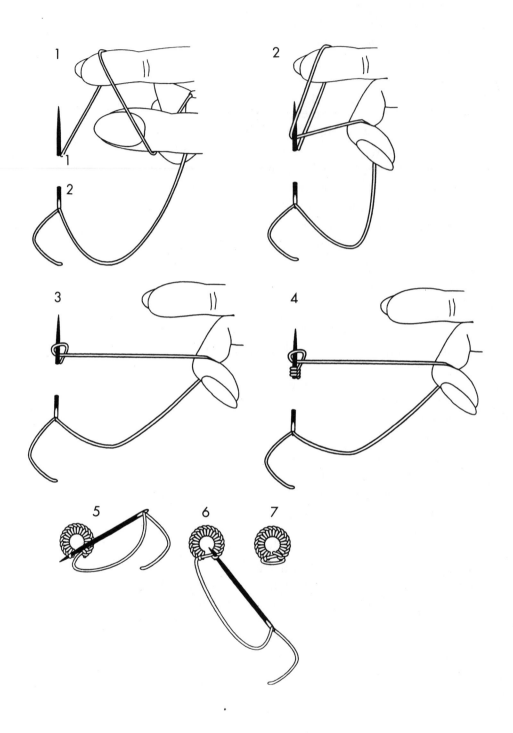

DOUBLE-SIDED DETACHED BUTTONHOLE STITCH — THREAD

W   I/C   M

- Thread the needle with a long thread and knot the two cut ends together to form a double thread.

- Bring the needle up at point 1, back stitch to 2 and up again at 1. Bring the point of the needle out at point 1 between the two threads so that one lies on each side of the needle (diag. 1). Do not pull the needle right through the fabric.

- Work one loop with the right hand as described for detached buttonhole stitch, with the thread on the right side of the needle.

- Work a second loop using the left-hand thread in the left hand, pulling the knot to the left side of the needle (diags 2 and 3).

- Work alternate right- and left-hand loops up the needle for the required length.

- Hold the loops gently between the left thumb and first finger as you pull the needle through the fabric.

- Ease the loops down, tighten the core thread carefully and anchor the stitch by passing the needle to the back of the work at point 2 (diag. 4).

The points to remember listed on page 225 for the detached buttonhole stitch also apply to this stitch.

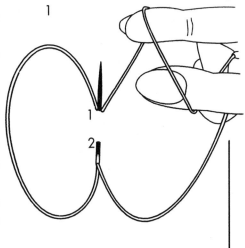

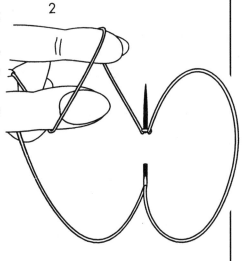

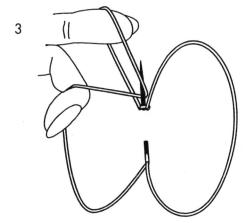

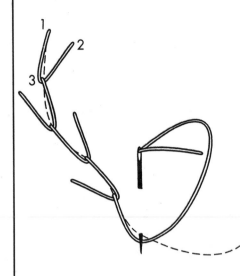

FEATHER STITCH — THREAD
W I Cr

This stitch is useful for defining a shape that will be embroidered with a random selection of flowers. It can also be very useful as a background fill of fern-type leaves.

- Bring the needle up at 1 at the top of the line to be followed.
- Take the needle down through the fabric below this point to the right of the line (point 2).
- Slant the needle down slightly and bring it back to the surface on the line with the thread looped under the needle. Pull the needle through (point 3).
- Repeat the stitch, inserting the needle to the left of the centre line. Continue working down the line, alternating the stitches from side to side.
- This is a 'one-way' stitch, so take care that all the stems point in the right direction on a design.

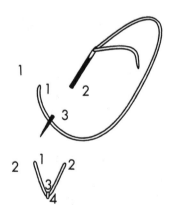

FLY STITCH — THREAD
W I Cr

- Bring the needle up at 1, then down at 2 and out again at 3. Keep the thread from point 1 looped under the needle at 3 and pull the needle through (diag. 1).
- Anchor the stitch by passing the needle to the back of the work at 4 (diag. 2). Note that a small stalk can be created by moving point 4 further away from point 3.

FRENCH KNOT OR HALF COLONIAL KNOT — RIBBON
W I Ch or T H

This knot is the second half of a full colonial knot.

- Bring the needle up through the fabric at point 1.
- With the needle pointing towards you, pick up the ribbon as shown in diag. 1.

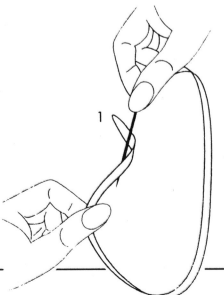

- Turn the needle clockwise over the ribbon held in the left hand. Pass the needle back through the fabric at point 2.

Pull down gently on the ribbon to ensure the knot rests on the fabric as the needle is passed to the back of the work. This is essential for neat compact knots.

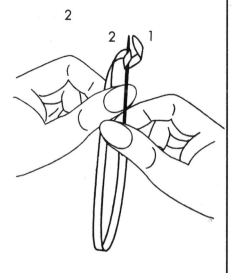

FRENCH KNOT — THREAD

W I M H

Work as described above.

JACQUARD STITCH — CANVAS WORK

T F

This stitch is made up of alternating rows of diagonal stitches.

- Work the stitches in the first row over two inter-sections of the canvas as detailed in diag. 1.
- Work the stitches in the second row over one intersection as shown in diag. 2.
- Repeat these alternating rows over the design area.

Note that small compensatory stitches will be required around the edges of the design to fill in the area.

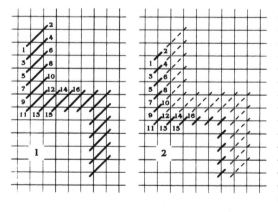

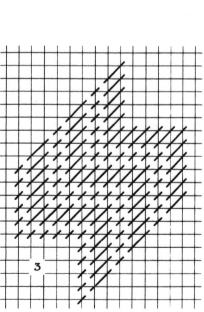

KNOTTED LOOP STITCH — THREAD

W/C N/I T H

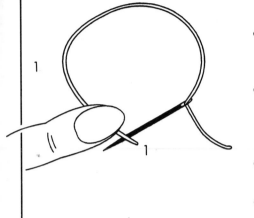

- Bring the needle up at point 1. Form a small loop with the thread, holding it in place under the left thumb.
- Slide the needle under the thread close to point 1 and pull through gently until the loop of thread is of the desired size (diag. 1).
- Anchor the loop by passing the needle to the back of the work just inside the loop made and close to point 1 (diag. 2). Do not pull the knot too tight at this point or the loop may slide.
- Bring the needle up to the right of the completed loop and in line with the outer edge of that loop.
- Pass the needle through the finished loop to link the stitches together as you form the next loop (diag. 3).
- Slide the needle under the thread at point 1, adjusting the size of the loop carefully to match the previously worked loop. Pass the needle to the back of the work at point 1 as before.
- When working this stitch into a circle, the final loop of each row must be linked by passing the needle through the stitches to the right and left of the loop being worked (diag. 4).

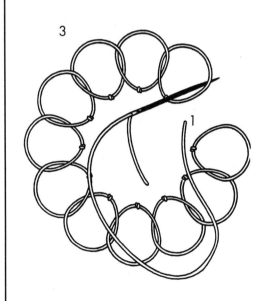

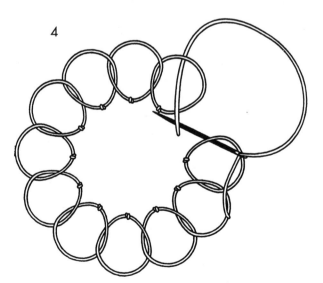

LADDER STITCH — THREAD

W   I   Ch or Cr

This is a simple and neat way to close seams left open for turning, and for invisibly joining two sections of work together.

Pick up a few threads of fabric along the seam line on one side, then pick up the same distance along the seam line of the other side of the opening. The crossover thread represents the rung of the ladder, the pick-up sections the side supports.

As long as a strong enough thread is used, several stitches can be worked and then tightened really firmly to pull the two sides together securely.

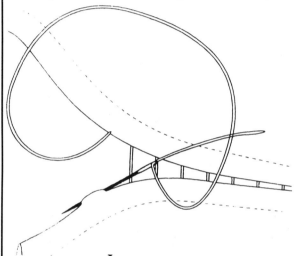

LAZY DAISY STITCH — THREAD

W   I   M or Ch

- Bring the needle up at 1, take it back down at 1 and out again at 2, looping the thread under the point of the needle.

- Pull the needle through the fabric, tightening the thread gently. Anchor with a small stitch at the point of the stitch.

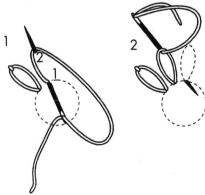

LONG AND SHORT STITCH — TAPESTRY

N T F

It is necessary to keep the working threads untwisted and spread as evenly as possible.

The stitch may be worked evenly over the same number of threads every time to give a symmetrical pattern, or as a random pattern, filling in the area.

Work two rows at a time. Half the stitches of each row are worked in one direction (diags 1 and 2), the work is then turned and the spaces filled by working back to the starting point (diags 3 to 6).

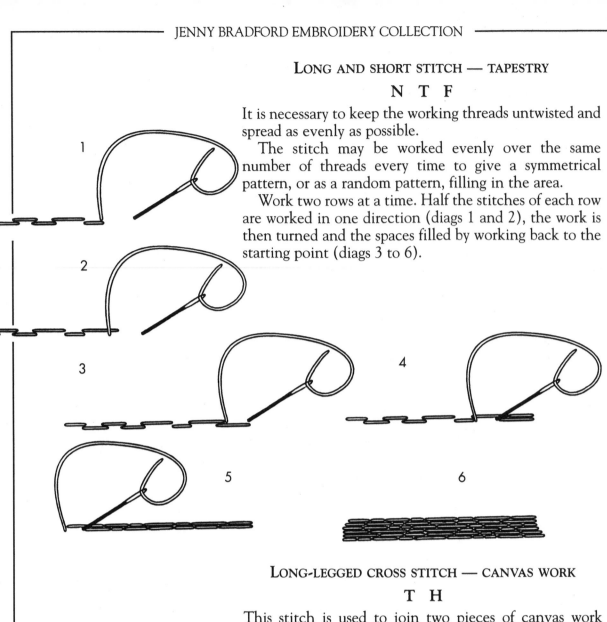

LONG-LEGGED CROSS STITCH — CANVAS WORK

T H

This stitch is used to join two pieces of canvas work together.

- Fold under the edges, leaving an unstitched thread on the edge of each piece.
- Place the edges together, lining up the threads of the canvas.
- Work across the edges, following the sequence of stitching shown in the diagram.

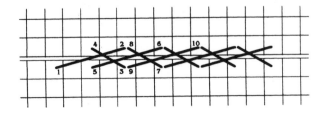

PALESTRINA OR DOUBLE KNOT STITCH — RIBBON

W I/C T

- Working from left to right, come up at 1 on the line to be covered. Take a small vertical stitch, going down at 2 (above the design line) and back out at 3 (below the design line). The distance between 1, 2 and 3 should be equal and approximately equal to the width of ribbon used (diag. 1).

- Keeping the ribbon to the right, slide the needle under (from top to bottom) the bar stitch formed in step 1. Pull the ribbon through (diag. 2).

  Note that the ribbon should be spread flat for this step, and not tightened too firmly.

- Slide the needle under the top corner of the original bar stitch a second time, keeping it to the right of the stitch worked in step 2. Bring the needle out over the top of the ribbon loop formed as this step is worked (diag. 3). Pull the needle through and tighten the ribbon to the desired tension.

- Continue stitching along the design line by inserting the needle at 4, coming up at 5 and working over the resulting bar stitch (diag. 4).

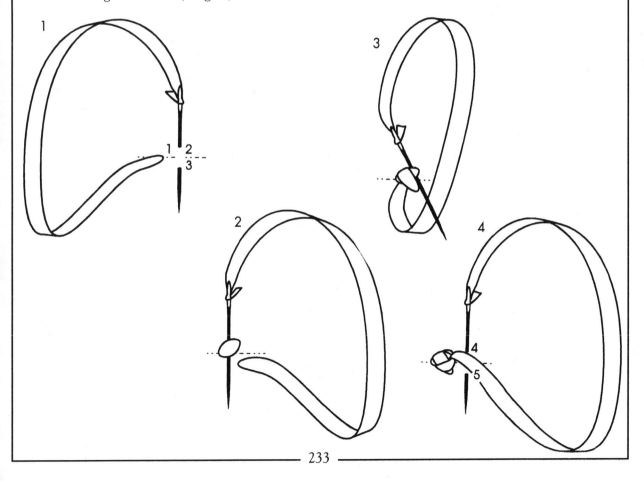

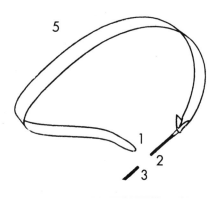

To work single stitches as buds or tiny flowers, start each stitch at the tip of the bud (diag. 5) and finish each stitch by taking the needle to the back of the work at the base of the bud where it joins the stalk (diag. 6).

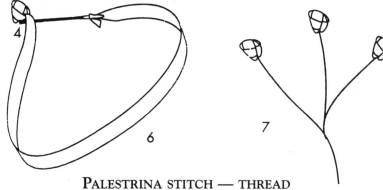

PALESTRINA STITCH — THREAD

W I/C T

For good results when working with thread the stitches must be spaced according to the thickness of the thread used. The finer the thread, the closer and smaller the stitches will need to be.

Details for working are exactly as described for ribbon.

PEARL STITCH — RIBBON

W I T

- Working from left to right, come up at 1. Take a tiny vertical stitch across the design line to be followed (from 2 to 3 in diag. 1).

  Note that the distance between 1 and 2 should be approximately the same as the width of the ribbon used.

- Pass the needle under the starting stitch formed in step 1. Pull the needle through, adjusting the tension and taking care not to tighten the wrap stitch too firmly (diag. 2).

- Continue stitching along the design line by inserting the needle at 4 and working over the resulting bar stitch (diag. 3).

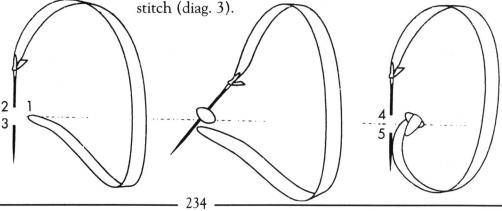

PISTIL STITCH — THREAD

W I M H or F

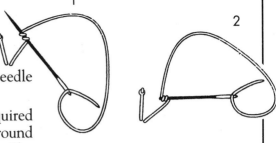

- Bring the needle up at point 1.
- Pick up the thread once or twice around the needle (diag. 1).
- Return the needle to the back of the work the required distance from point 1, pulling the thread taut around the needle as it is passed through the fabric (diag. 2).

PORTUGUESE STEM STITCH — RIBBON

W I T

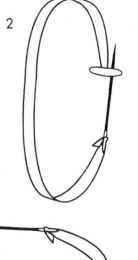

A lovely stitch with a cord-like texture based on the more familiar stem stitch.

- Working from the bottom up and stitching directly over the marked design lines, bring the needle up at point 1.
- Keeping the ribbon on the right-hand side of the needle, take the needle down at 2 and up again at 3.

The distances 1 to 3 and 2 to 3 should be equal and approximately the same as the width of the ribbon being used.

- With the ribbon *below* the needle pass the needle from right to left *between* the straight stitch just formed and the fabric, keeping the ribbon between 2 and 3 (diag. 2). Gently tighten the ribbon round the straight stitch, ensuring that it does not twist or curl.
- With the ribbon *above* the needle add a second wrap around the straight stitch below the first wrap and gently tighten as before (diag. 3).
- With the ribbon to the right of the needle work another stem stitch from 4 to 5. Wrap as before (diags 5 and 6).

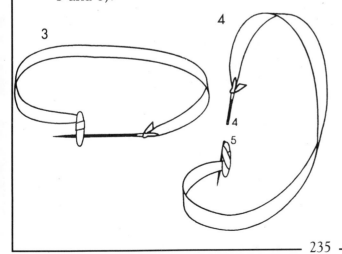

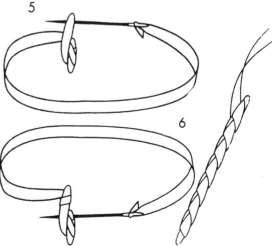

PORTUGUESE STEM STITCH — THREAD

W I T

Keep the stitches the same size as you would work for ordinary stem stitch (the finer the thread, the smaller the stitch). Work as given for ribbon version.

RIBBON STITCH — FLAT — RIBBON

NW Ch or Cr

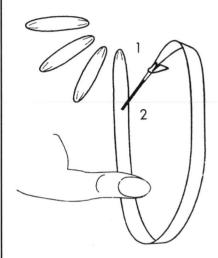

Always spread the ribbon carefully.

- Come up at 1.
- Pull the ribbon towards you, laying it directly over the petal or leaf position.
- Pass the needle through the centre of the ribbon, and pull the ribbon through very gently until the tip of the stitch curls over to form a point.

RIBBON STITCH — LOOPED — RIBBON

NW Ch or Cr

A variation of ribbon stitch.

- Pass the needle through the ribbon *only* at the tip of the petal to be formed.
- Then pass the needle to the back of the work, 1 to 2 mm ($^1/_{16}$") from point 1, to form a looped petal that stands away from the fabric.
- The petals must be held firm with colonial knots or pistil stitch.

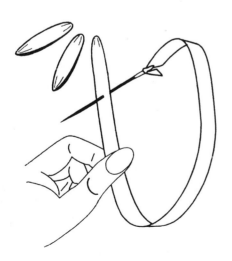

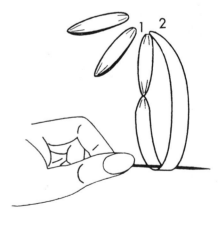

ROSETTE CHAIN — RIBBON

W I T

A traditional embroidery stitch, this versatile stitch makes a pretty braid-type edging to collars and cuffs when worked in a continuous line. It can also be used to form tiny flower buds by working each stitch individually or as a flower by working the stitches in a circle. It is not necessary to spread the ribbon for this stitch.

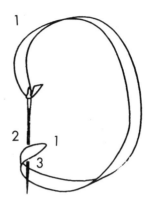

- Working from right to left, bring the needle up at point 1. Form a small anti-clockwise loop of ribbon, passing the needle through the fabric above the loop at 2, level with but to the left at point 1.

- Bring the needle back to the surface at point 3 inside the loop of ribbon and directly below point 2 (diag. 1). The distance between points 2 and 3 should be slightly less than the width of ribbon used.

- Tighten the stitch before passing the needle upwards under the ribbon between points 1 and 2 (diag. 2).

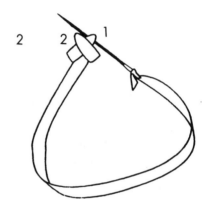

- To work a line or circle of stitches, form the ribbon loop at this point and insert the needle at point 2, the required distance away from the preceding stitch (diag. 3).

- For individual buds, finish each stitch by passing the needle to the back of the work between points 1 and 2 (diag. 4).

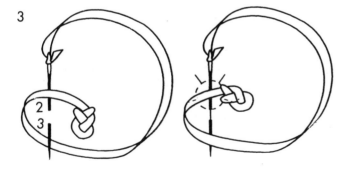

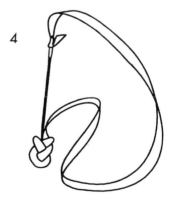

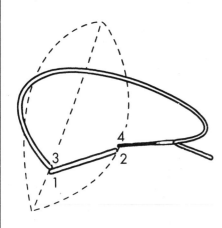

SATIN STITCH — THREAD
W I Cr F

Satin stitch will look smoother and more even if it is worked with a fine thread and needle. Use one or two strands and lay each strand side by side, avoiding any crossover threads.

It is usually easier to lay the first stitch across the body of the area, thus achieving a good angle for the main stitching area. Build the stitching up on either side of this foundation rather than starting at an odd angle across a corner.

- Start by anchoring the thread with tiny running stitches across the area to be covered. Bring the needle through from the back at point 1, and take it to the back of the work at point 2.

- For the second stitch, come up at 3 and down at 4, working as close to the first stitch as is necessary to cover the background fabric completely.

STEM OR OUTLINE STITCH — RIBBON
W/C NI Ch

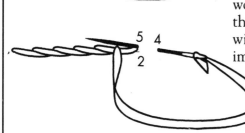

- Bring the needle out at 1, down at 2 and out again at 3 (where 3 is halfway between 1 and 2) with the ribbon below the needle (diag. 1).

- Keeping the ribbon below the needle, take the needle down at 4 and back out at 5 (diag. 2).

Note that stem stitch may curve more smoothly if worked with the ribbon above the needle, depending on the direction of the curve. Whether you choose to work with the ribbon above or below the needle, it is important to keep it consistent in each line.

STEM OR OUTLINE STITCH — THREAD
W I Cr

Worked exactly as given for ribbon.

STRAIGHT STITCH — FLAT — RIBBON

W   I   Ch or Cr   H

- Bring the needle up·at point 1.
- Hold the ribbon flat against the fabric, under the left thumb, directly opposite the required position of the stitch.
- Spread the ribbon.
- Making the stitch the required length, pass the needle down through the fabric at point 2.
- Keep the left thumb in position as long as possible, forming the ribbon loop over it. Pulling the ribbon firmly at this point should remove the twists from the ribbon. Slide the thumb from the loop and gently tighten the stitch to the desired tension.

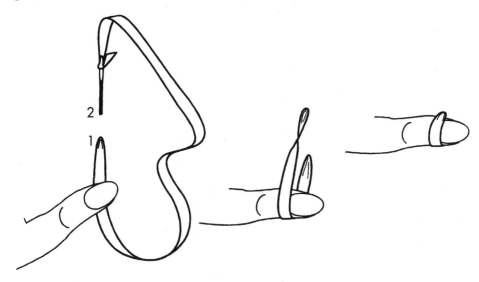

STRAIGHT STITCH — LOOPED — RIBBON

NW   Ch or Cr   H

Looped straight stitch flowers are more difficult to work than most of the other flowers because the petal loops are not secure and can easily be distorted until after the centres have been worked.

Always spread the ribbon and take care not to disturb and distort the stitches as you work.

You may need a second tapestry needle or a cable knitting needle to slip through the ribbon loops to hold them evenly as you work.

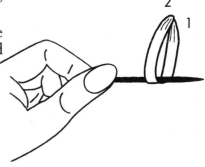

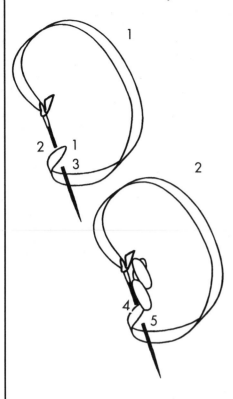

TWISTED CHAIN — RIBBON
W I/C Ch

- Work from the top of the design down directly over the line to be covered.
- Bring the needle up at 1.
- Form a small anti-clockwise loop of ribbon and pass the needle down at 2 and out again at 3.

Note that point 2 is level with and close to 1 but to the left of 1, so the ribbon crosses over at this point. The distance between 1 and 3 will vary according to the thickness of the ribbon being used. To maintain even stitching, distances between 1, 2 and 3 must be consistent with every stitch. When working a continuous line, be sure to keep the needle very close to the design line at points 2 and 4 (diags 1 and 2).

TWISTED CHAIN — THREAD
W I Cr

Work as for ribbon, remembering that the finer the thread, the smaller the stitches will need to be.

LONG-LEGGED TWISTED CHAIN — THREAD
W I Ch H

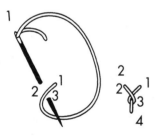

- Bring the needle up at 1 and form a loop of thread as for twisted chain. Pass the needle down at 2 and out at 3 (diag. 1).

Note that point 2 is in line with point 1 but about 4 mm ($^1/_6$") to the left of 1.

- Pull the needle through over the thread loop to tighten the stitch.
- Anchor the stitch by passing the needle to the back of the work at 4.

Note that the distance between points 3 and 4 may vary according to the shape of the flower being worked.

WHIPPED RUNNING STITCH — RIBBON

W I Cr + T H

This stitch is used for outline work and is based on a line of even running stitches placed along the design lines.

The surface stitches should be even in length and each stitch should be about one and a half times the width of the ribbon being used.

The gaps between the stitches should be as small as you can comfortably make them depending on the width of the ribbon and the type of fabric being used.

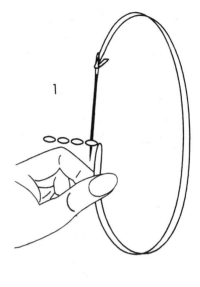

- Place the design area in a hoop and, using a crewel needle, work a row of running stitches along the design lines.

- Using a tapestry needle and working from right to left, start the wrapping ribbon just before the start of the first running stitch. Lay the work down and use both hands on top of the work to manipulate the ribbon. Hold the needle *above* the line of running stitches and pass it down behind the first running stitch. Pull the needle through and then slip the needle into the ribbon loop formed to hold the ribbon flat as the loop is tightened with the *left* hand.

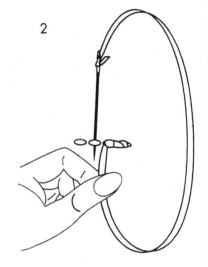

- Repeat a second time through the same stitch. Tighten this stitch to wrap firmly around the foundation stitch.

- Pass the needle down behind the second running stitch in the same way, but take care to leave this stitch more relaxed to allow the ribbon to spread and cover the gap between the foundation stitches.

- Pass the needle behind this second stitch again, laying this stitch firmly around the foundation stitch.

- Continue this sequence along the line of running stitches, alternating tightly wrapped stitches around the foundation stitching with more loosely wrapped stitches covering the spaces between each foundation stitch.

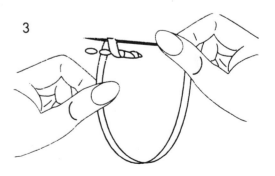

WHIPPED STITCH — SINGLE — RIBBON

W I T H

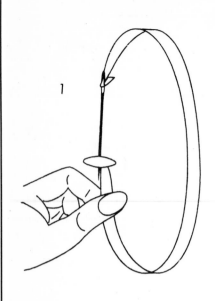

Similar in character to the whipped running stitch but each straight stitch is wrapped six or seven times, or until it is covered sufficiently for your purpose, as it is laid on the fabric.

- Work a straight stitch (1 to 2) the required length and pull it *very* firmly as the needle is brought back to the surface at 3.

- Lay the work down and use both hands to manipulate the ribbon as described in the second step of whipped running stitch.

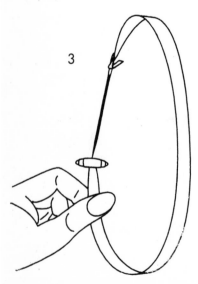

- Repeat the wrapping process, tightening each wrap firmly around the foundation stitch and positioning each wrap a little further along the foundation stitch until it is completely covered (3 to 4 wraps).

- Change direction and wrap from left to right over the previous row, working another 2 or 3 wraps.

- Finish the final wrap in the *centre* of the stitch. Pulling gently on the ribbon will then form the stitch into a curve. To anchor the stitch into this curved position, pass the needle through the centre of the ribbon close to the wrapped stitch (diag. 2).

- To anchor the stitch without a curve, pass the needle to the back of the work *above* the wrapped stitch (diag. 3).

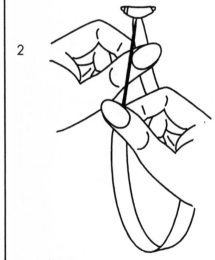

This stitch will not work successfully unless the wrapping is carried out as directed. The needle must be passed *down* from above the foundation stitches in order to have the ribbon in the correct alignment for anchoring the stitch.